ALSO BY WALTER J. ONG, S.J.

Frontiers in American Catholicism (1957)
Ramus, Method, and the Decay of Dialogue (1958)
Ramus and Talon Inventory (1958)
American Catholic Crossroads (1959)
Darwin's Vision and Christian Perspectives (1960)
The Barbarian Within (1962)
In the Human Grain (1967)
Knowledge and the Future of Man (1968)

The Presence of the Word

Some Prolegomena for Cultural and Religious History

by Walter J. Ong, S.J.

A CLARION BOOK
PUBLISHED BY SIMON AND SCHUSTER

A Clarion Book
Published by Simon and Schuster
Rockefeller Center, 630 Fifth Avenue
New York, New York 10020

Reprinted by arrangement with Yale University Press

First paperback printing, 1970

SBN 671-20549-8
Manufactured in the United States of America

THE DWIGHT HARRINGTON TERRY
FOUNDATION LECTURES

ON RELIGION IN THE LIGHT OF SCIENCE AND
PHILOSOPHY

The deed of gift declares that "the object of this foundation is not the promotion of scientific investigation and
discovery, but rather the assimilation and interpretation
of that which has been or shall be hereafter discovered,
and its application to human welfare, especially by the
building of the truths of science and philosophy into the
structure of a broadened and purified religion. The
founder believes that such a religion will greatly stim-
ulate intelligent effort for the improvement of human
conditions and the advancement of the race in strength
and excellence of character. To this end it is desired that
a series of lectures be given by men eminent in their
respective departments, on ethics, the history of civilza-
tion and religion, biblical research, all sciences and
branches of knowledge which have an important bearing
on the subject, all the great laws of nature, especially of
evolution . . . also such interpretations of literature and
sociology as are in accord with the spirit of this foundation, to the end that the Christian spirit may be nurtured
in the fullest light of the world's knowledge and that mankind may be helped to attain its highest possible welfare
and happiness upon this earth." The present work constitutes the thirty-fourth volume published on this foundation.

For
John and Simone Brown
who speak so many tongues
so many places
so well

Preface

The Terry Lectures have to do with religion in the light of science and philosophy, and traditionally have commanded from the lecturers contributions from their own special fields of competence which are relevant to religion in the broad sense of this term. The present work, an expansion of the lectures given at Yale University April 27, 28, and 29, 1964, is concerned with a matter of evident religious implication: with the word, chiefly the spoken word, but also its interior, imaginary, and intellectual counterparts. From Old Testament times, concern with the word of God (where "word" is far from a casual metaphor) has marked the Hebrew tradition, and in the New Testament man is confronted with the announcement of the Word made Flesh.

Ancient Hebrews and Christians knew not only the spoken word but the alphabet as well, as their devotion to the sacred scriptures makes plain. But for them and all men of early times, the Word, even when written, was much closer to the spoken word than it normally is for twentieth-century technological man. Today we have often to labor to regain the awareness that the word is still always at root the spoken word. Early man had no such problem: he felt the word, even when written, as primarily an event in sound. Today there has grown out of and around the spoken word a vast network of artificially contrived media—writing, print, electronic devices such as sound tapes or computers in which informational content is implicitly or explicitly tied in with verbal explanation far beyond the experience of early man—and other complex contrivances. These media are a great but distracting boon. They overwhelm us and give our concept of the word special contours which can interfere with our understanding of what the word in truth is, and thus can distort the relevance of the word to ourselves.

Paradoxically and fortunately, these same media have brought history into being and opened the past to us, making it possible to discover the word with new explicitness, if less directness, in its original and still natural habitat, the world of voice, of sound. The present work attempts to further such discovery. We wish here to pursue the story of the word among men as a natural mystery, a key point at which Christian revelation (and, preceding it, Hebrew revelation) establishes contact with human existence.

The word shares all the richness of human life and it can be studied from countless different standpoints, most of them complicated by the fact that they are intimately related to one another. One can, for example, examine the word as name, as term, as concept, or as a part of speech, perhaps taking up in this last case the fascinating difference between the word as name or noun (from the Latin *nomen,* which means also name) and the word as substitute-for–name or pronoun (Latin *pronomen*). But these concerns, however intimately connected with the present concerns, would enlarge this work beyond all bounds. I am therefore restricting this treatment of the word by focusing on some of its relationships to sound, its native medium, and incidentally to other senses and to the ways these relationships change as the word moves through history.

In addition to my auditors at Yale University, I am indebted to many other friends, particularly to James D.

Collins, Alden L. Fisher, Francis T. Severin, S.J., and
students at Saint Louis University, Indiana University,
and New York University who have read or listened to
versions of some of this and, by lending their sympathy
and understanding, have contributed to whatever value
this book may have. Research incorporated into the present study was in part made possible by a travel grant from
the Penrose Fund of the American Philosophical Society,
for which I am grateful.

Some of the material here explored in depth I have
touched on in chapters 1 and 4 of an earlier book, *In
the Human Grain.*

Contents

Erfahrungen ersten Grades, ersten Ranges, werden nicht durch das Auge gemacht. [Experiences of the first order, of the first rank, are not realized through the eye.]

—EUGEN ROSENSTOCK-HUESSY, *Die Vollzahl der Zeiten* (1957), p. 33.

I

The Word and the Sensorium

THE SHIFTING SENSORIUM

Man communicates with his whole body, and yet the word is his primary medium. Communication, like knowledge itself, flowers in speech.

The fact that man communicates with his whole body through all his senses is evident enough to us today. Modern psychology has underscored the way in which the child constructs his first world under the influence of touch (including kinesthesia), of taste, and of smell, as well as of sound and sight. The child's physical contact with his mother's body and hers with his is already communication, a sharing through touch, which will influence not only his feeling but his thought throughout his life. Taste and smell attract and repel him in his relations with persons and things around him, helping him ultimately to shape his life-world in which his thought itself will take form. Sight, at first perhaps less informative, soon becomes in many ways the most informative of the senses, commonly in connection with kinesthesia and other senses of touch, for the tactile senses combine with sight to register depth and distance when these are presented in the visual field.

Finally sound, a medium of communication since the child's first cry, manifests new potential of meaning as the child passes through the lalling stage, where he constructs around himself a vast bubble of sound, burbling, gurgling, playing with his diversifying vocal powers—and with his lips at the same time, for sound, both in speaking and in hearing, is closely linked with touch and kinesthesia. One "mouths" words quite literally, and our hearing is partly feeling, as Ilse LeHiste and Gordon E. Peterson have shown. The term "seesaw," to take an example related to theirs, seems to our hearing to have the accent on the first syllable, even though the last syllable may actually be pronounced to produce more volume (this can be tested on a moderately sensitive oscilloscope), for we have to work harder to produce the sound "see-," constricting our oral muscles and pushing air through a small space, and we interpret this greater effort (whether we make it ourselves or by listening share in the effort of others) as greater noise.

The oral–aural world of words is a highly complex and mystifying construct, but as he passes through the lalling stage the child learns to insert himself into it, and this world of words soon becomes paramount in the communications process. By the same token it becomes paramount in the child's thinking processes, since human thought apparently cannot arise at all outside a communications setting, either proximate or remote.

This is not to say that for the child or the adult all communication is lodged in speech or even, in the deepest sense of communication, in other bodily activities as apprehended by the senses. It is quite true, as Heidegger in *Being and Time* (Pt. I, sec. 34) and other existentialist thinkers like to insist, that language itself is at its deepest level not primarily even a system of sounds. There is a primordial attunement of one human existent to another out of which all language comes. Man is rooted in "speaking silence." All this is true, and in a certain sense commonplace, but it is noteworthy that when we thus think of silence as communicating, we are likely to think of it as a kind of speech rather than as a kind of touch or taste or smell or vision—*"speaking* silence," we say. The reason is plain: silence itself is conceived of by reference to sound; it is sound's polar opposite. Thus even when we conceive of communication as a transaction more fundamental than speech, we still conceive of it with reference to the world of sound where speech has its being, and thus attest in a reverse way to the paramountcy of sound and the oral–aural world in communication.

Because words are always primarily spoken things—writing transposes language to a spatial medium, but the language so transposed has come into existence in the world of sound and remains permanently a part of this world—to a certain degree the oral–aural world, the world of voice and hearing which the child enters in learning verbal communication will retain its paramountcy for good. But only to a certain degree. For, as we have lately learned, the world of sound itself does not have always the same importance in all cultures with relation to the worlds of the other senses.

Cultures vary greatly in their exploitation of the various senses and in the way in which they relate their conceptual apparatus to the various senses. It has been a commonplace that the ancient Hebrews and the ancient Greeks differed in the value they set on the auditory. The Hebrews tended to think of understanding as a kind of hearing, whereas the Greeks thought of it more as a kind of seeing, although far less exclusively as seeing than post-Cartesian Western man generally has tended to do. Thorlief Boman has brought together massive evidence of the Hebrew–Greek contrast, and, although James Barr

has contested some of Boman's interpretations and procedures, the contrast itself remains clear enough. The
work of Benjamin Whorf with the Hopi Indians has
shown how, in the Hopi life-world, time is retained as a
sense of duration (with a base which appears largely
kinesthetic) and how this life-world contrasts with that
built into and out of what Whorf styles Standard Average
European languages, which present time as "long" or
"short" (as though it were a stick) and as discontinuously
quantified, with one minute or hour or day broken off
from the next as on a clock face or calendar, as time itself
never is.

Some cultures, similarly, make more of the tactile than
do others. In his *Art and Geometry* (pp. 1–13), William
M. Ivins, Jr., has pointed out that ancient Greek geometry
differs from most modern geometry in that the ancient
Greeks thought more about the way the various shapes
felt (they tended to imagine themselves fingering their
way around a geometrical figure), whereas modern geo-
metricians think more about the way the various shapes
look. Ours, consequently, is a spectator's geometry, theirs
was a participator's.

Some cultures make more of taste than do others.
Whereas modern English, for example, has only a hand-
ful of concepts formed directly from gustatory sensations
(concepts such as sweet, bitter, sour), complementing
these with analogies borrowed from other sensory fields
(a taste is flat or sharp) or with crude similitudes (it tastes
like an overripe pineapple), the Korean language, I am
told by Korean friends, has many more concepts referring
more directly to taste.

Taste provides a good example of a sensory field which
even the same culture attends to with different intensity
at different points in its history. In the eighteenth century

through much Western culture, questions concerning taste somehow or other became extraordinarily urgent. In England Pope cried out against vulgar "taste"; Dr. John Armstrong published an important poem entitled *Taste* (1753); and Hume wrote an essay "Of the Standard of Taste" (1757). The questions agitated did not concern the sense of taste directly in any obvious way, it is true, but rather its analogical extensions into other areas of life—taste in poetry, art, style of living. Nevertheless, this analogical taste had indubitable, real connections with the sense of taste. That is why the term taste rather than smell or hearing or touch or vision came into play.

Some reasons for the ascendancy of taste in the eighteenth century can readily be seen. The sense of taste is basically a discriminatory sense as the other senses are not (Hume's title registers this fact: taste provides a standard or norm). Taste is a yes-or-no sense, a take-it-or-don't-take-it sense, letting us know what is good and what is bad for us in the most crucial physical way, for taste concerns what we are inclined to take into ourselves by eating, what will by intussusception either actually become ourselves or refuse to be assimilated and perhaps kill us. Undoubtedly the eighteenth-century concern with taste, analogously understood, derived in great part from the growing number of acts of discrimination which men were having to make. As feudal society finally bowed out, the individual and even a whole society were being forced to make decisions which an older, more tradition-bound culture used to provide ready-made. With democracy, the concern with taste wanes, as "public opinion" is formed to take over regulatory functions, the crises of decision assume other shapes, and the relationship of the human life-world to the complex of the senses changes once more.

The relationship of sound and of the word itself to the human life-world varies, too. Sound and the word itself must thus be considered in terms of the shifting relationships between the senses. These relationships must not be taken merely abstractly but in connection with variations in cultures. In this connection, it is useful to think of cultures in terms of the organization of the sensorium. By the sensorium we mean here the entire sensory apparatus as an operational complex. The differences in cultures which we have just suggested can be thought of as differences in the sensorium, the organization of which is in part determined by culture while at the same time it makes culture. Freudians have long pointed out that for abstract thinking the proximity senses—smell, taste, and in a special way touch (although touch concerns space as well as contact and is thus simultaneously concrete and abstract)—must be minimized in favor of the more abstract hearing and sight. Growing up, assimilating the wisdom of the past, is in great part learning how to organize the sensorium productively for intellectual purposes. Man's sensory perceptions are abundant and overwhelming. He cannot attend to them all at once. In great part a given culture teaches him one or another way of productive specialization. It brings him to organize his sensorium by attending to some types of perception more than others, by making an issue of certain ones while relatively neglecting other ones. The sensorium is a fascinating focus for cultural studies. Given sufficient knowledge of the sensorium exploited within a specific culture, one could probably define the culture as a whole in virtually all its aspects. Such full or exhaustive knowledge is not easy to come by, and we are a long way from it at present. But to say we are far from knowing all about the sensorium is not to say we know nothing about it.

A recent seminal book by Marshall McLuhan, *The Gutenberg Galaxy,* shows, among other things, how widespread the interest in the sensorium has become today, often among authors who do not even think of the sensorium as such under that name. McLuhan's work connects closely with that of Harold A. Innis, as McLuhan himself has always graciously insisted, though few of his admirers or critics seem aware of the connection. In addition to Innis, McLuhan quotes from scores of scholars in vastly different historical fields—art history, literature, economic history, sociology, anthropology, religion, and many others—who have lately been turning up more and more material relevant to variations in the ratio or balance between the senses. The interests of most of these authors are not technically psychological but historical or cultural. Vast as McLuhan's spread of citations is, one could enlarge it indefinitely. There is, for example the well-known interest of the French *symboliste* poets in the transposition of the senses (assigning specific colors to specific sounds, as Baudelaire and Mallarmé do). The work of a number of recent philosophers enters into or touches on the organization of the sensorium. One thinks of Bergson's misgivings in *Time and Free Will* about the tendency of the past few centuries to overspatialize the universe so that everything is reduced to models picturable in space, and what is unpicturable ("unimaginable" is often the term invoked) is discarded as impossible or unreal). Or one thinks of Whitehead's subsequent comments in *Process and Reality.* Louis Lavelle and Jean Nogué elaborate discussion of the sensorium far beyond Bergson. Others concerned in one way or another with what we are here styling the sensorium include of course Freud and his followers, linguistic historians such as Jespersen and Sapir, psychologists such as Jean Piaget and

Jerome Bruner, and a number of phenomenologists. Many in these last three groups can be identified through the comprehensive bibliography in John W. M. Verhaar's valuable recent work, *Some Relations between Perception, Speech, and Thought: A Contribution toward the Phenomenology of Speech.*

Whitehead, in his *Modes of Thought* (1938), was one of the earliest to call rather specific attention to the need for study of the effects of changes in the communications media on the organization of the sensorium (without, however, naming the sensorium as such). Today there is a common awareness of the general pattern of these changes as man has developed his verbal communications media out of the initial spoken word. In general, before the invention of script man is more oral–aural than afterward, not merely in that his words are all spoken and heard words, never visually perceived marks on a surface, but in that his whole response to actuality is thereby organized differently from that of typographic man. Writing, and most particularly the alphabet, shifts the balance of the senses away from the aural to the visual, favoring a new kind of personality structure, and alphabetic typography strengthens this shift, as I pointed out at length some years ago when assessing the significance of Ramism in *Ramus, Method, and the Decay of Dialogue.*

The greater visualism initiated by script and the alphabet is given more and more play in the West through the Middle Ages and then suddenly is brought to a new intensity in the fifteenth century and thereafter with the invention of alphabetic typography. As will be seen, this new intensity involves much more than print—the word literally locked in space—for at approximately the same time that alphabetic typography appears, painting is being swept by a revolution in its treatment of perspective, and the mechanical reproduction of instructional (as against decorative) illustrations and diagrams becomes widespread. Historians of art and design, such as Erwin Panofsky and Gyorgy Kepes, have traced this and other developments in the use of vision. The visualism encouraged by print connects also with the increased use of maps and with the actual physical exploration of the globe (dependent on visual control of space in maps and imagination) which opens the modern age.

The modern age was thus much more the child of typography than it has commonly been made out to be. And, largely by reason of this fact, the modern age is now a thing of the past. Our own age today, as has by now frequently been pointed out, is marked by a new stress on the auditory. We live by telephone, radio, and television (which is never mere pictures, but is unequivocally a sound medium quite as much as it is a visual one), as well as by rapid transit, which expedites physical presence, and the use of voice to a degree unthinkable for typographic man.

But this is not to say that we are returning to an earlier oral–aural world. There is no return to the past. The successive verbal media do not abolish one another but overlie one another. The present sensorium is dismayingly mixed and we are hard put to understand it, but for the first time in the history of mankind the possibility of some kind of understanding is opening up. This itself gives us a unique opportunity to become aware at a new depth of the significance of the word.

RELIGION AND THE SENSORIUM

It is tempting to reduce religion to a particular condition of the sensorium. Man is religious when the sensorium has a certain type of organization, and when it changes he is no longer so. Religion has to do somehow with the invisible, and when the earlier oral–aural world, with its concentration on voice and sound, finally yields to the more markedly visual world incident to script and print, one may be tempted to argue, religion finally must go. Even if it were true, however, that the visible is non-religious, the visualist world has by no means exterminated the oral and the aural. The senses other than sight still operate today, and if they compete with sight less than was once the case, contact with actuality may be by that very fact less effective and real. Only a rampantly visualist culture, such as that in the West has tended to be in certain of its sectors over the past few hundred years, could suppose that vision alone gives satisfactory access to the real or that the rise of the visual should mean the suppression of all the other senses and what they stand for.

Nevertheless, there are problems concerning the relation of religion to the sensorium. Lest we become lost in the vagaries of the term religion itself, we can turn immediately to what will be our principal concern here, the Christian religion, together with its Hebrew foundations. This religion is, or has claimed to be, a revealed religion. It is unique among the larger religions of the world on several scores, one of them being its peculiar relation to history. Unlike most other religions, or perhaps all of them, it does not encourage its devotees to flee from time but tells them that in time they can be redeemed. Christianity, like the Hebrew religion before it, grows out of its own history with a strange self-consciousness. The currently popular and always true idea of Christian "witness" shows this self-consciousness. From the time of the Acts of the Apostles to the present, Christians have testified to something that has *happened* in the datable past, that is, to Jesus Christ's presence on earth, and they have done so even to the point of laying down their lives rather than deny this happening. The birth of Jesus is carefully situated in historical time in Luke's Gospel, as the events of Jesus' life are elsewhere in the New Testament. Even the Old Testament is unmistakably historical in import, although often, especially in its earlier books, it is not history quite in our modern sense. And because of its belief in God's personal entry into history through the Incarnation, Christianity, even more than the Hebrew religion, not only is situated in time but also feels itself unequivocally as situated in time, though it looks to eternity.

Seen, then, even from within the Christian faith, as well as from without through the eyes of secular history, God's communication to man in the Hebrew religion, terminating in Christianity, came about in a determinate culture. In our present perspectives this is to say that divine revelation itself, whether seen from within by the eyes of faith or considered from without as a series of events in secular history, is indeed inserted in a particular sensorium, a particular mixture of sensory activity typical of a given culture. Even when it is presented as destined to live through all of subsequent history, it must be thought of as first given to a people with a particular sensory organization in their life-world and thus with certain more or less specialized ways of thinking and knowing. Since its appearance, moreover, Christian revelation has survived vast changes in the sensoria of the cultures in which Christians have lived. Indeed, today it asserts its effects simultaneously on quite diverse sensoria, from the highly visualist sensorium of technological cultures now veering toward new organizations in sound, to the sensoria of primitive cultures which have not yet crossed the threshold of literacy.

The Sensorium and the Word of God

The question of the sensorium in the Christian economy of revelation is particularly fascinating because of
the primacy which this economy accords to the word of
God and thus in some mysterious way to sound itself, a
primacy already suggested in the Old Testament pre-
Christian tradition. Many religions make much of the
word of God or of gods, or simply of the word as a source
of wisdom. But the distinctively personal cast of the relationship between man and God in the Hebreo-Christian
tradition heightens from the earliest Old Testament
times the importance of the word as the focus of personal
communication. God calls to Abraham, "Abraham!" and
Abraham answers "Here I am" (Gen. 22:1). A similar
thing happens to Jacob, who is called by an angel of
God (later recognized to be God himself), "Jacob!" and
who likewise answers, "Here I am" (Gen. 31:11). As
Erich Auerbach has made clear in the first chapter of his
Mimesis, this direct and unexplained confrontation—a
verbal assault on a given person by God—is not the sort
of thing one meets with in Greek or other nonbiblical
tradition. God's word impinges on the human person as a
two-edged sword.

In the prophets, the sense of the word of God reaches
particular intensity. The primacy of the Hebrew feeling
for the word suggests a highly auditory sensorium, for
word here means primarily the spoken word (in a way in
which, as we have earlier indicated, it seldom does today).
The word is not an inert record but a living something,
like sound, something going on. The current dispute,
already noted above, between James Barr and Thorlief
Boman as to how far the Hebrew *dabar* means not only a
spoken word but also an action or event could perhaps be

focused better by more attention to the nature of sound as sound.

The New Testament goes even farther than the Old in what it makes of the word. It presents the word of God as even more the center of its teaching, announcing that the Word was made flesh and dwelt, a Person, among us. As is the case in no other religion, the Word is here the proper name of a Person, the Son of God, himself God— *eo verbum quo filius,* runs the classic theological logion: "He is Word by the fact that he is Son." The designation Word thus belongs to the Son directly and immediately, just as the designation Son itself does. It is his divine name. The visually grounded titles such as the "Light of Light" of the Nicene Creed are applicable to him, but they are second-level designations, less meaningful than "Word" or "Son."

The Word of God, moreover, is reciprocating. If the Word who became man is God's communication to man, he is also man's response to God. The Christian approaches the Father "in his name": "If you ask the Father anything in my name, he will give it to you" (John 16:13; cf. Eph. 5:20, Col. 3:17). As a human being, with his human name, Jesus Christ is thus the Word whereby man addresses God the Father: *per Ipsum et cum Ipso et in Ipso,* the Church prays, "Through him and with him and in him."

The New Testament Gospel or Good News about the Word is itself likewise tied to the spoken word of man. For it is the business of those who know this truth to make it known to all other men by use of the word in preaching, where the human word exists in a mysterious connection with the divine. The Christian Church is thus inevitably a missionary Church, committed to sharing its good news with all men, driven by the Word to maximum communication, and in all this, through the personal contacts effected most basically by the spoken word. *Fides ex auditu,* "faith comes through hearing," we read in the Epistle to the Romans (10:17).

But the word of God in both Old and New Testament is also involved in writing, and thus in man's shift from a primitive oral–aural culture to one organized through a more visualist sensorium. In the scriptural account the Old Testament public revelation was first given to the ancient Hebrews, one of the peoples actually possessing the alphabet, at a time when the alphabet was new and rare. Jesus himself, the Word of God, could read and write, as we know from several incidents in the New Testament, although sometimes his opponents were nonplussed as to how he had learned to do so: "How does this man know letters without having studied them?" (John 7:15). Gradually through its history the Hebrew people had become more and more a people of the book, the Law and the Prophets, and the Christians if anything were a people of the book even more decisively. Their glory in their unity, and their shame when they fell out among themselves, had often to do with what they made of the Holy Scriptures. Nevertheless, despite this addiction to literacy, the spoken word retains always for the Christian some special value. In Catholicism this is manifest by, among other things, devotion to nonwritten tradition as well as to the Scriptures. In Protestantism it is manifest by a special stress on preaching the word of God, a stress of course not unknown in Catholicism and growing stronger in Catholic circles today, though less uniquely dominant there.

The history of religion thus far has built relatively little on understanding or investigation of the history of the word as such. The human word has migrated far from its original habitat in early oral–aural preliterate cultures, with their addiction to "fame" (from *fama,* which means talk) that marks the heroic age, through early script culture, where once "wingèd words" came to be stored like things, to alphabetic manuscript culture, typographic culture, and beyond into our present trans-typographic electronic age. The classic, and invaluable, accounts of religious history have most of them been brought to a kind of head in the work of Mircea Eliade, who has shown quite beautifully the roots of religion in special attitudes to time and space, which have both sacred and secular moments or faces. This kind of study cannot be replaced, but it can be supplemented by another which sees religion in terms of man's relation to sound.

The relationship of man to man, of man to society, of man to his entire life-world, which includes his religious state, can be seen in new and refreshing detail if we attend to the history of the word itself, that is, to the history of communications. Only we must be clear that by communications we understand here not simply new gimmicks enabling man to "contact" his fellows but, more completely, the person's means of entering into the life and consciousness of others and thereby into his own life. Communications in this sense obviously relate to man's sense of his own presence to himself and to other men and to his sense of God's presence.

But the study of the word is a complex matter. In our own day the word takes on a seemingly limitless number of new forms. Long given visual extension by writing and print, it is now given artificial oral–aural public presence through the electronic media of radio and tapes and loudspeakers. It is projected on television with special visual accompaniment, not only dancing men but also dancing cigarettes and bars of soap, such as could not be realized without this or other spatial media. It is towed visibly through the skies behind aircraft and bounced invisibly off satellites.

In this milieu the question of man's relation to the word of God or to the bearing of the term "word" becomes of crucial importance. Could the cry of Nietzsche's madman, "God is dead," derive from the fact that He cannot be readily found by the old signs in the newly organized sensorium where the word stands in such different relationship to the total complex of awarenesses by which man earlier situated himself in his life world? Could the late Martin Buber's more sensitive suggestion that this is an age in which God is "silent" reflect the same state of affairs? Could it be that God is not silent but that man is relatively deaf, his sensorium adjusted to the post-Newtonian silent universe?

If so, the situation is not hopeless. If we have moved far from the original culture in which the word acquired its basic meaning, yet we still do use the word, we still talk. How much is the word the same and how much different? To understand ourselves and the religious question as it exists in the modern world, we have somehow to understand man's past in which the word existed in a sensorium by now grown utterly strange to us. What was the word like to men of old, more particularly to men before the word was put into writing? The past is, after all, ourselves, and it is our future. Our possibilities themselves are what they are because of what we have been.

2

Transformations of the Word

THE STAGES OF THE WORD

Over the past few decades, as indicated earlier, it has become evident that, in terms of communications media, cultures can be divided conveniently and informatively into three successive stages: (1) oral or oral–aural (2) script, which reaches critical breakthroughs with the invention first of the alphabet and then later of alphabetic movable type, and (3) electronic. If these stages do not have to do exclusively with verbal communication, since at certain points in the evolution of the media nonverbal visual devices such as diagrams and illustrations increase in use and effectiveness, and if much else can be said about verbal communication outside this framework, nevertheless these three stages are essentially stages of verbalization. Above all, they mark transformations of the word.

Awareness of the succession of the media stages and wonder about the meaning of this succession are themselves the product of the succession. We have come into this awareness only as we have entered the electronic stage. I do not mean by this simply that we have become aware of how different the electronic stage is only as we have entered into it. This would be only a truism. I mean much more: only as we have entered the electronic stage has man become aware of the profundity of differences, some of which have been before his eyes for thousands of years, namely, the differences between the old oral culture and the culture initiated with writing and matured with alphabetic type. Apparently it is impossible for man to understand the psychological and cultural significance of writing and print and of oral expression itself, with which writing and print contrast, until he had moved beyond print into our present age of telephonic and wireless electronic communication. As late as the 1930s, when the Chadwicks were completing their monumental work on the origins of literature from oral performance, which they called *The Growth of Literature,* the differences between speech and writing were still impossibly occluded for even the most astute scholars. Work such as that of Milman Parry on survivals of sophisticated oral culture in Yugoslavia was beginning to effect a breakthrough, which was made decisive chiefly by the studies published by Lord and Havelock in the 1960s (these reported and built on work initiated by Parry and went beyond it). The result is that our entire understanding of classical culture now has to be revised—and with it our understanding of later cultures up to our own time—in terms of our new awareness of the role of the media in structuring the human psyche and civilization itself.

Our new sensitivity to the media has brought with it a growing sense of the word as word, which is to say of the word as sound. As yet, however, this sense is not very well worked out. Where it exists at all, our understanding of the word as sound is often more felt than articulated, or more implied than explained. It will be our business here to reflect on the sequence of the media with particular attention to the fact that the word is originally, and in the last analysis irretrievably, a sound phenomenon. Such reflection should lead to a deeper understanding of what the word as word is, and thus of what human life is, and in the light of our earlier suggestions here, of what some relationships of man to God are.

For present-day man the word is intimately associated with writing and thus with visually accessible permanence. In his *Modes of Thought* (p. 52), Whitehead has made the point that we habitually mingle speech and writing so much that when we discuss language we hardly know whether we refer to oral performance or to written work or both. The situation is in fact much worse than Whitehead suggests. We are the most abject prisoners of the literate culture in which we have matured. Even with the greatest effort, contemporary man finds it exceedingly difficult, and in many instances quite impossible, to sense what the spoken word actually is. He feels it as a modification of something which normally is or ought to be written.

We tend, for example, to think of early oral cultures before the invention of script as simply illiterate or pre-literate, that is, as cultures without writing or before writing. How much do we say when we thus define cultures in terms of things which we have and they do not? For hundreds of thousands of years such cultures had existed without anyone's thinking even of the possibility of script. To think of them in terms of their relationship to script is the equivalent of working out the biology of a horse in terms of what goes on in an automobile factory.

It is of course legitimate and informative to point out what in another culture is different from ours, but this is precisely what we often fail to do in treating of oral cultures. There are not a few scholars who still speak and write of "oral literature," as though oral epic, for example, performed by singers who had never heard of

writing as even a possibility, were something that should
have been written down but somehow was not. A glance
through the "Comments" in *Current Anthropology, 4*
(1963), 273–92, shows how widespread the term oral literature is among both anthropologists and folklorists.
Even in the great work of H. Munro Chadwick and N.
Kershaw Chadwick just referred to, *The Growth of Literature (1, 5)*, the authors state that they use literature to
include what never was and never will be written, because "there is no other term available, apart from cumbrous circumlocution." The difficulty is that cumbrous
circumlocution often signals an inadequate or malformed
concept. Book titles themselves can display such concepts,
as in Melville Jacobs' fine study of Clackamas Chinook
myths and tales published in 1959, entitled *The Content
and Style of an Oral Literature.*

The problem has comic dimensions at times. I recall an
incident in St. Louis in 1964 when I heard a professional
American folk-ballad singer introduce a Caribbean ballad by explaining to his audience that the ballad was *not*
a literary ballad, that is, it had not come into existence
first on paper, from which it was subsequently sung, but
instead was "written [sic!] by the author while he was
first singing it to his audience." Even while explicitly denying the ballad's connection with writing, our literate
twentieth-century American singer could find no way of
conceiving of oral composition except as a variety of writing—nonwritten writing. His balladeer as he described
him was certainly one of the busiest men in history:
strumming his instrument or instruments, making up the
ballad, singing it, and, without slowing down his playing
or singing, writing it out at full tilt, all at the same time.

This kind of cultural squint shows how the communications media of our own culture impose themselves on us

surreptitiously as absolutes, with crippling effect. For centuries the inability of literate thinkers to conceive meaningfully of what the spoken word actually is has blocked our fuller understanding not only of epic and ballad but of the massive rhetorical tradition which underlies Western culture, of many political and social institutions (in the Carolingian Middle Ages much law was not what was written, but what the ruler *said orally,* the written documents being rather commentaries on the law, as Ganshof has shown). The same disability has interfered with our understanding of the nature of the Bible, with its massive oral underpinnings, and of the very nature of language itself.

We have been slow to note, although the linguistic experts remind us of it constantly now, that writing is a derivative of speech, not vice versa, and that speech in its original state has nothing at all to do with writing. Indeed, as will be seen, much truly oral performance such as epic not only arises with no reference to writing but seemingly cannot be performed in a way true to its original if the performer so much as knows how to write. For certain uses of language, literacy is not only irrelevant but is a positive hindrance.

In view of these facts, it will not help to minimize our habitual obtuseness by saying that the term literature indeed did first mean what was written (*litera* means a letter of the alphabet) but that the meaning has long been extended to include oral performance. This precisely confirms our point, that our concept of oral performance has long been derived from our concept of literature despite the fact that in actuality it is literature which grows out of oral performance. A parallel, again, would be to refer to a horse never as a horse but always as a four-legged automobile without wheels.

In the past few years a fairly adequate set of concepts and terms has been coming into currency to get us through this impasse. We shall use them, speaking of oral performance when we mean verbalization which has no direct connection with writing, and referring to early cultures before script as oral cultures or oral–aural (voice-and-ear) cultures. Of course, long after the invention of script and even of print, distinctively oral forms of thought and expression linger, competing with the forms introduced with script and print. Cultures in which this is the case can be referred to as radically oral, largely oral, residually oral, and so on through various degrees or admixtures of orality. Finally, we can use verbalization or artistic verbalization or skilled verbalization to refer to oral performance and writing conjointly or generically. In none of these cases are special definitions of these terms particularly called for. The terms will be used to mean what in context they seem to mean. They are worth mentioning here, however, because they are not so common as they should be.

FIRST STAGE:

THE UNRECORDED WORD—ORAL CULTURE

A basic difficulty in thinking about words today is our tendency to regard them largely or chiefly or ideally as records. We are inclined to think of words as records because we are inclined to think of them as, at their optimum, written out or printed. Once we can get over our chirographic–typographic squint here, we can see that the word in its original habitat of sound, which is still its native habitat, is not a record at all. The word is something that happens, an event in the world of sound through which the mind is enabled to relate actuality to itself. To understand more fully what this implies, we must examine in some detail what an oral–aural culture in general is like.

The differences between oral–aural culture and our own technological culture are of course so vast and so profound as to defy total itemization. We can here hope to touch only on some points relevant to our present interest in the word itself as sound.

Perhaps one of the most striking and informative differences is that an oral–aural culture is necessarily a culture with a relationship to time different from ours. It has no records. It does have memory, but this is not by any means the same as records, for the written record is not a remembrance but an aid to recall. It does not belong to us as memory does. It is an external thing.

In an oral–aural culture one can ask about something, but no one can look up anything. As a result, in an oral–aural culture there is no history in our modern sense of the term. The past is indeed present, as to a degree the past always is, but it is present in the speech and social institutions of the people, not in the more abstract forms in which modern history deals. In verbal accounts of the past in an oral–aural culture, the items that we should isolate as facts become inextricably entangled with myth —to be disentangled partially and with great difficulty perhaps only thousands or tens of thousands and even hundreds of thousands of years later, after the advent of writing develops our curious latter-day probes into preliterate ages.

There is no doubt that many oral–aural societies nourish among some of their members, and even to a degree among virtually all of them, memory skills which are beyond those cultivated in present-day technological cultures. Frances A. Yates shows in *The Art of Memory* the gargantuan mnemonic apparatus originating in the mists

of antiquity and built into all Western culture, from
rhetoric to the layout of buildings. Albert B. Lord's book,
The Singer of Tales, building on massive studies of Yugo-
slavian epic singers by Lord himself, Milman Parry, and
others, explains (pp. 26–29, 98, etc.) how, after listening
to it only once, a trained singer can repeat from memory
an epic of hundreds of lines even though he had never
heard the particular epic at all before. But it is a mistake
to think that such a skilled singer memorizes or repeats
the way persons using texts do, or even the way many of
those studied by Miss Yates might do. His memory, so far
as we can find, is never verbatim. In the thousands of recordings which Parry and Lord and their associates have
on hand, they find that never is an epic sung by either the
same singer or by different singers in exactly the same
words, even though the singers themselves may protest
vehemently that they do sing in the same words. The conservation of incident and narrative structure is nevertheless surprising—the general story varies little from one
telling to another. But the words always do.

The opposite impression is created among literate
listeners and even scholars by the fact that the epic in
question is sung in highly structured verse. Most persons
who can recite verse orally in our literate, technological
society have learned what verse they recite by rote study
of a text. The illiterate oral epic singer has no text and no
need for a text; if he had one, he could not read it. If he
is in a purely oral–aural culture, no one he knows has
ever used a text. His memory is thematic and formulaic,
and his formulas are prefabricated metrical units.

All epics are structured of certain themes—the sum-
moning of the council, the arming of the hero, the description of the hero's mount, the messenger, the challenge, the journey, the battle between heroes, the ban-

quet, and so on. The number of themes is vast, but finite, and each epic singer has his own massive store of them which he can weave together with ease. Moreover, he has an even more massive store of thousands of often repeated formulas (such as Homer's "rosy-fingered dawn" or "wine-dark sea") or formula-like elements not exactly the same but virtually so ("roan-red steed," "coal-black steed," "snow-white mount," "steel-gray mare"), all of which are metrically manageable. That is to say, as anyone who speaks a language has a vocabulary of words, the oral–aural singer has a vocabulary of metrical phrases, fragments of verse, a huge store of verbal equipment prefabricated to fit into his verse structure, and often slightly malleable ("steel-gray steed," "steel-gray stallion") so that the fragments can fit into the meter in various ways. Hearing a new story, he does not try to memorize it by rote. He digests it in terms of its themes (Lord reports that a singer asked to sing a story he has heard only once often prefers to wait a few days before performing), which are essentially the themes of all the singers in his tradition. He then verbalizes it in the formulas or formulaic elements he has in stock, which are also essentially those of the other poets in his tradition except that each individual poet will have his own particular twists and turns of style, his own oral–aural "signatures" which mark his performance as his own. Oral singers are likely to favor striking visual imagery, Eric Havelock explains in his *Preface to Plato* (p. 188), not merely because these are aesthetically pleasing but also because they serve as storage and recall devices—the ocular equivalents of verbal formulas.

Once texts are in use, this economy of memorization changes, and most particularly for verse. Lord has shown this clearly in *The Singer of Tales*. In *The Art of Memory*

Miss Yates reports (p. 15) that the memory systems deriving from classical antiquity make something of verbatim memory (memory of words) chiefly for retention
of poems and plays, which by that time consist in texts.
When concerned with the proper business of the orator, preparing or delivering a speech, these same systems
(pp. 9, 11, 18, etc.) minimize verbatim memory in favor
of thematic memory (memory of things). That is to say,
orators (for the memory systems are for them, not for
poets as such any more) favor properly oral techniques in
their own oratorical medium.

The fantastically organized memory systems explicated by Miss Yates deal with knowledge in a still highly
oral framework insofar as they imply that knowledge is
unrecorded and thus must be memorized even at exhausting cost to assure accessibility. They also make use of the
striking visual symbols fostered by epic poetry as just
mentioned, but they develop these by calculating iconographic elaboration, freighting images of gods and god-
desses, signs of the zodiac, and so on with the most bizarre
associations in fantastically organized detail. They also
arrange these figures in carefully contrived spatial patterns, often distributing them imaginatively around the
interior of a specific building. These memory systems are
intermediate between the oral and the chirographic–
typographic, presupposing that knowledge is something
necessarily to be memorized in full detail for instant recall (oral attitude) but also implementing memorization
with a "scientific" systematization of data which is quite
impossible without writing. They are a part of rhetoric,
which as a reflectively organized technique is the product
of a literate culture dealing with still urgent problems of
oral performance: neither Raymond Lull's *Ars Magna*
nor Aristotle's *Art of Rhetoric* could come into being

without writing. The fact that the memory systems favor verbatim memory for verse and thematic memory for oratory shows that these two great prechirographic verbal art forms relate somewhat differently to writing once this has made its appearance. Verse grows more directly dependent on writing than oratory does, probably because verse is the sort of thing that invites exact repetition more than does an oration. Writing expedites repetition for the many who have not mastered the extraordinary skills of the oral epic singer. But in implementing repetition for those without such skills, writing also changes the basic nature of repetition from the thematic to the verbatim.

Thematic and formulaic memory had of course affected much more than the epic. Havelock, in *Preface to Plato* (pp. 93–94, 139 and passim) has shown that in the completely oral culture of the early Greeks the ability to compose mnemonically in terms of themes and formulas was not a prerogative of professional singers. The professional singer simply exercised superlatively a skill which normally all persons in important positions of leadership were obliged to some extent to have mastered. If a military or civil official in an oral–aural culture wants to send a fairly complicated message, he is going to find it very serviceable to cast the message in some sort of mnemonic scheme which will keep it intact in his messenger's mind. Otherwise the message may not arrive. The practice in residually oral cultures of measuring the suitability of civil servants by demanding that they recite passages of standard verbalization (Homer or the Koran or Confucius) is not so cavalier as it appears to technological man. Pretechnological cultures, all relatively oral, need memorizers and reciters in strategic administrative positions. What information is kept alive in such cultures is largely dependent on mnemonic formulas such as those that have survived only sporadically in our society: "Thirty days have September,/ April, June, and November./" and so on. Such mnemonics were a regular part of formal education through the Middle Ages and the Renaissance, and, indeed, much later. Today, with incomparably more massive and efficient extramental storage arrangements, such as computers, we hardly need to know by heart even the arithemetic tables.

In a culture dependent on mnemonic techniques for its verbalized, intellectualized contact with its past and thus with itself, a poet like Homer serves not merely as an entertainer or even as a recaller but also as a repeater. If the poets were not at large, saying things over and over again, much of the knowledge in an oral–aural culture would evaporate. Homer was truly a textbook as well as an encyclopedia for his age. In prealphabetic Greece the closest thing to a manual on shipbuilding, for example, appears to have been in the songs of bards. The craft of shipbuilding, learned by apprenticeship, was not directly associated with much verbalization at all. Although craftsmen could build ships and did, we have no evidence that anyone could actually verbalize directions for shipbuilding or descriptions of ship structures more informative than the *obiter dicta* on these subjects in the *Iliad* and the *Odyssey*. Few plumbers, even highly literate ones, can write a manual on plumbing, even today, when models for manuals exist. There were of course no manuals in an oral–aural culture, and in a literate culture even as late and as practically oriented as that of Roman antiquity, descriptions of processes are very few and never very manual-like. Cato the Censor, Varro, and Columella on agriculture, Frontinus' work on aqueducts and his and Polyaenus' remarkably apothegmatic and anecdotal works on military strategems, Vitruvius on architecture, and a bit on military engineering—such are the typical works antiquity yields, often half philosophical or literary in preoccupation, socially oriented, and much concerned with conflicting opinions, rather than radically factual. Close to the oral tradition of formulaic codification of knowledge, Calumella does the tenth book of his *De re rustica* in verse and uses Virgil's versified *Georgics* as a major authority. Polyaenus shows clearly the nonobjective, virtue–vice tow of the old oral culture working against literacy in classical times by the way he wanders off from military matters to expatiate on the human qualities of valor and wisdom. Vitruvius is one of the most objective and technical, but the absence of a widespread tradition for this sort of writing has made his descriptions at times mystifying, both to Renaissance artists who tried to recreate some of the structures he described and to modern editors. The Middle Ages were somewhat more manual-minded, for they were technologically more advanced than antiquity, but the crafts were hardly put into manual form. A typical manual-like medieval production is Chaucer's *Treatise on the Astrolabe,* adapted from the work of the eighth-century Arab Messahala, strongly mathematical and academic rather than banausic in bent and appeal. Manuals would become fully objective and truly useful to tradesmen and artisans chiefly after the invention of typography. As Havelock has exhaustively shown, in prealphabetic Greece, epic poets were the closest thing to manualists the culture could produce and about the closest thing to abstract thinkers as well.

The fact that Homer's and other poets' seemingly pedestrian functions of storing, recalling, and reciting knowledge were performed in an atmosphere of relaxation and celebration—the singing of the epic—should not surprise us. In an oral culture, verbalized learning takes place quite normally in an atmosphere of celebration or play. As events, words are more celebrations and less tools than in literate cultures. Only with the invention of writing and the isolation of the individual from the tribe will verbal learning and understanding itself become "work" as distinct from play, and the pleasure principle be downgraded as a principle of verbalized cultural continuity. As Freud well knew, such hardships must be endured if civilization is to advance.

In an oral culture the mnemonic procedures which we today ordinarily associate with verse are not only part of ordinary extrapoetic verbalization but actually determine thought structures as well. Havelock has shown this for ancient Greek culture. There is ample evidence elsewhere—for example, in both the Old Testament and the New. The Beatitudes, like the Psalms and so much else in the Bible, are obviously mnemonically structured thought: "Blessed are the poor in spirit/ for theirs is the kingdom of heaven. Blessed are the meek/ for they shall possess the land." This is the nicely balanced symmetry which Père Marcel Jousse has throughout his works connected with the bilateral symmetry of the human body and with kinesthesia, and has shown is typical of "verbomotor" cultures. Such balanced structures are designed to be retained by being recited while one rocks back and forth, at least in imagination, as the Koran is retained in still highly oral Arab societies.

This economy of storage, moreover, demands that orally conditioned knowledge be relatively rigid or typical. Not only do formulas abound but characters themselves become types, not free-ranging and developmental as they can be in the novel, a product of print culture, but formalized. Odysseus is wily, Nestor is wise, Achilles is

brave. In *The Waning of the Middle Ages* (pp. 207–08)
Johan Huizinga notes how in the medieval mind "every
case, fictitious or historic, tends to crystallize, to become
a parable, an example . . . a standing instance of a general
moral truth. . . . Scripture, legends, history, literature
furnish a crowd of examples or of types." This is the oral
sensibility, still surviving in manuscript culture.

To say that he composed out of formulaic or typic elements is not to say that the epic poet had no occasion or
room for virtuosity. He had. A good epic poet (there were
certainly poor ones) was a man of tremendous skill, an
often dazzling performer. His virtuosity, however, lay
much less in creativity, the managing of new effects, than
in the extreme skill with which he performed with the
given tools of his craft. All epic poets used set formulas,
but a good epic poet could spin his formulas much better
than a poor one.

The formulary character of oral performance is responsible for the development of the doctrine of the commonplaces or *loci communes* which dominated skilled verbal
performance from oral–aural times until the maturing
of the romantic age. The *loci communes* were essentially
formulaic modes of expression derivative from oral practice and perpetuating oral psychological structures. They
were codified by the alphabetic but still highly oral–aural
ancient Greeks (Aristotle's *Rhetoric* indicates that the
Sophists made systematic use of them) and thereafter became a central part of Western culture. One could even
argue that they were in many ways *the* center of the culture. More will be said about them later in this chapter.

Formulaic expression places a high premium on memory, which literate cultures take to be at its maximum
when it is verbatim. But is it possible for memory in a
purely oral–aural culture to be verbatim, rote memory?

Obviously, short expressions can be. We have, however, seemingly no clear-cut instances of absolutely verbatim memory for any lengthy passages in completely illiterate cultures. The nearly worldwide research by the Chadwicks in *The Growth of Literature* turns up not a single verifiable case of truly verbatim memory for extensive utterances, say of three or four hundred words, among completely nonscribal peoples. The Chadwicks were particularly on the alert for instances of communal recitation of entire texts—not merely refrains or snatches—in a purely oral–aural setting. In the spring of 1962, consulting with Mrs. Chadwick in Cambridge, England, I learned that even then, twenty-two years after she and her husband had seen through the press the last of the three volumes, she still had found no verifiable instance of such recitation. It appears obvious that, in a culture enjoying no contact at all with writing, the only way to be sure that memorization is verbatim would be to have several memorizers recite the same passage simultaneously.

When it does not imagine oral–aural memory as verbatim in the way literate memory can be, a highly literate culture tends to regard the state of oral–aural memory as more disadvantageous than it actually is. This is because a literate culture tends to overrate verbatim repetition or record. In literature cultures the illusion is widespread that if one has the exact words someone has uttered, one has by that very fact his exact meaning. This is not true. In the last analysis, all our interpretation of the most exact verbal records of the past is dependent not on writing but on vocal exchange in the present. We know the meaning of words which we look up in a dictionary because we can connect them, directly or deviously, with words which we actually use or hear others use in real exchanges of speech. The word as record depends for its meaning upon the continuous recurrence of the word as event. We tend to think otherwise because in our technological culture we can spin out in print endless skeins of arcane terminology at greater and greater distances from the vocal world on which their entire meaning ultimately depends. Highly mathematicized operations are carried on in terms which psychologically are light-years away from the ordinary speech in relation to which mathematics, too, has all its meaning.

An oral–aural culture has nothing to correspond to such verbalization. It can never get far away from the word as a vocalization, a happening. The expression of truth is felt as itself always an event. In this sense, the contact of an oral culture with truth, vague and evanescent though it may be by some literate standards, retains a reality which literate cultures achieve only reflexively and by dint of great conscious effort. For oral–aural man, utterance remains always of a piece with his life situation. It is never remote. Thus it provides a kind of raw, if circumscribed, contact with actuality and with truth, which literacy and even literature alone can never give and to achieve which literate cultures must rather desperately shore up with other new resources their more spatialized verbal structures.

These perspectives make it possible to see as never before the significance of Greek thought and particularly of Plato in the development of the human mind. For, as Eric Havelock has shown in his *Preface to Plato,* the Greek philosopher's thought is essentially the thought released by a rather thoroughly alphabetized culture taking issue with the thought of the old oral–aural world, newly superseded in Plato's day. Plato's banishment of the poets and his doctrine of ideas are two sides of the same coin. In banishing the poets from his *Republic,*

Plato was telling his compatriots that it was foolish to imagine that the intellectual needs of life in Greek society could still be met by memorizing Homer. Rather than deal in this verbalization, so much of a piece with the nonverbal life-world, one needed to ask more truly abstract questions. By mobilizing information in much greater quantity and detail than an oral culture could do, the alphabet has made abstract analysis possible as never before. Coming into use around 720–700 B.C., the Greek alphabet had at first simply created a new craft; one hired a scribe to write a document as one hired a mason to build a house. By Plato's day, some three centuries later, the Greeks had moved beyond this early craft literacy. Writing had finally become a general acquisition of the citizenry and was radically affecting the handling of knowledge and modes of conceptualization.

Under these circumstances a *paideia* or educational procedure which consisted in memorizing Homer was obsolete. Rather than devoting one's time to oral storage of knowledge organized in terms of the human life-world, one needed to face up to explicitly abstract questions. What is a couch? What is it that makes a couch a couch? What is the abstract idea of a couch?

In classic Hegelian thesis–antithesis fashion, Plato's ideas, the "really real," were polarized at the maximum distance from the old oral–aural human life-world. Spoken words are events, engaged in time and indeed in the present. Plato's ideas were the polar opposite: not events at all, but motionless "objective" existence, impersonal, and out of time. Forming the ultimate base of all knowledge, they implied that intellectual knowledge was like sight—despite Plato's well-known protests, discussed here later, in favor of the spoken word in his Seventh Letter and in the *Phaedrus* (274). Basically, the

Greek word *idea* means the look of a thing. It comes from the same root as the Latin *video* (I see), which yields the English "vision" and its cognates. The ideas were thus in a covert sense like abstract pictures, even though other things were only pictures or "shadows" of them.

In the older oral–aural society, encyclopedism had had to be a matter of poetry, combined with the other great oral–aural speech form, oratory, which in turn was largely poetic, as poetry was largely oratorical. For Plato, this world was gone. Like his master Socrates, in hitting out against the Sophists he hit out also against the other great oral form, oratory. Of course, these perspectives explain the Greek achievement only to a degree. There remains the question why, of all the alphabetized peoples, it was the Greeks who first reacted this way to the new structures, social and psychological, which the alphabet had brought about.

SECOND STAGE: THE DENATURED WORD— ALPHABET AND PRINT

The route to the alphabet had been long and devious. An oral–aural culture can take a variety of steps toward writing: stone monuments, totem designs, property marks, various primitive types of pictography, and so on. These and similar steps, insofar as they are not merely magical, serve as aide-mémoires. They encode little. The information storage remains almost entirely in the heads of those who use such creations, which are much more triggers than storage devices. This can be seen in one of the more intriguing aide-mémoires, the Inca quipu, a stick with suspended leather thongs which could be knotted at intervals with other leather strips of various colors to record information, for example, about the stores of maize in a granary. What was recorded was actually minimal. For different quipus the Incas had to have separate quipu-keepers to remember and explain to others what this particular quipu meant.

True scripts go beyond the earlier aide-mémoire devices. A script is an organized system of writing, not an assortment of more or less isolated signs, and a system which in one way or another undertakes rather to represent concepts themselves directly than merely to picture sensible objects around which concepts may play. We of course do not know when man first began to draw pictures; origins here reach far back into prehistory. And it is not always easy to say exactly when the borderline from primitive pictorial representation to a true script is crossed. But we do know that true scripts came late in man's existence, appearing first among urban Neolithic populations. The approximate dates of appearance (B.C.) are, to use Diringer's figures in *Writing* (pp. 35–119): cuneiform scripts among the Sumerians around 3500, Egyptian hieroglyphics around 3000, Minoan pictographs around 2000, Minoan (Mycenean) "Linear B" script around 1200, Indus Valley script around 3000 to 2400, and Chinese script around 1500, which was about the time when, in the Eastern Mediterranean region, the alphabet itself was developed. The Mayan script of the New World came into being only around A.D. 50 and the Aztec around A.D. 1400. If man has been on earth some 500,000 years, script of any sort is thus quite a new experience for him.

Pictures can be used as the basis of a true script and in fact many different picture-based scripts have come into being independently of one another. Picture writing, however, has limitations: as such it is not directly representative of words themselves for it does not directly represent sounds. The same picture of a bird will draw forth

any number of different words from various speakers—
pájaro, oiseau, Vogel, bird, and so on indefinitely, dependent on the language or languages familiar to the
individual speaker. Even when it becomes so supremely
sophisticated as Chinese character writing, picture writing does not at root work from words as sounds. Thus
Chinese characters, which basically are pictures, are used
not only for different Chinese dialects (really different
languages) but are also used by Japanese (in conjunction
with their syllabary) and in less abundance by Koreans
(in conjunction with their alphabet) to express words in
their own languages which have no more phonetic relationship to Chinese than English words have.

Some picture scripts in some languages develop special
orientations toward sounds as sounds, devious and cumbersome by comparison with the alphabet. In a language,
for example, like Chinese, which has many homonyms,
a given character originally picturing one object can be
used for another object with a homonymic name (as in
English one might use a picture of a sole of a foot also for
"sole" meaning the fish, "sole" meaning alone, and "soul"
as against body). Pictograms used in this primitively
phoneticized way are known as phonograms. Like Mesopotamian cuneiform (also basically pictographic), Chinese character writing has developed also a system of
determinatives or radicals, that is, special characters to
distinguish the various senses in such homonymic use of
characters (as in English one might place a picture of dry
land alongside a picture of the sole of the foot to indicate
that in this instance the sole referred to was simply the
sole of the foot itself, or a picture of water alongside the
picture of the sole of a foot to indicate that this meant
the fish, a picture of an isolated human figure alongside
to indicate that here the symbol meant alone, or a picture

of the sky to indicate that the soul as against the body was being referred to, and so on). In a sense homonymic characters thus manipulated come to represent sounds. But they do so incidentally, remaining essentially pictures which have become puns. Writing systems such as the Chinese are filled with many other elaborate and often unexpected ideological or phonemic ties between various characters so that the writing itself as writing develops a life of its own different from speech, becoming imaginatively supercharged to a degree totally unfamiliar to users of the alphabet. When you can draw a picture of "however" or "nevertheless," you are working pictography very hard indeed.

Alphabetization of language is quite a different thing from picture writing or character writing even of this hypersophisticated sort. The alphabet is related to picture writing, from which it is doubtless derivative, and forms intermediate between pictures and the alphabet occur, such as syllabaries. But syllabaries are of limited serviceability, are more effective in some kinds of languages than others, and call for unhandy quantities of signs. The alphabet is a more efficient and frugal code.

It is also a code which was very hard to hit on. In fact, the alphabet was so hard to discover that it was invented only once or, just possibly, twice in quick succession in almost the same place. This is perhaps the most striking feature about the alphabet, although certainly the next most striking feature is the small number of scholars, even in the fields of language or literature, who are aware of this entirely incontestable and uncontested fact. With the possible exception of the Ethiopian and the few scripts related to it, every alphabet known ever to have been in use—Hebrew, Greek, Roman, Cyrillic, Sanskrit, Tamil, Arabic, Korean, and the rest—is derivative from the linear alphabet which was known, however it may have been invented, among the North Semitic peoples by around 1500 B.C.

The possible exception is not much of an exception at all. Diringer suggests in *Writing* (pp. 121–22) that the South Semitic alphabet, from which a few and only a few present-day scripts are derived (the Ethiopic alphabet and its descendants Amharic, Tigré, Tigriñya, and other alphabets of modern Ethiopia) may have been developed independently of the North Semitic, from which all other alphabetic writing descends. But the contiguity in time (around 1500 B.C. for North Semitic, 1000 B.C. or earlier for South Semitic) and the similarity of languages involved would seem to make it impossible to consider the South Semitic a totally independent development. The idea of the alphabet can be borrowed without borrowing or adapting the existent alphabetic symbols, although it is usual to borrow or adapt the symbols, too. One can see, for example, the relationship between the forms of the Hebrew aleph, the Greek alpha, the Roman letter A, and the Russian letter A. But in the case of the Ugaritic cuneiform alphabet, discovered in 1929 at Ugarit in Mesopotamia and also discussed by Diringer (pp. 115–16), we have letters which were designed by some person or persons who knew the North Semitic alphabet but who formed only six of the letters to resemble this alphabet, apparently designing the others under the influence of other sign systems and always with a view to their serviceability for writing with a stylus on wet clay. The oghamic script of the Celtic population of the British Isles is a comparable alphabet, more or less arbitrarily designed with a view to its serviceability for use on a particular medium (stone) but in conscious imitation of the idea, though not the letters, of an earlier alphabet.

By 1500 B.C. a good many populations were using scripts, and it does seem strange that only at one point (or virtually one point, if the South Semitic alphabet should prove to have some relative independence) the supreme system of sound writing was achieved. Diringer (p. 121) suggests that just possibly a single man may have invented the alphabet, demonstrating the same kind of individual genius shown later in Newton. But this appears quite unlikely, for oral cultures, as we shall see, hardly produce individual thinkers or inventors as do cultures where writing, and particularly the alphabet, has become deeply interiorized and given the individual relative independence of the tribe. In earlier cultures, highly oral even though they possessed one or another script, thought moved ahead in a communally structured glacier where individualized activity was quickly encysted if indeed it ever appeared. Whatever the case, we do not know and probably will never know the full story of how the alphabet came about. We can, however, know something about reasons for its tardy and nonce appearance if we reflect on the relationship of the alphabet to the spoken word and on the psychological distance between the spoken and the alphabetized medium. Such reflection throws much light on the nature of the oral medium itself.

Speech itself as sound is irrevocably committed to time. It leaves no discernible direct effect in space, where the letters of the alphabet have their existence. Words come into being through time and exist only so long as they are going out of existence. It is impossible, as Augustine notes in his *Confessions* (iv. 1) to have all of an utterance present to us at once, or even all of a word. When I pronounce "reflect," by the time I get to the "-flect" the "re-" is gone, and necessarily and irretrievably gone. A moving object in a visual field can be arrested. It is, however, impossible to arrest sound and have it still present. If I halt a sound it no longer makes any noise. I am left only with its opposite, silence.

Other sensory phenomena are of course also in time, but they do not have the built-in progression which sound has. Sight can follow motion through time but it seeks to fix its objects. To view something closely by sight, we wish to stop it for inspection, and we do so when we can, studying even motion itself, or so we pretend, in a series of still shots. Smell loses its sensitivity to odors protracted in time and thus can be weakened by time's progression and indeed typically is so weakened. Moreover, it lags in time. We cannot register a succession of different odors at the rate of five or six per second as we easily register sound in attending to speech. Taste and touch linger within time rather than progressing through it. The necessary progression of sound through time appears to be one of its central properties, differentiating it from the objects of the other senses.

It is of course true that duration is involved in the subjective experience of all the senses. When I taste something and discover it to be salty, the taste itself persists for a discernible period. Moreover, we know from scientific studies that all sensation is process, that in all sensation there is actually something going on outside the organism and within—the movement which we call light "waves" for sight, chemical reactions for taste and smell, molecular movements for the feeling of heat, and so on. But in the case of senses other than hearing, we know that something is going on from scientific study, not directly from the sensation. None of the other senses gives us the insistent impression that what it registers is something necessarily progressing through time. Hearing does. Sound is psychologically always something going on, something active, a kind of evanescent effluvium which exists only so long as something or someone is actively producing it. Sound implies movement and thus implies change. Elementary reflection, such as that caught in folklore and proverbs, notes this fact about sound: *verba volant, scripta manent*—words fly away, what is written stays put.

A later chapter will discuss how this same progression through time makes the oral–aural world more than the world of the other senses immediately exploitable in connection with our mental processes, how these processes themselves are not only registered by sensible words but are set in motion by flows of sensible words, and how intellectual activity appears to have an immediate affinity with the auditory which it does not have with visual, olfactory, gustatory, or tactile activity. For the moment, we shall note only that the economy of a world of sound is violently disrupted by the alphabet.

Operations with the alphabet imply that words—not the things which words refer to, but words themselves as sounds—can somehow be present all at once, that they can be somehow dissected into little spatial parts called letters of the alphabet which are independent of the one-directional flow of time and which can be handled and reassembled independently of this flow.

The world of words which results from this alphabetic fiction is quite different from the sound world. It is possible in it to reverse letters in ways in which it is impossible to reverse sound. Thus I can write the letters in the word "over" from right to left, putting down the r first, and nevertheless pronounce the resulting inscription to yield the sound "over." Or I can reverse the letters in "pot" to yield "top." There is no equivalent for this in the world of sound. Even if I pronounce the word pot on

a recording tape or disk and then reverse the tape or disk,
I do not get "top" but simply a different sound. I have,
in fact, not reversed the sound, but only the tape, a
mechanism producing sound. There is quite simply no
way to reverse a sound. I can, of course, reverse the sequence of two different sounds—oooh-aaah to aaah-oooh.
This reversal of the temporal sequence, of the order of
production of two sounds, however, is not a reversal within sound. One might think of registering the oscillographic pattern of a sound and then of producing a sound
which would in turn register in an exactly reversed oscillographic pattern. Again, this is a reversed sound simply
in the sense that it results in a reversed spatial pattern. A
person apprehending such a "reversed" sound would
not necessarily experience it as a reversal of the original
sound it matched.

The difficulty here is that the concept of reversal itself
is taken from the spatial field and that we apply it to sound
insofar as sound can be represented or fictionalized in a
spatial field. In other words, we cannot find a meaning for
"reversing" sound unless we first reprocess sound spatially, as on a chart or oscillograph or disk or tape. But the
diagram on the spatial field or the print on the disk or
tape is precisely not sound. It makes no noise.

Sound cannot be reversed, because of the way in which,
as we have just seen, it rides in time. Time is entirely
irreversible. This fact enables science fiction to generate
some of its weird effects by pretending that time is reversed. The maneuver here is simple: one adopts a spatial
equivalent of time (perhaps more or less disguised, as in
The Time Machine of H. G. Wells), and one reverses (or
speeds up or slows down) the spatial equivalent, considering this operation to be an operation in time itself.
The pretense is convincing in our culture since we are

elsewhere so accustomed to spatializing time (on calendars, on the faces of clocks, in the countless expressions which bring us to speak of a long time or short time, instead of older or younger time, by analogy with long or short extensions in space, though time is actually not long or short). English, like modern Western languages generally, is impoverished in qualifiers derived directly from time, such as old and young or enduring or permanent. The Hopi Indians, Benjamin Whorf has explained in *Language, Thought, and Reality* (pp. 142–43, 146) do not think of today as a part or section of time as coming after another part or section of the time-mass designated yesterday. They do not picture today as "next" to yesterday (as on our calendars) but rather think of time in terms of its perpetual "getting later."

We are as accustomed to spatializing sound as we are to spatializing time. Our physics treats sound in terms of space, measuring it in waves and wave "lengths" and representing it by fascinating oscillographic patterns. Of course these measurements are necessary, exact, and even beautiful, and they most assuredly apply to sound and inform us about it. But they are not sound. Although something of what happens when a sound occurs can be thus represented, sound itself in its full existential actuality cannot. These representations in space suggest inevitably a quiescence and fixity which is unrealizable in actual sound. And of course, they make no noise, for noise comes only with direct involvement in time such as we have described, which measurement and spatial patterns do not entail. Strange though it seems to us, sound in its own actuality cannot be measured. Its reality eludes diagrammatic representation. This is a hard truth for technological man to accept: to him the measurements in space appear to be what is real in sound, though quite the opposite is true—the diagrams are unreal by comparison with sound as a psychological actuality.

Independence of this engagement with sound in time is achieved once one has the alphabet. This independence, moreover, is not merely a matter of permanence as against impermanence. Picture writing assures a kind of permanence, but a permanence like that of objects, not a permanence imputed to words. A picture of a bird, as we have seen, will call forth hundreds of different words— *Vogel, pájaro, oiseau, bird,* and so on—depending on the language of the viewer. Pictures do not deal with sound as such. Alphabetization does. The letter sequence in "bird" does not generate the same sounds as those in *Vogel, pájaro,* or *oiseau.* The alphabet irrupts into sound itself, where the one-directional flow of time asserts its full power, and it neutralizes this flow by substituting for sound immobile letters.

The sense of order and control which the alphabet thus imposes is overwhelming. Arrangement in space seemingly provides maximal symbols of order and control, probably because the concepts of order and control are themselves kinesthetically and visually grounded, formed chiefly out of sensory experience involved with space. When the alphabet commits the verbal and conceptual worlds, themselves already ordered superbly in their own right, to the quiescent and obedient order of space, it imputes to language and to thought an additional consistency of which preliterate persons have no inkling. Any script, even picture writing, gives some such sense of order, but no other does so in so radically simplified a fashion. It appears no accident that formal logic was invented in an alphabetic culture.

The order imposed by the alphabet remained generally convincing and satisfactory until the advent of modern linguistics, which is concerned primarily with speech in its primary state, as sound, and with writing as a special development subsequent to vocalization. Linguistics has made us agonizingly aware of the deficiencies of the alphabet, which proves to be like Newtonian physics: it works admirably until you get down to details, then it does not work very well at all. Modern linguists regard even the International Phonetic Alphabet as at best an approximation. The study of language today uses the alphabet, of course, but it relies heavily also on the tape recorder and other ways of dealing more directly with sound as such.

The alphabet is responsible for many illusions and delusions deriving from associations of meaning with a visual field. The most common are probably those generated around the term "literal meaning." This term frequently implies that meaning which is literal, or according to the letter, is necessarily trim and easily manageable. As philosophers and lexicographers well know, it is virtually impossible to assign to literal meaning a significance any more definite than the first or most obvious meaning of a passage as apprehended by one familiar with the language and context; this is what thoughtful definitions come to, from Aquinas (*Summa Theologica*, I, 1, 10, c.) to *Webster's Third New International Dictionary*. Aquinas points out that just because a meaning is literal it is not necessarily simple but can be manifold. Often in discourse the first or most obvious meaning is quite complex or even more or less purposefully occluded. The fixity of space, however, and the possibility of segmentation suggested by "literal," continues to foster the contrary impression, namely that literal meanings, meanings according to the letter, are all fixed and neatly segmental too. Since letters are so clear and distinct, literal meaning must be the same. But a complex and polysemous utterance is no clearer when it is written down, nor is its meaning any simpler. We are surer that we can recover it word for word. That is all. But word for word, it may convey only a very obscure sense.

An alphabetic culture, which puts a premium on visualist qualities such as sharp outline and clear-cut sequence, is likely to regard the literal meaning, in the sense of plain or definite meaning, as something altogether wholesome and altogether desirable, and to regard other remote, perhaps more profoundly symbolic, meanings with disfavor. Augustine, closer to an oral culture, felt quite otherwise in *The City of God* (XIII, xxi) and elsewhere. To him the literal meaning was all right, but far less interesting and far less important than the profound resonances in the symbolism, the more remote implications. In Chinese, where literal meaning is ordinarily not conceived of, since the writing system provides no *literae* or letters on which the concept literal can be built, the roughly equivalent concepts are "according to the surface of the word," "according to each word in each utterance," "according to the dead character." These are hardly laudatory expressions. Here too in a chirographic but analphabetic culture, the first or most accessible meaning appears in an at least vaguely depreciatory light. The rich suggestiveness of Chinese characters favors a sense of a fuller meaning lying much deeper than the literal.

The spatialization of sound initiated with the development of the alphabet was reinforced and intensified by the typographical developments in fifteenth-century Western Europe commonly referred to as the invention of printing. What was crucial for this ultimate locking of sound in space was the invention of movable alphabetic type cast from matrices which had been made with punches. When this development was matured it entailed a large number of steps in fixed sequence. One started by cutting punches in a hard metal (iron or steel), one for each letter of the alphabet, with the letter raised on the end of the punch as a letter is on a typewriter key. These punches were struck into pieces of softer metal to form matrices (that is, if we translate this Latin word, "wombs"). Still softer metal, molten, an alloy of lead, was then brought into contact with the matrices to cast types, which were made in large quantities for each letter. A font (that is, a pouring) of these types was stored in a case, a large tray with box-like compartments, one for each letter. The typesetter took his copy to the case and set type on a composing stick (a small tray-like holder), later transferring it to a galley (a larger tray), proving it and correcting the proof sheets and subsequently the type in the galley. The type was moved onto the composing stone with other type from other galleys and locked in a form or chase. This chase was transferred to a press into which it itself was further locked. After makeready, the type was inked, the inking apparatus (originally daubers, later rollers) moved aside, paper brought into contact with the locked-up type, the platen of the press squeezed down on the paper, the platen then removed, and the printed sheet taken off the type. Some twelve to sixteen steps, dependent on how one figures the units, intervene here between the written word (already one remove from the spoken) and the printed sheet. All these steps are matters merely of local motion—the sort of processes that can be automated and are being more and more automated, producing newspaper strikes today. To perform them, knowledge of the language concerned is not necessary (although it is certainly helpful). The commitment of spoken words to space here in typography has a depth and intensity continuous with but far exceeding that achieved by alphabetic chirography.

Significantly, like the alphabet itself, printing from movable alphabetic type was a nonce invention. And even more than the alphabet, it was a tardy invention. All the individual component operations and materials necessary for the invention had in fact been known for centuries. Printing from dies and plates had been known from antiquity, and movable nonalphabetic type had been in use for some time. There was obviously some curious psychological block to the breakthrough to movable letters, as can be seen in some facts noted by Thomas Francis Carter in *The Invention of Printing in China and Its Spread Westward* (pp. 218, 228). By 1434 a book had been printed in movable type in the new Korean alphabet, but not in alphabetic type. It is in parallel columns of Chinese and Korean, and both appear joined on the same type: one Chinese character with its corresponding Korean phonetic symbols. Uigur Turks used both alphabetic writing and movable type, but word type, an unimaginative imitation of the Chinese system of movable character type. The breakthrough to full spatial maneuverability was not achieved, and thus the full potentiality of the alphabet was not realized. One might conjecture that this was because the alphabet was too new, at least in Korea and among the Uigur Turks, for its full implications to have worked themselves out in the consciousness. Letter-type printing developed only by spreading out from its one point of origin in fifteenth-century Western Europe.

The lodging of speech in space which culminated in the development of alphabetic typography was not an isolated phenomenon. It was, as the preceding chapter here mentioned in passing, part of a widespread reorganization of the sensorium favoring the visual in communication procedures, that is, favoring the visual in association with the use of words. We are not suggesting that typographic man used his eyes more than earlier man had. Even primitive man is highly visual in the sense that he is a keen observer, detecting all sorts of minute visual clues in his environment which civilized man misses. What happened with the emergence of alphabetic typography was not that man discovered the use of his eyes but that he began to link visual perception to verbalization to a degree previously unknown. The revolution which ensued has often been clumsily accounted for either as a movement from deduction to induction or as a movement from an authoritarian attitude concerning knowledge toward an observational attitude. Both these accounts probably occlude at least as much as they explain. For, apart from the fact that many of the historical data simply do not fit this description, the account has difficulty in saying why the change took place. Often resort is had to a conspiratorial theory of intellectual history: until the mind was "liberated," certain persons or groups of persons—churchmen, most likely, and possibly schoolteachers, or just ignorant people in general—imposed the deductive and authoritarian attitudes because this somehow or other served their purposes. We know that conspiratorial theories accounting for complex historical developments have their origin within the psyches of those who propose them rather than in verifiable fact.

It is much more informative to consider the state of affairs in the light of the organization of the sensorium of which we have been speaking. A great deal can be learned from examination of the relationship of pictorial illustration to the word and to communication in general.

In a manuscript culture, which has already committed the word to space but with relatively low intensity, very little exact information is deliberately communicated with the help of pictures, which, even when they contain exactly rendered representations of natural objects, tend to be decorative rather than informative in intent. In medieval manuscripts, illustrations do not generally demonstrate or clarify what is in the text but rather provide welcome distraction from the labor of reading. Medieval stained glass does convey some story-type and iconographic information, but it remains basically decorative, a far cry from the kind of information-bearing illustration which one finds in a post-typographic manual or, finally, in *La Grande encyclopédie* of Diderot and his associates, for which there is no equivalent and indeed no demand in a manuscript culture.

As the work of Lynn White, E. H. Gombrich, W. M. Ivins, and others makes clear, texts which verbally describe machines or processes, primitive though they may be, are steadier and more reliable and more viable than the explanatory illustrations which in a manuscript culture may occasionally accompany them. Technical illustrations are of course very difficult and expensive to reproduce by hand accurately and intelligently, even when concerned with such simple things as the difference between the leaves of white and yellow clover. In *Prints and Visual Communication* (pp. 14–16, 40–45, etc.), Ivins has shown the quick deterioration of significant detail inevitable when technical drawings are copied even by expert artists unfamiliar with the exact points being made in the illustration. Reproduced by a dozen draftsmen in succession from one another's drawings without reference to nature or supervision by a botanist, a sprig of white clover can end looking like a bunch of asparagus. Little wonder that the conveying of botanical information often becomes the mere listing of names of plants such as one finds from the ancient Greeks mentioned by Pliny down through Joannes Ravisius Textor's early printed Latin word book *Officina* (1520).

This problem is solved today by print. One painstakingly supervised design is made and then reproduced mechanically without variation. Strangely enough, this same solution, mass production of an illustration, had long been possible in manuscript cultures—in its essentials even from antiquity—for the printing of designs from various dies or blocks antedates Gutenberg by centuries. But, given the highly oral organization of the sensorium, the idea of using such processes to convey accurate information simply did not strike home. Communication was not much associated with the use of space, but rather with speech. When speech developed the massive commitment to space entailed in typography, the use of spatial design in conjunction with verbalization came into its own. Before the typographic reorganization of the sensorium, correlation between what was seen by the eye and verbalization remained by modern standards exceedingly low.

There is a kind of authoritarian set of mind here: one did tend to believe what one read in Aristotle or Pliny rather than what one saw. But this set of mind, as will be explained further below, is to a notable degree the correlative of an orally organized sensorium. What is effective here is not authority in the sense of commanding presence so much as it is the word itself. One prefers what is verbally reported to what is seen, correlating the two relatively slightly. "Everything we believe, we believe either through sight or through hearing," Ambrose of Milan notes in his *Commentary on St. Luke* (iv. 5). And, speaking out of the old oral tradition, he adds, "Sight is often deceived, hearing serves as guarantee."

The long-standing indifference to visual presentation of information is noted by Ivins, who points out in *Prints and Visual Communication* (p. 31), that the first "set of datable prints . . . that purported to be pictures of precisely identifiable and locatable objects" was issued only in 1467. The art of printing designs, it must be recalled, had been practiced for centuries before this. In *Art and Illusion* (pp. 68–69) Gombrich has called attention to a woodcut of a city by Dürer's teacher Wolgemut, which appears in Hartmann Schedel's so-called "Nuremberg Chronicle" four times as a picture of four different cities: Damascus, Ferrara, Milan, and Mantua. The illustration was not of a visually apprehended reality but of an orally processed one: it was a kind of visual commonplace on "the city" or "citiness." With typography, however, the change was under way, and what Ivins calls exactly repeatable visual statement—woodcuts and engravings which, like printed texts, could be reproduced without variation and which calculatingly provided circumstantial information—for the first time became a prime concern of thinkers and a means of learning inseparable from the development of the new post-Gutenberg science.

COMPLICATIONS AND OVERLAPPINGS

The movement through the sequence of media is of course not merely a matter of successive reorganizations of the sensorium. It involves a host of social, economic, psychological, and other factors. The first scripts arose because of the need for record keeping attendant on urbanization. In *The Hand-Produced Book,* Diringer notes (p. 56) that the earliest script served administrative purposes, not religious or literary. He reports (p. 80) D. J. Wiseman's observation that of the roughly 750,000 Mesopotamian cuneiform clay tablets known today, most deal with economic transactions. When the alphabet developed out of earlier scripts, it, too, at first served practical social and economic purposes almost exclusively. Its literary use came later. Modes of communication both result from social, economic, psychological and other changes and cause such changes. Thus the development of writing and print ultimately fostered the breakup of feudal societies and the rise of individualism. Writing and print created the isolated thinker, the man with the book, and downgraded the network of personal loyalties which oral cultures favor as matrices of communication and as principles of social unity. Though feudalism died slowly and from a variety of maladies, it was under serious threat from the time of the invention of script. Inevitably, record keeping enhanced the sense of individual as against communal property and the sense of individual rights. With printing, even words themselves could become property, as the principle of copyright came into being and was finally taken for granted.

In addition to being complicated on such scores, the movement through the sequence of the media is also complicated by the fact that the changes from one stage to the next are by no means abrupt. States of mind created by an earlier stage tend to persist stubbornly through the new stage in which they are in fact obsolete. Before going farther in our own account, it will be best to note here some of the complications and overlappings in the transition from oral communication to alphabet and print.

Oral–aural cultural institutions have been surprisingly tenacious. McLuhan has tended for this reason to assimilate scribal or manuscript culture to the oral rather than to typographical culture, a position tenable on some grounds but not very informative in our present concern with the word as word, as an event originally occurring in the universe of sound. We can, however, look briefly here at the continuity between oral and manuscript culture.

In antiquity the most literate cultures remained committed to the spoken word to a degree which appears to our more visually organized sensibilities somewhat incredible or even perverse. Living more than a millennium after the invention of the alphabet and in a culture which had used the alphabet for some three hundred years, the philosopher Socrates left none of his philosophy in writing. Despite the fact that Plato's philosophy, as we have seen, was the product of literacy, Plato was deeply and explicitly committed to the spoken word. He wrote down some of Socrates' teachings in a tight, pointed style far removed from oral modes, but he calculatingly used the dialogue form to give the teachings something like their original oral cast, protesting in his Seventh Letter that one cannot put what is really essential to wisdom in writing, for this is to falsify it, and noting in the *Phaedrus* (274) that writing serves merely recall, not memory or wisdom.

Aristotle, Plato's pupil, soon abandoned the dialogue form in which he also began, but it is quite wrong to think that the texts of Aristotle which we have are texts all written as an author today might write a book. Aristotle's *Metaphysics,* as Jaeger showed in his *Aristotle* (pp. 168 ff.), is a collection put together only after Aristotle's death under conditions that leave us puzzled as to what in it is Aristotle's own fresh writing, what his own accommodation of parts of his earlier works, and what adaptations of his earlier or later work by editors. The

Aristotelian writings are in great part school *logoi,* as Joseph Owens puts it in *The Doctrine of Being in the Aristotelian Metaphysics* (pp. 74–77), not "works" set down for an indeterminate and indeed fictional general public but observations directed to a specific group of followers. There is more real dialogue embedded in the *Metaphysics* than one might think. Perhaps it is not irrelevant that Aristotle and his school were called the Peripatetics, that is, the Walkers. Walking while philosophizing is hardly compatible with taking philosophy to be a textually based enterprise in the way that modern philosophers commonly do, including even an existentialist such as Karl Jaspers, who, in his reflections "On my Philosophy" (p. 135), considers a philosopher as necessarily a student of texts. Antiquity hardly had such an idea. In *The Ancient Greeks* M. I. Finley has pointed out how little, by our standards, the Greeks were addicted to reading even in the most literate and literary periods of their culture.

The ancient Romans, literate too, continued the Greeks' preference for the spoken word. To learn Greek philosophy, Cicero did not simply read Greek authors; he went to Greece to listen to Greek philosophers. Both from Sallust's history, *The Conspiracy of Catiline,* and from Quintilian's *Training in Oratory* (*Institutiones oratoriae*) as well as from Torsten Petersson's painstaking analysis in his *Cicero: A Biography,* we know that Cicero wrote his orations after he had given them—in the case of the Catilinarian orations, it appears, several years after.

In working up orations Cicero used writing, but only to a limited degree. Like other orators of antiquity generally, he carried in his mind a vast stock of commonplaces, in the sense of purple patches on set themes such as treachery, loyalty, honesty of character, decadence.

O tempora! O mores!—this piece which Cicero put down
in the Catilinarian orations he must have used elsewhere
any number of times. It was the "things-are-going-to-pot"
topos or "bit."

In an age when facts and statistics were less functional
than today because they were harder to come by, orations
consisted largely of such commonplace considerations,
only occasionally interspersed with matter peculiar to the
particular issue, after the fashion still followed—necessarily, not perversely or perfidiously—by political leaders
in oral cultures today. These commonplaces were got up
in part with the help of writing, at least Quintilian urged
this practice in his day. Cicero also took notes, we know,
during the trial or other procedures in which he was
participating, but when he stood up to speak it was without manuscript and without memorization in our sense
of the word.

Like epic song, a Ciceronian oration was not a rendition of a text, it was an oral performance. Though more
"logical" than poetry, it remained largely thematic and
formulaic, if we take the commonplaces as formulas. As
noted earlier, in *The Art of Memory* (pp. 9, 11, 18, etc.)
Frances Yates points out that classical rhetoric favored
not verbatim but thematic memorizing (memory of
things rather than of words). The oration was admired
not as a recitation but as an oral composition. Sophists
were scorned for providing their clients with speeches
written out in advance, and not simply because selling
speeches was venal but because speeches which were not
truly oral, a response to the living moment, were taken
to be insincere.

The oration and the epic were the two great verbal art
forms of oral and residually oral society in the West.
They deeply affected all verbalization in practice as in

theory. History itself was oral to a degree which to us appears weird: vast stretches in ancient historians are made up of speeches attributed to historical characters, and historians themselves, such as Livy, often wrote their histories in order to read them to little gatherings of auditors. Even lyric poetry was commonly described well through the Renaissance as a variety of rhetoric (that is, of the art of oratory).

Through antiquity and the Middle Ages, and much later, most written matter itself remained associated with the oral to a degree seldom appreciated today. In antiquity, reading was normally aloud, even when it was to oneself. In his *Confessions* (vi. 3), Augustine makes special note of the fact that when he once dropped in on Ambrose, Bishop of Milan, he found Ambrose reading to himself without making any sound. Augustine's note shows that silent private reading was not entirely unknown, but it also shows that it was certainly singular and deserving of comment. Studies by Francis P. Magoun, Robert P. Creed, Ronald A. Waldron, and others cited in Lord's *The Singer of Tales*, as well as additional studies such as those by Ruth Crosby and Jess B. Bessinger, have made it common knowledge today how profoundly oral were modes of composition and literary forms in the Middle Ages and have opened up the way for much further work. Indeed, the oral tradition projects itself well beyond the Middle Ages. Abraham Keller has made clear how Rabelais paces his anecdotes in the way an oral performer does and, more recently, I have attempted elsewhere to show how heavy an oral residue underlies Tudor literature.

Even academic education did not foster writing to the extent we would consider normal today. University instruction through the Middle Ages and the Renaissance retained a dominantly oral–aural bent. The schoolboy used writing to learn the Latin in which his schooling would all be conducted (even his Latin grammar for learning Latin was already in Latin). But once he was passed this stage, all further testing and performance was entirely oral. The student in the university proved his ability in logic, physics or natural philosophy, ethics, metaphysics, law, or medicine as well as in theology by disputation and possibly a final oral examination in a disputation-like form. There were no written papers, written exercises, or written examinations at all. Writing was used a great deal, but in connection with oral expression. All too often, despite efforts at reform, teaching a subject in the arts faculty consisted of no more than dictating to students who copied down what their masters had copied down before them and were now droning out, if they were better teachers, in improved form. And teachers committed to writing what they said in the lecture halls. But always, writing was subordinated to the oral: one esteemed it, István Hajnal shows in *L'Enseignement de l'écriture aux universités médiévales* (p. 64), for the reason that "one saw in it the proof of a solid oral formation." In this culture, Hajnal likewise points out, brief written notes were in much less common use than now. Writing was not taught for such offhand, rapid work: memorization served instead.

Little wonder that the art of structuring thought was taken to be dialectic, an art of discourse, rather than pure logic (although this latter was highly developed, too). Thought itself was felt to take place typically in an oral exchange. Aquinas organizes his *Summa theologica* in this tradition, presenting his material in what to typographical man is a roundabout, residually disputatious form, a kind of inside-out debate. He thinks of his matter as "questions," which he handles by giving, first, objections to his proposed solution, then the solution itself, and finally answers to the objections. He falls into this mode of presentation unself-consciously and without the need for elaborate theoretical justification. This world of dialectical exchange was the assumed natural habitat of thought through the Middle Ages. Only later would thought be taken typically to be something that went on silently, and perhaps even without words, which were thereupon taken to be clothing supplied to naked thought generated in the presumed privacy of one's own consciousness independently of any social context such as the very existence of a language signals.

Nevertheless, the Middle Ages were far more text-centered than antiquity had been. The Christian religion, which influenced so much in medieval culture, was profoundly scriptural even though oriented to the word as word. And medieval scholarly work, even in secular matters, was largely a recovery enterprise, necessarily concerned with texts directly or indirectly derivative from classical antiquity and themselves often commentaries on other texts, as the *Sentences* of Peter Lombard. The *scholae dictaminis* or secretarial schools were vital institutions for medieval intellectual, political, and economic life, as such schools had never been in classical antiquity. Under these circumstances, for medieval man reading became a status symbol much more than it had been in antiquity, as can be seen in the nickname which a famous twelfth-century rector of the University of Paris proudly bore—Petrus Comestor or, in English, Peter the Eater, understood by all to mean Peter the Eater of Books. Bookworms perhaps existed in classical antiquity, but they were not cultural heroes of the sort that Peter was and delighted in being.

The commonplaces and formulas of various sorts which

had been the stock in trade of ancient oral culture were still in use in the Middle Ages and through the Renaissance, but more and more they were garnered in and learned from written (and, later, printed) collections of *exempla* and other sententious material hundreds of times and perhaps thousands of times more extensive than such written collections had ever been in antiquity.

As Beryl Smalley has pointed out in her *English Friars and Antiquity in the Early Fourteenth Century* (pp. 37–38), the medieval sermon favored the use of writing, though it was itself clearly an oral genre. More than secular orations, which were normally fitted to a particular occasion, the sermon dealt with recurrent situations in life. For this reason it tended to exploit commonplaces even more than did the political oration in the tradition bequeathed from antiquity. The ancient political orator typically used commonplaces in infinitely varied configurations, determined by the occasion to which his address was shaped. The Christian preacher found himself often addressing himself to the same situation over and over again: the general human propensity to pride, covetousness, or lust. Thus, unlike the ordinary political oration shaped to a special set of circumstances, a whole sermon having to do with permanent human dispositions could often be used over and over again, as Chaucer's Pardoner well knew. Hence the motive to write out the sermon for oneself or others was increased. The Christian stress on preaching, oral though the genre was, thus curiously favored the growing emphasis on literacy.

The Renaissance fell heir both to the medieval preoccupation with texts and to its lingering predilection for oral performance. In terms of the presence of the word to man, the Renaissance is one of the most complex and even confused periods in cultural history, and by the same token perhaps the most interesting up to the present in the history of the word. An exacting devotion to the written text, a devotion which has been the seedbed of modern humanistic scholarship, struggled in the subconscious with commitment to rhetoric and to dialectic, symbolic of the old oral–aural frames of mind, and maintained the old oral–aural anxieties and a sense of social structure built to a degree intolerable today on personal loyalties rather than on objectification of issues. Humanist rhetoric as such was opposed to scholastic dialectic, and yet both belonged to the oral–aural culture which typography was destined to transmute.

The relationship of rhetoric to both the spoken and the written word was as insistent as it was confused. The humanists' ideal of *copia* (free flow, fluency, abundance) in speech was rooted in oral performance, not in written: the oral performer fears having to pause while composing, the writer need have no such fear. Humanists implemented the achievement of *copia* by cultivating the commonplaces, which are a residue of oral culture, as will be seen (pp. 79–87) below. Letter-writing manuals in the Renaissance tradition, such as those of William Fullwood (1595) or Angel Day (1595), frequently impose on letters the organization of an oration: exordium or introduction, statement of matter to be proved, proof, refutation of adversaries, and peroration or conclusion. The humanists' emphasis on epithets and other formulas is clearly derivative from oral performance. Commonplaces, devices primarily for oral performance, serving the orator as his stock in trade, were never so carefully cultivated as by Erasmus and his followers, who broke down virtually the whole of classical antiquity into these bite-size snippets or sayings (adages or proverbs, and apothegms or more learned sayings) which could be introduced into discourse as they stood or could be imitated. Yet these commonplace sayings were collected by Erasmus from written and printed works and were fixed by him forever in print.

Through all this melee Latin was in the ascendancy—a symbol of the old oral–aural world where the orator was the perfectly educated man—but at the same time a language which, as will be seen in the next section here, had been deprived of any oral–aural roots of its own for an entire millennium. This mixture of the old and new in the Renaissance was not unproductive, but from the point of view we are taking here it was rare and strange. It certainly imposed curious new pressures on the psyche. At the time when the long-impending breakthrough to typography was achieved and the religious crisis of the Reformation took form, the word was present to man in most curious and confusing guises.

In the West by the eighteenth century the commitment of sound to space initiated with alphabetic script and intensified by movable alphabetic type had discernibly altered man's feeling for the world in which he lived and for his way of relating to his surroundings. The world of intellect and spirit and the physical universe itself became curiously silent in man's way of conceiving of them.

By the eighteenth century Descartes' logic of personal inquiry, silent cerebration, had ousted dialectic, an art involving vocal exchange, as the acknowledged sovereign over human intellectual activity. The new logic was not the art of discourse (*ars disserendi*) as earlier ages, following Cicero, had commonly taken dialectic and/or logic to be. Rather, it was the art of thinking—that is, of individualized, isolated intellectual activity, presumably

uninvolved with communication (as thought in fact can
never be, since it is always nested in language even when
it is not overtly verbalized in the interior consciousness or
exteriorly).

Views of language themselves had grown more and
more spatialized. Language belonged essentially to the
world of writing, not to speech. Despite the survival of
so much from the oral set of mind, even by the seventeenth century, as R. F. Jones has shown in *The Triumph
of the English Language,* the concept of languages has
become inextricably tied to writing. Even the most well-
intentioned scholars dealing with the English vernacular
were unable to work their way through the relationships
and tensions between sight and sound introduced by the
alphabet, so that often their work is sheer gibberish.
Linguistic theorists contrive unbelievably contorted and
fantastic explanations about how the nature of a given
letter equips it to represent the sound (or, more embar-
rassingly, sounds) associated with it. Sir Thomas Smith,
in a 1568 Latin work on English orthography, discussed
by Jones (p. 145), maintains that writing is somehow a
"picture" of speech or sound as painting is a picture of
the body or features, assimilating the world of sound
from the beginning in a bizarre fashion to the world of
vision. John Hart in a 1569 English work and others
followed Smith in "painting" the voice with letters. A
century later, John Wilkins' *An Essay towards a Real
Character and a Philosophical Language* (1668) continues
the same stubbornly visualist and spatial approach to
verbalization. Wilkins (p. 385) maintains that writing
may be subsequent to voice "in order of time" but not
in the "order of nature," which is to say, language is of
its very nature primarily a written, not a spoken phe-

nomenon. By the mid-eighteenth century such views are in clear possession of the field, as can be seen in James Harris, whose *Hermes, or a Philosophical Inquiry Concerning Universal Grammar* (1751) explains that writing "causes" reading and reading causes oral speech.

The eighteenth century is the great age of dictionaries in English and most other European vernaculars. These dictionaries almost universally undertake to regularize or control the vernaculars in such a way as to give them the same kind of inflexibility that Learned Latin was reputed to have. Such undertakings are of course nothing more than an attempt to establish total written control over the spoken word. Latin, as will be seen in the following section here, had for over a thousand years been a chirographically controlled language in which all oral performance had been forced to conform to written models. The members of the Académie in France, Samuel Johnson in England, and their confreres elsewhere had ambitions for this same sort of control for their mother tongues. They were unaware that their model for language was shaped by the condition of the media in their own cultural background.

The development of concepts adapted to thinking of language as something spoken, concepts such as phones, phonemes, morphs, morphemes, and the rest of the apparatus of modern linguistics, was to have to wait for almost two hundred years after Harris' work. For it is hardly an exaggeration to say that language was never effectively described as a spoken medium until the past few decades, and that, even now, we have not fully succeeded in so describing it. The eighteenth century seemingly did not even try very hard to do so. The drive toward painstaking description of natural phenomena had been intensified by writing and print, which brought the scientific mentality into being. But words as sounds eluded all description. The effort to force a sense of visual space into sound had been so gargantuan that the ability to conceive of language as sound had been almost totally inhibited, and still remains so for almost all literates today.

Nevertheless, the subconscious rebels against the effort to force sound into a spatial format. By the eighteenth century, the printed book becomes the object of hostility, shown in satire. One of the *topoi* or commonplaces of the Renaissance book preface had been the expression of hostility toward the printer—he was careless, too demanding, stupid, and so on. But the book itself was not yet the object of recrimination. By the eighteenth century it was. Swift pokes fun at books in "The Battle of the Books" and in *A Tale of a Tub* more particularly at the practice of footnoting. Numbers of other writers of the period do the same. Sterne's *Tristram Shandy* parodies printed book format, allowing the reader, for example, to fill in pages himself here and there. It is obvious that the printed text as such is in obscure ways getting on the eighteenth-century reader's nerves. The satirists teach him to grin and bear it.

If the eighteenth century found the word itself thoroughly committed to space, it found the human consciousness out of which the word was once spoken committed even more in the philosophy of John Locke (1632–1704), which dominated so much thinking not only in the British Isles but in all Western Europe. In "An Essay Concerning Human Understanding" (Book II, chapter 11), first published in 1690, Locke assimilates the entire sensorium to sight and converts consciousness into a *camera obscura,* a hollow into which and through which light rays play. The visual simplicity of Locke's model is matched only by the naivete of his assumption that the model is adequate to the real state of affairs.

> *Dark room.*—I pretend not to teach, but to inquire: and therefore cannot but confess here again, that external and internal sensations are the only passages that I can find of knowledge to the understanding. These alone, so far as I can discover, are the windows by which light is let into this dark room. For methinks the understanding is not much unlike a closet wholly shut from light, with only some little openings left to let in external visible resemblances or ideas of things without: would the pictures coming into such a dark room but stay there, and lie so orderly as to be found upon occasion, it would very much resemble the understanding of a man in reference to all objects of sight, and the ideas of them.

It is painful to recall the enthusiasm with which this description was hailed. The age could extract seemingly limitless satisfaction from contemplation of such simple spatial models presented as the equivalent of most puzzling psychological activities. Locke of course did not initiate the popularity of such models; in *Leviathan* (1651) Thomas Hobbes had found them quite titillating for the representation of social processes. But Locke carried them almost to their extreme limits. Psychology becomes for him maneuvers in space, the mind a tidy container, and the conceptual world out of which words are spoken a construction yard in which unit building blocks, shipped in from "outside," are physically assembled. Chapter 7 of the same book of "An Essay Concerning Human Understanding" explains all this and makes it quite clear that Locke's concept of human understanding is closely associated in his own mind with the alphabet itself (I italicize some of the more telling terms):

> Nor let anyone think these too *narrow bounds* for the *capacious* mind of man to *expatiate* in, which *takes its flight farther* than the stars, and cannot be *confined* by the *limits of the world;* that *extends* its thoughts often even *beyond the utmost expansion of matter,* and makes *excursions* into the incomprehensible *inane.* I grant all this; but desire anyone to assign any *simple* idea which is not *received* from one of those *inlets* before mentioned, or any *complex* idea not *made out* of those *simple ones.* Nor will it be so strange to think these few *simple* ideas sufficient to employ the quickest thought or *largest capacity,* and to *furnish the materials* of all that various knowledge and more various fancies and opinions of all mankind, if we consider *how many words may be made out of the various composition of twenty-four letters;* or, if, going one step farther, we will but reflect on the variety of *combinations* that may be made with barely one of the above-mentioned ideas, viz., *number,* whose *stock* is *inexhaustible* and truly *infinite;* and what a *large and immense field* doth *extension* alone afford the mathematicians.

The concepts of outlets for sexual "drives" used by Freud, Kinsey, and others have been criticized for reducing psychology to a plumbing system. But neither Freud nor Kinsey at all approaches the crude equations which underlie Locke's blueprint of understanding. This is not to say, of course, that spatial analogies are useless in considering the work of consciousness or even the nature of the word. But it is to say that if in using them one thinks he is saying as much about actuality as Locke appears to think he is saying, one is quite wrong.

Locke's well-known opposition to rhetorically centered schooling, explicit in his treatise *On Education,* accords with his diagrammatic conception of the universe, commented on by Ernest Tuveson in "Locke and the Dissolution of the Ego." What is, however, even more fascinating apropos of our present concerns is the fact that his penultimate appeal to validate his model in the passage just quoted here is to the alphabet itself, which, as an operation in space, he rightly observes is only "one step" away from mathematics. During this same age, Thomas Sprat, in the well-known passage in his *History of the Royal Society* (1667), would call for reducing the use of words themselves to "as near the mathematical plainness as possible."

It must not be thought, of course, that, because the eighteenth century was a significant watershed dividing residually oral culture from typographical culture, it thereby eliminated all oral residue from Western society. In many cases oralism persisted much later and with great force. A delightful story, "El buen ejemplo," by the Mexican writer Vincente Riva Palacio (1832–96) pictures a late nineteenth-century school in a little Mexican village as a place which hummed busily all day with the murmur of the children reciting everything in every subject over and over and over again—learning here was close to what "studying Homer" was in pre-Platonic Greece, the oral memorizing of texts. The Mexican schoolmaster's parrot escapes and, at large in the woods, proves to be so saturated with what he had been hearing that he infects a whole flock of parrots, who trail after him through the trees and recite what he is reciting, to create the illusion of a traveling sylvan schoolroom. Tech-nologized man regards such parroting as a debasement of intelligence, although it was originally the foundation of all learning before the devocalization of the word. Its persistence testifies to the fact that the typographical or technological psychological structures have not estab-lished themselves everywhere even yet. Where they have, however, devocalization is unmistakable.

In the devocalized world it is little wonder that the Muses, patrons of the old world of voice and sound, lan-guish and die. In *The Nature of Narrative* (p. 52), Robert Scholes and Robert Kellogg have shown how Homeric invocations of the muse belong to oral performance, where they "are a movement in the direction of authorial self-consciousness, providing a very slight and a highly stereotyped exception to the general rule that traditional oral narrative is told by an 'objective' and authoritative narrator." The Muses, moreover, not only typify the role of sound in an oral culture but also advertise the place of celebration and pleasure in the pursuit of knowledge such as oral cultures possess: they belong to the era before the pursuit of knowledge took on the trappings of "work," and indeed to an era when work and play are less clearly distinct than they are in an alphabetic, tech-nologized culture.

In his *European Literature and the Latin Middle Ages* (pp. 228–46), Ernst Robert Curtius has explained some of the details of the gradual retirement of the Muses over the centuries. He notes the relationship between the Muses and the harmony of the spheres but does not advert to the connections between the obliteration of the Muses and the shift in the communications media, although he quotes Blake's lament over the sisters:

> How have you left the ancient love
> That bards of old enjoy'd in you!
> The languid strings do scarcely move,
> The sound is forced, the notes are few.

Blake is aware that something has changed in the acoustic system, and, since he is speaking for his own age, he reminds us that the eighteenth century was the critical period in the silencing of this once convincingly vocal group. Invocation of the muse had, in fact, not been very convincing even in Milton's *Paradise Lost* (1667), and by the time of Alexander Pope's *The Rape of the Lock* (1712) can no longer be taken seriously, remaining only as a satiric, mock-epic device. Thomas Gray's attempt to summon the muse in his 1754 ode on *The Progress of Poetry* raised no real response. By the nineteenth century, John Stuart Mill actually makes clear what is wrong, for he explicates the new mode of existence of the poet, nonvocal and withdrawn, a "loner"—quite the opposite of the gregarious oral bard. In his essay "What Is Poetry?" in the *Monthly Repository* for January 1833, Mill explains (without catching the historical implications at all) that "Eloquence is *heard;* poetry is *over*heard" (Mill's own italics). The poet has retired from the oral–aural world. He is no longer singing, or even talking, to anybody.

Mill's poet was only suffering from the curious silence which had fallen over not only the world of intellect and spirit but the physical universe itself during the century preceding his own. By the eighteenth century the old acoustic syntheses had lost their appeal. "Observation" ruled—and observation, we must recall, is something only the eyes can perform. For sounds cannot be truly observed, only heard; odors are not observed, but smelled, flavors not observed but tasted, and heat and cold, wetness and dryness, with the other objects of the senses other than sight are observed only by analogy with sight itself and thus by adjusting their own proper being to something it is not. The sensorium had been narrowed somehow to the sense of sight as never before. Inevitably, "individualism" came into its own as the socializing effects inherent in voice as sound were minimized.

The devocalization of the universe extended to outer space. The harmony of the spheres, part and parcel of the earlier orally conceived cosmos, becomes irrelevant in the Newtonian world. In the *Spectator* for August 23, 1712, Joseph Addison simultaneously mourns and rejoices about the new state of affairs:

> The Spacious Firmament on high,
> With all the blue Etherial Sky,
> And spangled Heav'ns, a Shining Frame,
> Their great Original proclaim:
>
> . . .
>
> What though, in solemn Silence, all
> Move round the dark terrestrial Ball?
> What tho' nor real Voice nor Sound
> Amid their radiant Orbs be found?
> In Reason's Ear they all rejoice,
> And utter forth a glorious Voice,
> For ever singing, as they shine,
> "The Hand that made us is Divine!"

Addison retains some oral–aural apparatus here—"proclaim," "Reason's Ear"—but reduces it clearly to the metaphorical, since he finds no more "real Voice nor Sound." For all the truth in Newtonian physics, this account of a silent universe is actually no improvement over the old auditory syntheses for the cosmos. If the spheres do not, strictly speaking, sound in harmony, we know that as a matter of fact neither is the extraterrestrial universe by any means silent. Massive collisions occur, and many stellar bodies give off sounds of a volume which would certainly destroy the human ear. Addison's account of a silent universe is not scientifically supported. It is an illusion, induced by a complex of causes, no doubt, among which we must place the shift in the eighteenth-century sensorium from preoccupation with sound to preoccupation with space.

This neutralized, devocalized physical world has in a profound sense moved out of relationship with man's own personal, social, vocal world. It is really beyond man's ken. Henceforth, man will be a kind of stranger, a spectator and manipulator in the universe rather than a participator. Certain theological implications are clear. This world knows nothing of the power of the word caught in one of the accounts of creation in Genesis (1:3): "God *said*, Let there be light. And there *was* light." The concept of God is itself affected. Eighteenth-century Deists, following the recipes favored for man the isolated thinker and following also the spatialized accounts of language which make it a phenomenon rather than a communication, tend to think of God himself as no longer a communicator, one who speaks to man, but as a Great Architect (a typical eighteenth-century concept), a manipulator of objects in visual–tactile space, or possibly as a "force," a kinesthetically based concept, also spatial in its implications. They are likely to consider this idea of God to be a notable improvement.

The fuller implications of this devocalization will manifest themselves spectacularly at the end of the eigh-

teenth century in Kant, who thinks of intellectual knowledge itself in terms of "phenomena" and in doing so
climaxes in a new way the centuries-old tendency to deal
with intellection more and more exclusively by analogy
with vision. *Phainomenon,* "appearance," comes from
phainein, "to show," "expose to sight." The essential
Kantian problem thus connects with Kant's use of the
sensorium. If intellection or understanding is conceived
of by using a model from the field of vision, the phenomenon–noumenon problem automatically emerges from
the model, the problem whether apprehension can get
beyond surfaces. In vision, it never can, as we shall see.
Sight reveals only surfaces. It can never get to an interior
as an interior, but must always treat it as somehow an
exterior. If understanding is conceived of by analogy
with sight alone (which includes some inevitable admixture of touch), rather than by analogy also with hearing
(which gives interiors as such, as will be seen), as well as
with smell and taste, understanding is ipso facto con-
demned to dealing with surfaces which have a "beyond"
it can never attain to. As soon as one sets up the problem
of intellectual knowing in terms of a visualist construct
such as "phenomena," the question of "noumena" thus
automatically arises. From this point of vantage, a basic
question about Kantian philosophy would seem to be:
How much of the problem Kant poses is really in the
understanding or intellectual process itself and how much
of it is in the model for understanding which the history
of his culture made available to him?

The persistence and slow transformation of oral styles
of existence and states of mind through cultures which
have long had knowledge of writing has been sketched
here solely in terms of Western culture. This persistence
has been even stronger in Asia and Africa, where modern

technology, the congener if not the child of alphabetic
print, is not a native growth but an import. Despite the
absence of detailed studies, it is nevertheless evident
enough that in general Asian and African cultures remain
to this day far more radically oral than those of the West,
far less penetrated by writing and print even when they
have known script or the alphabet itself for centuries.
The same is true of indigenous American cultures apart
from European influences. Commonplace instances to
illustrate this point can be cited without end—the facility
with which Arab illiterates can resort to vocal composition of song; the Hindu insistence that for true wisdom
it is essential that one learn not merely from books but
from the spoken word received personally from a guru;
the Chinese civil-service examinations, only recently
abolished, involving recitation of Confucius; widespread
identification of learning with ability to recite orally long
stretches of the Vedas or the Koran or to sprinkle one's
speech with apposite quotations; schools where study of
the Koran means reciting it while rocking back and forth
(the state of learning which Plato decried in the Greece
of his day); and so on.

Modern Asian and African creative writers as well as
sociologists call constant attention to this active oral
heritage. One beautiful example is a short story by Pupul
Jayakar, an Indian writer with a profound social as well
as literary concern for her own culture. In "The Girl and
the Dark Goddess," she pictures an Indian family on an
outing. As the family drives along, the grandfather in the
group spends his time trying to get the others to chant the
Vedas after him. He rolls off the verses with insistent enthusiasm and succeeds in getting his granddaughter to
join in. She soon tires, but he continues, forgetting her,
totally possessed by the recitation, "entombed in the

sound of his own voice, in rolling the words, in tasting their texture, in feeling them beat against his conscious mind—shattering its awareness." This kind of total response to vocalization, which Homer would have understood, can still be found also outside Asia and Africa where the alphabet has not penetrated too deeply into a culture's fabric. I have encountered it, for example, in highly schooled West Indians. But it is doomed, by and large, with the growth of technology. Not that technologized man is necessarily hostile to such manifestations—he is often quite taken with them, for he studies them often with real love—but his psychological structures are different and he simply cannot respond as more directly oral persons do.

SOUND–SIGHT SPLIT IN THE LEARNED LANGUAGES

One of the hitherto neglected factors involved in the shift from an oral to a chirographic culture in Western Europe through the Middle Ages and the Renaissance was the condition of the word in Latin, the language used for learned thinking and expression. From the end of classical antiquity the whole existence of this language had depended on script. It was spoken by millions, but by no one who could not write it. So far as the learned world was concerned, the oral word no longer had any existence independent of the written.

Ancient Latin had in fact split into two separate lines of development. The one followed sight, the written word: here ancient Latin remained for all practical purposes unchanged. The other line followed sound, the spoken word. Somewhere between the sixth and the ninth centuries (dependent on what locality or social group one is considering), the dialects of Latin which have grown into modern Italian, Spanish, Portuguese, French, and other Romance tongues had moved so far along in their own development that the old Latin was quite incomprehensible to their ordinary users. The natural tendency of spoken languages to evolve new verbal forms and structures had here been helped by the influx of non-native speakers of Latin all through the Western Empire at the end of antiquity. Latin was "misused" by these non-native speakers; that is to say, its forms were speedily simplified.

At the same time, however, the old Latin remained in the schools. At first it had struck the schoolboys as merely a quaint old form of the way they spoke at home. But as their vernaculars veered farther and farther from Latin, in Western Europe around the sixth century and later, boys whose great-grandfathers could understand the old Latin in school without too great difficulty found that they themselves could not understand it at all. They had to study it as a foreign language. Still, there was no effective desire on anyone's part to substitute any of the vernaculars in the schools. There were no works in the vernaculars comparable to the Latin works which had always been read in Latin from elementary school through the highest reaches of education. The thought of translating these Latin works into the hundreds of fluid vernaculars—whether the Romance vernaculars deriving from Latin or the Teutonic vernaculars such as English or German—could hardly be entertained seriously. Most of the vernaculars were seldom if ever written. When they were, there was no standard way to write them. Moreover, there were no accepted words in the vernaculars for the technicalities of the arts and sciences studied in the classroom. The few medieval vernacular translations of standard or semistandard Latin works, such as the translations made or fostered by King Alfred in ninth-century England, met with little general acceptance. Latin remained the school language.

In the course of the sound–sight split, the great age of Latin rhetoricians around the turn of the Christian era (Quintilian died about A.D. 95) was succeeded by the age of such great Latin grammarians as Victorinus, Donatus, Priscian, Cassiodorus, from the fourth to the early sixth century of the Christian era. Rhetoricians were concerned primarily with the spoken language. Grammarians focused on writing; *gramma* means in Greek a letter of the alphabet. The rise of grammarians to prominence signaled a marked shift away from an oral economy of speech to a written economy as Latin fell under total chirographic control. Writers of the language determined not only how it should be written but also how it should be spoken.

Latin from this period on is sometimes called a "dead" language, but this it hardly was, for those actually using it for communication have invented new words and new meanings for old words by the thousands up through the present day. Latin is not a dead language but a chirographically controlled language: the formation of new words has been governed entirely by written usage.

Only a part of Latin, however, came under strict chirographic control. The other part continued normal oral linguistic development and formed the various Romance languages which continue today (and others which have died out). Latin had, in fact, undergone a sound–sight split, forming two streams. One was the orally developing stream of vernaculars which only around the eighteenth century were to be brought under effective typographic, visual control by dictionaries and grammars (which standardized written presentation primarily). The other was the chirographically controlled glacier, Learned Latin, governed in everything by the way it was written, more and more isolated from the spontaneity of the oral world, even when it was itself spoken aloud.

This sound–sight split is a major phenomenon of linguistic and cultural history, although it is hardly mentioned as such by the historians. It marks an epoch in the development of the word across much of the world. We find it not only in Latin but in Greek, Hebrew, Sanskrit, and, with allowance made for the vast differences between the economy of character writing and that of the alphabet, in Chinese, to mention only a few tongues preserving the older form in the written tradition while the spoken tongue continues active evolution into a diversity of vernacular dialects and finally languages. Such sound–sight splits, moreover, occur everywhere at about the same time: after the alphabet or other script has been in use a few hundred years and before the intrusion of typography or the later electronic media. The split has to do often with the conservation of religious texts, but by no means always or entirely; Greek and Latin classics are far from being all religious. Today the split is passé. Most of the learned languages now are vernaculars. At the same time, they are to a large degree subject to written control as early vernaculars were not, but to a control less despotic than that exercised over Learned Latin and becoming still less despotic daily as modern linguistic study and the electronic media (telephone, radio, television) call more and more attention to the oral base of all verbalization.

COMMONPLACES AS ORAL RESIDUE

For centuries after the invention of writing and of print, the modes of information storage and of conceptualization characteristic of oral culture were preserved with surprising directness in the doctrine and use of the commonplaces, or *loci communes*. These were also intimately connected with the history of Latin as an oral and written medium, for they were taught chiefly in rhetoric, which in the academic world well into the nineteenth century was concerned in principle with Latin expression. To an extent, the commonplaces were also the concern of the related subject of dialectic or logic. Rhetoric and dialectic as such are treated later in chapter 6 in connection with the polemic structures surrounding the use of the word. Since, however, the commonplaces are so directly connected with what I have said about oral culture, particularly as this has been analyzed by Lord and Havelock, they will be treated here.

The doctrine of the commonplaces picks up and codifies the drives in oral cultures to group knowledge of all sorts around human behavior and particularly around virtue and vice. In one sense of the term, a commonplace or *locus communis* was what we would think of as a "heading," but, instead of being so conceptualized, it was thought of as some kind of "place" (*locus* in Latin; *topos* in Greek, whence our word "topic") in which were stored arguments to prove one or another point. Whether this place was taken to be in the mind or in one's notes or elsewhere remained always quite vague and unsettled. In his *Topica* (ii) Cicero defines a *locus* as "the seat of an argument," a definition which Quintilian follows in his *Institutio oratoria* (v.10.20). In any event, such headings or places were "common" when they could be used for all subjects, not merely for certain specific ones. Thus, for example, whether one was orating on the worth of loyalty or on the loathsomeness of treachery or the beauties of a city or the innocence of a client accused of a crime or almost anything else, one could betake oneself to headings such as causes, effects, contraries, comparable things, related things, and so on through the various lists of "common" places. Commonplaces thus understood we might style here the analytic commonplaces, since they in effect analyze a subject in terms of various headings.

Another sense of commonplace or *locus communis* met with in both Greek and Latin antiquity had also been noted by Quintilian in his same work (x.5.12; cf. i.11.12). In this second sense a commonplace was a prefabricated passage for an oration or other composition (the oration was regularly taken as the prototype of any and all literary forms, including poetry). Such passages were got up in advance on a multitude of more or less standard subjects, as has already been explained, and, since they were stored in the mind or in writing, we might style them cumulative commonplaces by contrast with analytic. Cicero's passage on social decadence beginning *O tempora! O mores!* and mentioned on p. 57 above might be taken as a typical commonplace in this sense of the term, usable on any number of occasions with only minor adjustments. An oral culture puts a premium on such expected performances, as we have seen, looking not precisely for originality but rather for superlative proficiency in executing a familiar figure. As I have attempted to show in a study on "Oral Residue in Tudor Prose Style," collections of commonplaces in this sense of prefabricated purple passages were common in residually oral cultures, where writing made it possible to accumulate even more of them than a purely oral speaker might have at his command, although addiction to writing simultaneously cut down on fluency in their use. Commonplace books, such as that of John Milton, are essentially such collections of passages which might prove useful later. Since such books helped assure *copia,* the fluency or free flow of speech so touted by humanists, they were also called *copia* books or copiebooks, whence our "copybook." To copy something is thus in this sense to enter it in a commonplace collection as *copia* for future exploitation.

Rhetoric shared the doctrine of the commonplaces with dialectic, the art of disputation or of discourse (often equated with logic). For in disputing or merely "thinking," one could run through headings to find something to say by way of argument and one could have recourse to previously prepared material. Rhetoric and dialectic shared the doctrine also with particular disciplines such as medicine and law, for there were books of medical and legal "places," too. Strictly speaking, if one followed Aristotle's theory in the *Art of Rhetoric* (i.2, 1358a), a theory which partly coincided and partly conflicted with actual linguistic usage in his day and later, places such as those for law and medicine were not "common" places but private or special places, since they furnished arguments only for their particular subjects; they were not sources common to all subjects. But the general idea of special places was the same as commonplaces: a set of headings enabling one to analyze a subject or an accumulated store of readied material, or both, previously composed or excerpted, to which one resorted for "matter" for thinking and discoursing.

The connection of the doctrine of the places with oral modes of expression has been explicated and should be evident: the oral performer, poet or orator, needed a stock of material to keep him going. The doctrine of the commonplaces is, from one point of view, the codification of ways of assuring and managing this stock, a codification devised with the aid of writing in cultures which, despite writing, remained largely oral in outlook and performance patterns.

In the vast amount of commonplace material and discussion which the doctrine of the commonplaces generated, one would expect to find a little about everything under the sun, and one does. The amount of commonplace material, first in manuscript, and then, with the invention of typography, in print, is so vast that it is probably impossible even to make a complete survey of it all. But we do have access to more than enough to enable us to generalize a bit. It is true that one finds a great deal of material on almost everything in the commonplace literature. But the overwhelming impression one gets in working through masses of it is that it tends to cast up issues in terms of virtues and vice. In particular, the cumulative places, whether consisting of the collector's own compositions or of excerpts from other authors, tend to have to do with virtue and vice.

In antiquity one could prepare what we have here called the cumulative commonplaces on an indeterminate number of unclassified subjects, but the tendency was already marked to think of these previously readied bits of discourse (such as Cicero's *O tempora! O mores!* passage) as having to do primarily with praise or blame, and hence with virtue or vice, as Sister Joan Marie Lechner, has shown in *Renaissance Concepts of the Commonplaces* (p. 102, etc.). The tendency was accentuated almost beyond credence in the medieval collections of exempla, such as those which Chaucer's Pardoner as well as more sincere preachers ransacked for their sermons, for these collections were got up precisely in order to illustrate virtue or vice. Biography was warped on a virtue-and-vice framework in collections of exemplary

saints' legends on the one hand (the saints were generally
made out to be paragons of undiluted virtue from birth
or even conception through death) or on the other in the
de casibus stories about the fall of the mighty, of which
Chaucer's "Monk's Tale" is one of the well-known examples.

The commonplaces were used in true oral fashion not
merely as formulas but as themes which were strung together in traditional, and even highly rationalized patterns to provide the oral equivalent of plot. Various
formulary rhetorics dating from antiquity and in regular
use through the seventeenth century, such as the *Pro-
gymnasmata* of Aphthonius (fl. ca. A.D. 315), set down
fixed sequences of commonplaces which were to be used
for various parts of an oration (or, by extension, other
writing; Shakespeare uses these formulas regularly in his
plays). Thus, to praise or vituperate an individual, one
could proceed regularly through a sequence praising or
vituperating his family, descent, fatherland, sex, age,
education, physical constitution, state of life, character,
and occupation. The formulary rhetorics in use in England, which were the same as, or of a piece with those
used all over Europe, have been treated in detail by
Wilbur Samuel Howell in his *Logic and Rhetoric in
England, 1500–1700.*

What one finds in the doctrine and use of the commonplaces are thus the essential tendencies which an oral
culture, as described by Lord and Havelock, develops because of its information storage problem: a tendency to
operate verbally in formulas and formulaic modes of expression combined with a tendency to group material for
memory and recall around action in the human life-
world, thus around interactions between persons and
around questions of virtue and vice, plus a tendency,

which combines the two foregoing tendencies, to make individuals themselves into types, thereby shaping them to formulaic treatment.

Oral culture had generated the commonplaces as part of its formulary apparatus for accumulating and retrieving knowledge. Script gave further play to the formulary drive, making it possible to assemble and classify the commonplaces by fixing them in one way or another on the surface of a written page. The result was first the theoretical codifications of "analytic" commonplaces (that is, the lists of headings or *loci*) by the Sophists, by Aristotle in his *Topics,* and by Cicero, Quintilian, and others. This initial organization, made possible by writing in the still powerfully oral literate culture of antiquity, was followed in the next stage by the vast float of collections of the "cumulative" commonplaces which, after modest beginnings in antiquity, distinctively mark the more chirographic culture of the Middle Ages. The best known of these are the collections of exempla, brief moralizing stories excerpted from countless sources.

Print gave the drive to collect and classify such excerpts a potential previously undreamed of. Getting together an assemblage of snippets on classified subjects culled from any and every writer now paid a thousandfold and more, for the results, the ranging of items side by side on a page, once achieved, could be multiplied as never before. Moreover, printed collections of such commonplace excerpts could be handily indexed: it was worthwhile spending days or months working up an index because the results of one's labors showed fully in thousands of copies. Through the sixteenth and seventeenth centuries editors compete valiantly with one another in the number and extent of their indices. Thus, to take random samples at hand, the collection of legal places, *Loci argumen-*

torum legales by Nicolaus Everhardus of Middelburg appeared in a 1591 Frankfurt-am-Main edition with a title page advertising a "double index" (*geminus index*), a modest offering already outbid some years earlier when in a 1562 Lyons edition the title page of Franciscus Valleriola's medical commonplaces, *Loci medicinae communes,* announced a triple index, and again later when a 1603 Ursel edition of Paulus Manutius' revision of Erasmus' *Adagia* boasted on its title page more sweepingly, "a great number of most ample indexes" (*cum plurimis locupletissimis indicibus*). In a manuscript culture, indexing never amounted to this much for it was too tedious; each separate copy of a work demanded a separate index, and thus seldom had one.

The result of the opportunity offered by print was the thousands upon thousands of editions of commonplace books in various guises which flooded the market for some two hundred years after the invention of alphabetic typography and which certainly come to far more than even the float of medieval collections, for the early typographic age printed the greater bulk of the medieval collectors' work and added more. That this mass of printed material exists virtually unattended by scholarship appears due to two facts. First, it is so extensive that the very thought of trying to survey it immediately diverts the most intrepid scholar's attention elsewhere. The chief service to learning rendered by the prolific Erasmus was in the mainstream of the commonplace tradition, where we find his *Adages,* his *Apothegms,* his *Colloquies,* and his countless other collections and editions of collections; his work alone ran to over six thousand editions, most of which had appeared by the mid-seventeenth century. But Erasmus was only one of many. Theodor Zwinger, in the introduction to his *Theatrum humanae vitae*

(1604 edition), lists over one hundred collectors on whom his own collection draws.

Second, the printed commonplace collections are neglected because they are likely to appear completely irrelevant to anything we esteem or use. They are the flotsam and jetsam of the old oral culture to which the Western world bid adieu in the age of romanticism, as we shall see in chapter 5. The Renaissance humanists and their epigoni were unaware that their appetite for producing collections was the final upsurge of the old oral, formulary culture which writing had long before doomed and to which alphabetic typography had given the fatal blow. But the blow had a delayed effect. Commonplace collections, we now know on grounds noted in my study of "Oral Residue in Tudor Prose Style," were a major factor in producing Montaigne, Bacon, Shakespeare, and most of the major writers and thinkers pretty well into the age of romanticism. The tradition lingers peripherally today, as in the late Burton Egbert Stevenson's *Home Books* of quotations (30,000 pages) and Mortimer Adler's *Syntopicon*.

THIRD STAGE: ELECTRONICS AND THE SENSORIUM TODAY

The past century has seen the word enter into a new stage beyond orality and script and print, a stage characterized by the use of electronics for verbal communication. There has been a sequence within this stage, too: telegraph (electronic processing of the alphabetized word), telephone (electronic processing of the oral word), radio (first for telegraphy, then for voice; an extension first of telegraph and then of telephone), sound pictures (electronic sound added to electrically projected vision), television (electronic vision added to electronic sound), and computers (word silenced once more, and thought processes pretty completely reorganized by extreme quantification).

How can the status of the word in such a world be described? The changes in today's sensorium as a whole have been too complex for our present powers of description, but regarding the fortunes of the word as such one fact is especially noteworthy: the new age into which we have entered has stepped up the oral and aural. Voice, muted by script and print, has come newly alive. For communication at a distance, written letters are supplemented and largely supplanted by telephone, radio, and television. Rapid transportation makes personal confrontation, interviewing, and large-scale meetings or "conventions" possible to a degree unthinkable to early man. Sound has become curiously functional with the development of sonar, which is used even to catch fish for commercial purposes. Sound has become marketable, if indirectly so, through the use of (nonelectronic) disk recordings and, even more, through the use of electronic tapes. Recordings and tapes have given sound a new quality, recuperability.

Relying on the theorem that tribal life was basically oral–aural and thus rooted in constant interchange of communally possessed knowledge, and that writing and print isolate the individual or, if you prefer, liberate him from the tribe, Marshall McLuhan has described our present situation as that of a global village. And that it is. But a global village is not a tribal village.

There is a vast difference between tribal existence and our own, for tribal man either did not yet know or at least had not yet fully assimilated writing and print. Present electronic culture, even with its new activation of sound, relies necessarily on both. For the media in their succession do not cancel out one another but build on one another. When man began to write, he did not cease talking. Very likely, he talked more than ever; the most literate persons are often enough extraordinarily fluent oral verbalizers as well, although they speak somewhat differently from the way purely oral man does or did. When print was developed, man did not stop writing. Quite the contrary: only with print did it become imperative that everybody learn to write—universal literacy, knowledge of reading and writing, has never been the objective of manuscript cultures but only of print cultures. Now that we have electronic communication, we shall not cease to write and print. Technological society in the electronic stage cannot exist without vast quantities of writing and print. Despite its activation of sound, it prints more than ever before. One of the troubles with electronic computers themselves is that often the printout is so vast that it is useless: there are not enough attendants to read more than a fraction of it.

Nevertheless, it is true that what is said and written and printed may be determined more and more by the shape which electronics and sound give to social organization and to human life generally. What we are faced with today is a sensorium not merely extended by the various media but also so reflected and refracted inside and outside itself in so many directions as to be thus far utterly bewildering. Our situation is one of more and more complicated interactions. The radio telescope is an example. It has largely supplanted the earlier more direct-sight instruments. Yet it does not exactly return us to a world of sound. Rather, it provides data for a basically visual field of awareness, but does so by elaborate indirection. One looks at charts instead of at a galaxy. The code transmission of a picture of Mars is another example: the picture is constructed on earth from electronic impulses transmitted from outer space and recorded as a series of numbers. Vision here is more and more disqualified as providing direct access to information. The electronic processes typical of today's communications world are themselves of their very nature infravisible—not even truly imaginable in terms of sight. To think one knows what an electron looks like is to deceive oneself. It is not something like the things we see, only smaller; rather, it is the sort of thing that cannot be registered directly at all in visual terms, or, indeed, directly in any sensory terms, although it is part of the substructure of the sensory world.

When we say that the present age validates voice again in a new way, as it certainly does, we must also add that the visual or the visual–tactile, which were so intensified with the emergence of alphabetic script and print, are being further intensified as never before. Quantification, reduction to parts outside parts in space, is the key to the computer's operations. And, although the computer is far from being the dominant factor in human life which the popular mythologies make it out to be, it is certainly a characteristic and critical factor. Computers are manipulators; they juggle items in space, quantified items only. What cannot be reduced to a spatial arrangement directly or indirectly cannot be digested in computer "language."

Furthermore, while the present age has in a new way validated the use of sound and thereby in a new way validated time, since sound is time-bound, existing only when it is passing out of existence in time, the present age has also established man in a radically new relationship to time. Developing further his theorem of the global village, McLuhan has pointed out in *The Guten-*

berg Galaxy that a sense of simultaneity is a mark of both early oral culture and of electronic culture, a sense of sequentiality (one-thing-after-another) with a related stress on causality is the mark of chirographic and typographic culture. Certainly, living in an oral–aural universe, the village consciousness has to live in simultaneity in the sense that it lives in the present to a degree unknown to man who can relate to the past circumstantially through writing and concomitantly to the future through highly controlled and sophisticated planning. Primitive life is simultaneous in that it has no records, so that its conscious contact with its past is governed by what people talk about. As Havelock has pointed out, if Homer and his associates had stopped singing, the knowledge their works impart would have largely disappeared in Homer's Greece. But today's simultaneity is not due to absence of records, to the need to keep talking about our conscious possessions acquired in the past in order not to lose them. Rather, it is a simultaneity based on the most massive accumulation of records ever known. Today, with our knowledge of history and need for planning, the past and the future are forced into the present with an overpowering explicitness unknown to early man. Compared with that of earlier man, our sense of simultaneity is supercharged, and our reflectiveness supercharges it even more. Moreover, unlike earlier man, we achieve our sense of simultaneity in a sequential fashion. The computer is actually the most quantified and most highly sequential or linear of all instruments: it creates a sense of simultaneity only because its inhuman speedup of sequences makes it appear to annihilate them.

For all this to have happened, something must have happened to the word. To bring us where we are, the word must have been transplanted from its natural habitat, sound, to a new habitat, space. Writing and print and, later, electronic devices must have reshaped man's contact with actuality through the word. Only through the patterned sequences of shifts in the media and corresponding changes in the sensorium can man come into possession of his past. The word in its purest form, in its most human and most divine form, in its holiest form, the word which passes orally between man and man to establish and deepen human relations, the word in a world of sound, has its limitations. It can overcome some of these —impermanence, inaccuracy—only by taking on others —objectivity, concern with things as things, quantification, impersonality.

The question is: Once the word has acquired these new limitations, can it retain its old purity? It can, but for it to do so we must reflectively recover that purity. This means that we must now seek further to understand the nature of the word as word, which involves understanding the word as sound. What earlier man possessed instinctively and confusedly, we must possess more explicitly and clearly. But before we continue the exploration of the word as sound, a special question concerning the sequence of the verbal media must be looked into.

COMMUNICATIONS MEDIA AND THE FREUDIAN PSYCHOSEXUAL STAGES

The sequence of orality, anality, and genitality which since Freud has come to be so widely made use of to interpret the psychosexual development of individuals obviously needs at least some brief attention here. For the question arises whether the verbal communication sequences we have just been treating, which likewise begin with an oral stage and have proceeded through two others, are related to the psychosexual sequence.

Certain parallels immediately suggest themselves. One feature of the oral psychosexual stage is permissiveness, by contrast with the stage following, the anal stage, when control becomes a central issue. The oral stage, as Erik H. Erikson points out in *Childhood and Society* is by no means entirely permissive, for the child has to learn to suckle in a way gentle enough that the mother does not withdraw her breast. He has to learn reciprocity, and, to this extent at least, control. Moreover, as Erikson likewise explains, nursing involves for the infant the oral powers of retention and elimination (regurgitating and spitting out). By contrast, however, with the anal stage, the oral stage is permissive. The anal stage, when the child is brought to manage his fecal and urinary elimination processes, involves retention and elimination more centrally than the previous stage had; Erikson styles the sphincters the "modal zone" for these conflicting muscular activities.

It is easy to assimilate the world of oral verbalization to the oral psychosexual stage if we think in terms of permissiveness and lack of constraint. Spoken words flow. The great educational ideal of oral–aural cultures has been the *copia* or "abundant flow" of the orator, touted by classical antiquity and its Renaissance humanist heirs. Spoken words are free-moving, essentially, and so much so as to be fleeting. Homer's culture thinks of them approvingly as "wingèd words." Manuscript cultures regard their mobility more disparagingly. *Verba volant, scripta manent:* words fly away, what is written stays put.

Writing "retains" words. This, indeed, is its raison d'être. It is a record. It holds words so that they do not escape. The analogy with the retention of urinary and

fecal matter—which of themselves flow, like words, unless restrained—is obvious enough. Many concepts normally associated with chirography or handwriting present
it as involving constraint, by contrast with oral verbalization. The notion of fluidity is indeed still present in
writing—a script is supposed to flow. But as applied to
writing, this notion competes with another, plainly that
of constriction. Writing is fixed in space, confined, bound,
unvarying, subject to inspection and reinspection, and
thus firm, controlled. "This letter will confirm what I
said on the phone." *Scripta manent.*

Less spectacularly than print, but quite really writing
is also created by a squeezing process. To produce script,
one normally applies quite consciously the pressure of
a pen or crayon or other instrument under what for a
beginner is the most arduous discipline. It is perhaps
significant that the earliest scripts are cuneiform, made by
pressing a stylus into the surface of a still soft clay tablet.
If writing is with a brush, so that there is less pressure on
the writing surface, muscular constraint is still in evidence since the deliberate muscular constrictions controlling the brush are, if anything, even more arduous
for lack of a surface to brace the strokes against.

Speech of course involves muscular activity, too, and
thus some contraction and constraint. But it comes about
with far less anguish than does writing. Indeed, one of
the reasons, although probably not the most basic reason,
why sound is so serviceable for communication is that
vocalization involves minimal muscular effort and does
not interfere with much other muscular activity, as
gesture, for example, does. Vocalization can be carried on
while one uses the hands, feet, eyes, and other members
for other purposes. Speech is easy. It grows out of the
child's natural lalling stage, when sounds are spontane-

ously produced. It is not drilled into the child with the grim determination that often marks the teaching of writing. Speech develops out of simple play with sounds, by gradual specialization in the sounds useful in the language of the child's culture and gradual neglect and atrophy of the sounds not useful. Writing, on the other hand, is learned by concentration or application, and it rarely becomes for any individual, even professional writers, so spontaneous or flowing as speech. Few persons can write while carrying on other activities—walking, riding horseback, playing baseball, washing dishes. One can talk during all these activities and many others besides.

The muscular activity producing speech, moreover, does not result in fixity, in a "product." Quite the contrary, for the spoken word vanishes immediately. Writing, however, terminates in fixity: it fixes marks in space, and by virtue of a rigid code of rules. The fixity of writing sets this medium at odds with the spoken medium which writing proposes to represent and which, as we have seen, never fully accommodates itself to fixity. The writer is constrained by the artificial rules involved in writing, and also by the fact that because what has been written is motionless, it can be returned to and corrected in a way that speech cannot; the possibilities of greater accuracy themselves generate the need for greater constraint. One can "hold" or "cling" or "adhere" or "stick" to the letter.

It may be that dealing with written texts especially fosters anxieties and constraint. One thinks of the great biblical textualist of classical antiquity, St. Jerome, a tense, demanding psychological type by contrast with his more expansive and sonorous friend Augustine of Hippo, who was a thoroughly oral man, a professional rhetorician even in dealing with the written word. Jerome's equivalent as a textual scholar in the Renaissance was Erasmus, a lively and creative person, but finicky and certainly less relaxed than his friend Thomas More, who was likewise interested in texts, as all humanists were, but was again, like Augustine, a celebrated orator. In "A Grammarian's Funeral" Robert Browning has memorialized a man who sacrificed himself to the written word. Today's textual scholars, however, are feeling the effects of the new orality. Whereas earlier textualists were perhaps somewhat compulsive about securing *the* text of an author, present-day editors are outspokenly aware that there may be no single text. In editing Emily Dickinson, Thomas H. Johnson does not hesitate to print poems for which there is no final version, but only a set of alternatives of which sometimes all have been rejected by the author. Textual scholars have in fact liberated themselves from much of the compulsiveness of writing and print, for they have been the ones who chiefly have awakened us to the oral substratum of many texts, in particular those of the Bible and of Homer.

But the parallels between constrictive anality and chirography remain. And between anality and typography the parallels become spectacular. For, if constriction is closely associated with writing, it is of the absolute essence of print. The concept of "print" itself necessarily involves pressure. The key instrument of printing is the press. A type (*typus* in Latin, from the Greek) means originally the mark of a blow, a stamp, print, or footprint, the product of pressure again. Type is "set," placed in rigid lines, by hand or by a machine. The lines, of uneven lengths, are "justified"—spaced out to the same length—which is to say forced to comply to a set measure. (Columns of such type are often lined up between "rules," as in newspapers.) The set type is then "proved" or tested to see if all the rigorous conventions have been complied with, and it is then "corrected." In the form or chase it is "locked up" with the aid of quoins—wedges which put the type and chase under extreme internal pressure and which are manipulated with a "key." The form or chase is in turn locked under pressure into a press, which itself presses the type onto the final printed sheet. Even afterward, when set type is taken out of a form and put aside in storage, it is tied up tightly.

All this appears natural enough to those used to dealing with printing. How else, one asks, could it be? And of course there is no other way. But this is the very point. How strange is this typographical world of compression and visually inspected, locked-up chunks of metal and wood when compared with the world of speech in its original, oral–aural habitat, where words "flow" and indeed must flow without constraint. Speech at its oral optimum must be free from all this sense of hindrance or pressure that is inseparable from print.

Once, however, we have noted a kind of parallel between the movement of the individual psyche from an oral to an anal stage and the movement of the media of verbal expression from an oral to a chirographic–typographic stage, we must also note how the parallel fails to be total. First, it fails in terms of assimilative activity. We have observed that the oral stage of psychosexual development is primarily assimilative: the mouth is used chiefly to take things in. The oral stage of verbalized expression is the opposite: the mouth is used primarily for emission (a function which psychosexually is basically anal), and corresponding assimilation takes place through an entirely different organ, the ear (whose relationships to sexuality have at the best been minimally explored).

One could argue, of course, that verbalization is essential for the individual to take in or assimilate the world around him in a truly human way: oral verbalization and thinking develop in deep dependence upon each other, so that insofar as thought can be conceived of as an "intake" of something outside the individual (in one way thought is such a thing, although this is not all it is), the verbalization which is the counterpart of thought can be conceived of as an assimilative process. One could argue, too, that by comparison with a chirographic or a typographic culture an oral culture is one of constant intake. It circulates proverbs, aphorisms, and other sayings constantly among its members, for if there were not a constant intake of such things, the store of knowledge in the culture would vanish. A manuscript or print culture, by contrast, sets visual symbols down on a surface as records for subsequent reassimilation only if and when need be. In this sense it is not so constantly assimilating. All this is true, and yet in an oral culture it is still the ear, not the mouth, which takes in what is assimilated. If we think of an oral–aural culture this way, in terms of the ear organ rather than the mouth organ (there are reasons for doing both one and the other), any parallelism with the Freudian psychosexual sequence becomes tenuous indeed.

The parallel between the two kinds of orality fails to be total on another score. For the orality of speech appears closely allied on certain scores to the genital psychosexual stage. One does not produce words in order to get rid of them but rather to have them penetrate, impregnate, the mind of another. This penetrating quality of words is due not merely to an intentionality deliberately given them (I *want* my words to penetrate your consciousness) but to the very nature of sound itself, which, as we have seen in the preceding chapter, proceeds from one interior to another interior, setting up responses even physically in inanimate objects which have the proper interior structures enabling them to respond (as the strings and sounding box of one piano will vibrate to the sound of another).

Is it possible to discern anything in the media sequence corresponding to the phallic stage? Apparently it is to some degree. Just as in the psychosexual sequences after the anal stage there comes a phallic stage marked by aggressiveness and intrusiveness, and preceding the more fully social genital stage, so in the media sequence once the chirographic–typographic stage has matured, typographic man apparently enters into a spectacularly aggressive period. In his *Empire and Communications* Harold Innis has shown the close interrelationship of communications media with imperial expansion. The late typographic age is the age of empire building and of laissez-faire economics; Adam Smith had begun his academic career at Edinburgh as professor of rhetoric and belles lettres, a typographic communications man with lingering oral commitments (rhetoric). In the United States this age culminates with the robber barons. It was also, in the United States, the age of "manifest destiny," which promised the literate Americans dominance over relatively illiterate, highly oral, Spanish-speaking, feudal populations. This aggressive late-literate or post-literate age is the age by contrast with which our present less aggressive, socialized age appears to have lost its nerve.

When we move beyond the phallic to the genital stage, does the correspondence between psychosexual and communications stages persist? Are we now in a final or "genital" stage, the post-typographic era of electronically diffused verbal communications? Again, some analogies may be found. If we think of mature genitality as directing the

individual out of himself, as social in bearing, antinarcis-
sistic, orienting man and woman toward each other and
both toward children, who in turn will be matured
through oral and anal stages to be in turn themselves
oriented toward others, we find perhaps the most productive parallels between genitality and the electronic verbalism of telegraph, telephone, radio, and television.

It is certain that our present electronic age is more
explicitly and programmatically social than any other age
man has known and that its socialization has been made
possible by developments in the media. The first of these
developments was the rise of the mass languages. Primitive man for hundreds of thousands of years lived in tiny
populations scattered and often lost to one another over
the surface of the earth. There were no widely shared
or "large" languages such as we take for granted today
(English, Russian, French, Spanish, Chinese, Japanese,
German, and so on), which provide common meeting
grounds within the psyches of millions of individuals.
Early man's languages were shared each by only a few
hundred or few thousand persons, as are the small-group
languages still typical today in the Americas among some
Indians, and in Africa, Asia, and even, as a kind of linguistic subculture, to a limited degree in Europe. Small-
group languages are treasure houses of often unique cultural developments and values. It would be well to
preserve them so far as possible. But today they are humanly inadequate. Effective representatives of small-lan-
guage groups must be able to think and feel in one or
more of the large languages, to which of course the smaller languages can contribute their own thought-forms
and awarenesses, for all languages can learn from one
another.

The drive toward shared experience earlier implemented by the large languages was further implemented
by print. But print is isolating and slow moving, and its
socializing force is thus far less than that of electronic
media. These, beginning with the telegraph (first demon-
strated in 1844), and progressing through the telephone,
radio, television, the computer, and now Telstar, have
brought virtually all parts of the globe into contact with
all other parts. Near-instantaneous transmission of information across the globe maximizes the social sense by
generating a sense of omnipresence.

The sense of presence and of participation results, however, not merely from the speed of communication today
but also from the ability of electronic media to deal with
verbalization as sound. Sound, bound to the present time
by the fact that it exists only at the instant when it is
going out of existence, advertises presentness. It heightens
presence in the sense of the existential relationship of
person to person (I am in your presence; you are present
to me), with which our concept of present time (as against
past and future) connects: present time is related to us as
is a person whose presence we experience. It is "here."
It envelops us. Even the voice of one dead, played from a
recording, envelops us with his presence as no picture can.
Our sense of global unity is thus due not merely to the
fact that information now moves with near-instanteity
across the globe. It is also due to the electronically implemented presence of the word as sound.

If we keep our frame of reference large and general, it
is possible to discern something in common between today's overpoweringly socialized world of vocal communication enlarged through the electronic media and the
Freudian genital stage of psychosomatic development.

By contrast with the earlier stages of communication, the present exhibits an explicit orientation toward others, a social drive marked by a good deal of self-giving, at least as an ideal, which suggests the ideal of the mature human being. Many of the social awarenesses and activities of our time tie in directly with communications activities; indeed, freedom-rides and freedom-marches and the countless other demonstrations which have become a regular part of technological existence are themselves communications devices and would be quite ineffectual unless they entered the national consciousness over the mass communications media. Moreover, with or without self-giving, willy-nilly, mankind is today entering on an age of shared experience more marked than ever before: agitation throughout the world over racism in the Republic of South Africa and Rhodesia contrasts strangely with the relative indifference to such matters a few generations ago, and protests in the United States about the Vietnam war show that in a technological society even enemies cannot be viewed as distinct from oneself in the way they once could (one of the complications in the Vietnam situation has been that a nontechnologized enemy does not experience the same drive to identify to a degree with his opponent; for him the world is more clearly and convincingly divided into "good guys" and "bad guys"). The development of depth psychology itself and of philosophies of intersubjectivity and personalism have registered and intensified relationships between persons.

All this suggests in some way the world of the adult, who has moved through the oral, anal, and phallic stages to the world of genitality or maturity. Still, it is apparent that the parallels are only approximate. The world marked by electronic communications, as we have seen, is also a world of renewed orality. Moreover, it is not clearly ordered to generation in the way that the genital stage basically is.

When we attempt to discern parallels between the media stages and the Freudian psychosexual stages, we are, furthermore, hung up on the matter of ontogenetic and phylogenetic relationships. Basically, whatever parallels exist appear to be of interest because they suggest something like the recapitulation theory of biologists, whereby the history of the individual organism (ontogeny) and the evolutionary history of the phylum or group (phylogeny) are seen to parallel each other. That is to say, as the first organisms were monocellular in form, lived in water, and finally gave rise to organisms with gills, so also the individual mammalian embryo originates in a single fertilized cell, lives in a watery medium in the womb, passes through a stage when it has gill-like structures, and so on. Ordinarily, the history of the individual is taken to recapitulate the history of the race: each individual runs quickly through the stages which the race ran through more slowly before the individual in question appeared.

If, however, recapitulation applies to the media–psychosexual similarities, it applies in a curiously reversed form. For here, instead of the individual following upon and recapitulating the history of the race, we find the history of the race recapitulating that of the individual. Individuals have moved through the psychosexual oral–anal–genital sequence for thousands of years before the group first advances beyond the equivalent of the oral (oral–aural communication) to the equivalent of the anal (writing and print). We are arriving at the equivalent of the genital (electronic stage) only now.

One might try a second recapitulary alternative, looking to the communications media sequence in the individual's life today (oral to writing-print to electronic) as being a recapitulation of the same sequence in the history of the race or group. This results in a second anomaly, for the individual runs through this sequence today in a quite confused order. He starts regularly enough in the sense that he learns to speak before he learns to write. But the electronic media irrupt all through the presumably previous stages: the child is exposed to electronic communication before he can write or speak. For most individuals in a technologically advanced society, the writing and print stage is entered into last. In this state of affairs, the only "normal" persons, those who follow the proper sequence, are those belonging to the generation during which electronic media first came into use in their culture; these alone will have learned the third step last.

It should be noted, however, that in one especially fundamental matter the verbal media sequence and the psychosexual stages do have much in common. This is in the interaction of successive sequences or stages with those that have gone before. Succeeding psychosexual stages do not do away with preceding ones. Erikson has shown in *Childhood and Society* how the anal reintegrates the oral, and the genital both the anal and the oral. Something like this appears in the media sequence, as was explained in the foregoing section: each succeeding stage does not destroy but builds on and thereby reorganizes and reinforces the preceding stage. This has been true successively of writing, print, and electronic media.

Both the psychosexual stages and the media stages are concerned with maturity, which includes always some kind of accumulation. Maturity does not escape from its past but rather structures it. It is noteworthy that the present electronic age, with its massive modes of storage and retrieval of what is essentially past experience, exhibits a kind of maturity resembling the psychological maturity of the individual.

The lack of exact correspondence between the verbal media stages and the psychosexual stages makes it clear that the two are not direct reflections of each other, although they have some things in common. Other correspondences could most probably be worked out in more detail. Thus far we have considered the psychosexual stages *grosso modo* in the large, general or simplified categories of oral through anal to genital (with the last stage initiated by the phallic). It would be possible, if this treatment were made fuller, to work with more complex elaborations of Freud's psychosexual stages such as those of Erikson in his *Childhood and Society*. Here we find a fuller schema of the eight ages of man: (1) oral–sensory, (2) muscular–anal, (3) locomotor–genital, (4) latency, (5) puberty and adolescence, (6) young adulthood, (7) adulthood, (8) maturity. (Stages 4 through 7 are in a fashion subsumed under the genital, of which they represent elaborations or fulfillment.) With each of these successive stages Erikson associates its own characteristic type of interior crisis or polarity: (1) basic trust vs. mistrust with the oral–sensory, (2) autonomy vs. shame and doubt with the muscular–anal, (3) initiative vs. guilt with the locomotor–genital, (4) industry vs. inferiority with the latency period, (5) identity vs. role confusion with puberty and adolescence, (6) intimacy vs. isolation with young adulthood, (7) generativity vs. stagnation with adulthood, and (8) ego integrity vs. despair with maturity.

Apart from the fact that Erikson himself suggests that

this charting "leaves details of methodology and terminology to further study," it would appear that attempts to match stages in the communications media too closely with this complex apparatus—deeply meaningful though it is in the individual's psychological development—would probably be largely a tour de force ending in an accumulation of elaborate trivia. There appears no particular reason why the psychological development of an individual human being should provide an exact model for describing the development of the communications media. Because the pattern of human life is immediately accessible and very real to us, we are drawn constantly to try to make it serve as such a model for any and all historical developments. We feel we "understand" something when we can find it resembles ourselves. Thus historians have always been tempted to explain developments in cultures, nations, empires, languages, and so on by selecting phenomena which make it possible to picture the culture or nation or empire or language as moving through a series resembling human birth, growth through maturity, and death, despite the fact that most of the great languages, cultures, nations, and empires have not died but have simply been transformed into something else in the course of events normal to them but impossible to individual human beings. This kind of selectivity is often more stultifying than illuminating.

What the communications media sequence and the Freudian psychosexual sequence have in common that principally invites the comparison discussed here would appear to be that both call for analysis in terms of very basic images involving the history of the sensorium. Why this should be true in the case of the communications media is obvious enough, for the successive stages in media development move from one sense or sense cluster (auditory or auditory–tactile in the oral–aural communication system) through another sense or sense cluster (visual or visual–tactile in the chirographic and typographic stages) and into a third (the indirectly visual and amplified auditory of our electronic culture today).

The relationship of Freudian thought to the organization of the sensorium is less obvious, but quite as real. Although Freud and his followers (who at times include his opponents) have given a great deal of attention to the roles of the various senses, much of the relationship of the inner economy of Freudian thought—its conceptualization system and the history of this system—to the sensorium needs closer inspection. When we view the psychosexual stages in terms of the sensorium, it becomes apparent that these stages are conceived of in Freudian theory typically by extreme specialization in one area of the sensorium, tactual experience.

It is not merely that Freudians talk about tactual experience, but rather that the terms in which they analyze experience generally tend to be tactually and kinesthetically based. The concept of oral activity as assimilation, anal activity as constriction, and genital activity as orgasm are all at root tactual and kinesthetic, so that analysis in these terms means largely the resolution of the human life-world in more or less covertly tactual and kinesthetic categories.

Moreover, the psychoanalytic description of characters identified with one or another of these stages regularly entails the use of similarly tactual and kinesthetic experience. This becomes apparent, for example, if one attends to the concepts of orderliness, parsimoniousness, and obstinacy, which are attributes of the anal character. All these concepts entail to a high degree elements of restraint, pressure, and constriction. They are concepts which are typically formed by resort to our experience of tactual sensations and most particularly of certain kinesthetic sensations and which are associated with or supported by other concepts similarly derived. When, for example, we say "orderly," we are ultimately saying "formed by working against some resistance or with some effort," which is to say working against some strain (which we know as something kinesthetically experienced), against some constraint (also kinesthetically cognized); the root of the Latin word *ordo,* out of which or around which our present concept took form, means to strive upward, which entails effort, muscular constriction. Concepts descriptive of orderliness are themselves often kinesthetically rooted. An orderly person is likely to be thought of as strict (*strictus,* drawn together, compact, tight), the opposite of a loose performer. In a similar fashion, parsimonious (from a variant of the Latin *parcimonius*) derives from *parcere,* to spare, desist, refrain, restrain oneself. The kinesthetic base of such conceptualization is plain enough: in "refrain" or "restrain" one senses a pulling back, which is a concept derived basically from one's own muscular sensations. The concepts that go with parsimonious are likely also to be grounded in kinesthetic perceptions. A parsimonious person pinches his money, we say; he is tight-fisted or just plain tight. "Obstinate" comparably derives from *obstino,* to stand against, to stand in resistance to—again a muscular rather than a visual or auditory or olfactory or gustatory experience. An obstinate person is likely to be thought of as hard-headed or stiff-necked or inflexible. Hardness, stiffness, and inflexibility are apprehended by tactual sensations involving a high degree of kinesthesia.

Thus when one says that an orderly, parsimonious, and obstinate character is anal, one is in a sense uttering a tautology, for one is saying that a character definable in terms designating in effect (if not always at first blush) muscular constraint can be defined in terms of a physiological activity involving control of a sphincter muscle. Hardly a startling observation! The significant content of the Freudian discovery would appear to consist chiefly in the awareness not that orderly, parsimonious, obstinate persons are anal, but that the use of this sphincter is indeed a focus of kinesthetic awareness. It is interesting that a sphincter is normally contracted and that control of a sphincter consists in not allowing it to change its ordinary, normal condition involuntarily. "Control" here is minimal, because it does not mean establishing control but rather means not losing control. In a sense, anal control is thus not only focal but also relatively minimal and easy—a likely point from which to begin mobilizing skills ultimately to be developed for more intensely organized control activity.

In parallel fashion, when one says that the processes of writing and printing, which can hardly be conceptualized without resort to kinesthetic experience of constriction, are anal, one again is close to saying that constriction is constriction. Still, to identify writing and printing as akin to anality does call attention to the constrictive element in them, which may otherwise be obscured.

These observations suggest certain intriguing side reflections. One of these is that the appeal, productivity, and, to some, threatening character of Freudian analysis is due not merely to its conscious attention to tabooed areas of human life, notably the excretory and sexual, but also to its subtle exploitation of a tactual and kinesthetic sensorium in a culture which, as Freudians themselves have noted, had previously by dint of great effort worked itself into massive and difficult exploitation of a highly auditory and visualist sensorium. For purposes proposed as scientific, psychoanalysis makes use of the very "proximity" senses which Freudian thought itself has advertised as prescientific and full of danger for abstract thinking. For psychoanalysis has pointed out that for the rise of civilization, taboos must be imposed on the senses providing greater bodily pleasures (touch most of all, as well as taste and smell), and more attention must be given to the more sublime (abstract, distancing) senses such as hearing and, especially, sight. The relationship of the rise of psychoanalysis to the history of the sensorium and concomitantly of the communications media certainly deserves more attention than there is room or reason to give it here.

What we need is a phenomenology of psychoanalytic concepts, and then a phenomenology of phenomenological concepts.

3

Word as Sound

AUDITORY SYNTHESIS: WORD AS EVENT

In discussing the phonetic alphabet we have treated the alliance of sound with the passage of time and the consequent irreducibility of sound to purely spatial categories. There are also other features of sound which give it special importance within man's life-world and which have strong religious significance but which are likely to elude us in today's still highly visualist culture. It is a commonplace that early man, strongly if by no means exclusively oral–aural, experiences words—which for him typically are spoken words—as powerful, effective, of a piece with other actuality far more than later visualist man is likely to do. A word is a real happening, indeed a happening par excellence.

Some are tempted to regard the primitive attitude toward the word as superstition, but there is an abiding truth about it which we can see if we reflect further on the implications of sound in terms of man's life-world and in terms of actuality in general.

Sound is more real or existential than other sense objects, despite the fact that it is also more evanescent. Sound itself is related to present actuality rather than to past or future. It must emanate from a source here and now discernibly active, with the result that involvement with sound is involvement with the present, with here-and-now existence and activity.

Sound signals the present use of power, since sound must be in active production in order to exist at all. Other things one senses may reveal actual present use of power, as when one watches the drive of a piston in an engine. But vision can reveal also mere quiescence, as in a still-life display. Sound can induce repose, but it never reveals quiescence. It tells us that something is going on. In his *Sound and Symbol,* writing on the effect of music, Victor Zuckerkandl notes that, by contrast with vision and touch, hearing registers force, the dynamic. This can be perceived on other grounds, too. A primitive hunter can see, feel, smell, and taste an elephant when the animal is quite dead. If he hears an elephant trumpeting or merely shuffling his feet, he had better watch out. Something is going on. Force is operating.

Hence cultures which do not reduce words to space but know them only as oral–aural phenomena, in actuality or in the imagination, naturally regard words as more powerful than do literate cultures. Words *are* powerful. We take them in tiny doses, a syllable at a time. What would the shattering psychological experience of the hearer be if all the knowledge written in books were somehow suddenly *uttered* all at once? What would it do to the nervous system and the psyche to assimilate all these words simultaneously? Being powered projections, spoken words themselves have an aura of power. In personal relations —and spoken words of their very nature entail real, not imagined, personal relations, since the audience is on hand and reacting—words do have real power: the king's statement that so-and-so is his representative makes him his representative as nothing else does. Words in an oral–aural culture are inseparable from action for they are always sounds. Thus they appear of a piece with other actions, including even grossly physical actions. The Hebrew use of the word *dabar* to mean both word and event is, as Barr would have it, probably not so distinctive a phenomenon as it has been made out to be. But, however common the usage may or may not be, this sense is perfectly consistent not only with the oral–aural state of mind but with the very nature of words themselves. For every word even today in its primary state of existence, which is its spoken state, is indeed an event.

In oral–aural cultures it is thus eminently credible that words can be used to achieve an effect such as weapons or tools can achieve. Saying evil things of another is thought to bring him direct physical harm. Charms and magic formulas abound. This attitude toward words in more or less illiterate societies is an anthropological commonplace, but the connection of the attitude with the nature of sound and the absence of writing has not until recently begun to grow clear.

Moreover, since sound is indicative of here-and-now activity, the word as sound establishes here-and-now personal presence. Abraham knew God's presence when he heard his "voice." (We should not assume that the Hebrews necessarily thought of a physical sound here, only that what happened to Abraham was more like hearing a voice than anything else.) "After these events God put Abraham to a test. He said to him, 'Abraham.' He answered, 'Here I am' " (Gen. 22:1). As establishing personal presence, the word has immediate religious significance, particularly in the Hebrew and Christian tradition, where so much is made of a personal, concerned God. Mircea Eliade has brilliantly discussed the relationship of religion to sacred time and sacred space. Religious awareness grows out of regard for sacred times and sacred

places. But sacred time and sacred space are space plus
and time plus. The divine presence irrupts into time and
space and "inhabits" them. Presence does not irrupt *into*
voice. One cannot have voice without presence, at least
suggested presence. And voice, as will be seen, being the
paradigm of all sound for man, sound itself thus of itself
suggests presence. Voice is not inhabited by presence as by
something added: it simply conveys presence as nothing
else does.

> My nerves are bad to-night. Yes, bad. Stay with me.
> Speak to me. Why do you never speak. Speak.
> What are you thinking of? What thinking? What?
> I never know what you are thinking. Think.

The distressed person in *The Waste Land* of T. S. Eliot
expresses the agony of one to whom presence is denied
because vocal communication is denied.

Only with writing, and particularly with the phonetic
alphabet, do words readily appear to be disengaged from
nonverbal actuality to the extent to which technological
man today commonly takes them to be. This is to say, only
when words are made out to be something different from
what they really are do they readily take on radically distinctive characteristics. We are faced with a paradox here.
Reduced by writing to objects in space, words can be
compared with other objects and seen to be quite different. But reduced by writing to objects in space, they are
one remove from actuality, less real (although more
permanent) than when they are spoken. In this sense the
spoken word, evanescent though it is and elusive though
it is and lumped with other nonverbal actuality though
it is, is nevertheless in the deepest sense more real and
more really a word than the word sensed, through writing

(and even more through print), as something different from "things."

The greater reality of words and sound is seen also in the further paradox that sound conveys meaning more powerfully and accurately than sight. If words are written, they are on the whole far more likely to be misunderstood than spoken words are. The psychiatrist J. C. Carothers, in a brilliant study, "Culture, Psychiatry, and the Written Word," on which I have drawn here, puts it this way (p. 311):

> Few people fail to communicate their messages and much of themselves in speech, whereas writings, unless produced by one with literary gifts, carry little of the writer and are interpreted far more according to the reader's understanding or prejudice.

That is to say, the spoken word does have more power than the written to do what the word is meant to do, to communicate. We are inclined to think of writing in terms of the very specially gifted and specially trained individuals, professional writers or literary artists who can use writing often in specially controlled or limited circumstances, in truly exceptional ways. We are also likely to forget how very small a part of spoken speech can be put into writing that makes sense. The ordinary individual who can manage dismayingly complicated situations—his relations to scores of other persons and things in the intricacies of day-by-day activities—quite well through oral communication, is utterly incapable of managing comparably complex situations in writing at all. He can fill out forms or, after a long telephone conversation in which the real understanding was worked out (as it could never have been worked out by correspondence alone), he can "confirm the conversation in this letter." The letter only seems to be the definitive action. In reality it is a mere footnote to a complex of interrelationships which he could never write down. Our literate and now electronically computerized culture relies on the recorded word as never before, and yet at the planning level turns to conferences and idea-exchange meetings as no earlier culture ever did. The technological age is the age of the convention and conference and discussion group, and of the oral brainstorming session.

Such are the special demands of the written and printed media that it is rare ever to get into writing an exact, unedited version of oral verbalization, and virtually impossible to get it into print. Stenotype operators and stenographers transcribing from tape inevitably edit. Editors of printed works do what their title of editor has come to suggest: they "edit," that is alter, the expression that passes through their hands. (Yale's editor altered the foregoing sentence!) The written medium simply will not tolerate all of what actually goes on in oral speech. It has rules. If you cannot fit what you want to verbalize into the rules of writing, you are obligated not to write it.

The spoken word thus lends itself in quite full pliability to virtually everyone, the written word only to the select few, and even these cannot transact in writing all the complexities they can handle with little trouble in speech. One reason for this situation is of course that the spoken word is part of present actuality and merges with a total situation to convey meaning. Context for the spoken word is furnished ready-made. In written performance the writer must establish both meaning and context. This is one of the most difficult tasks in communication simply because the person or persons being communicated with are not *there* at all: the writer has to project them totally out of his own imagination. And they themselves, the readers, have to learn the game of literacy: how to conform to the other's projection, or at least operate in terms of it.

Sound is a special sensory key to interiority. Sound has to do with interiors as such, which means with interiors as manifesting themselves, not as withdrawn into themselves, for true interiority is communicative.

Sound is a clue to interiors in the physical as well as in the psychological sense. More than other sensory phenomena, sound makes interiors known as interiors (although it is of course true that the *concept* of an interior is derived also from other senses, notably the tactile and kinesthetic senses).

Sight presents surfaces (it is keyed to *reflected* light; light coming directly from its source, such as fire, an electric lamp, the sun, rather dazzles and blinds us); smell suggests presences or absences (its association with memory is a commonplace) and is connected with the attractiveness (especially sexual) or repulsiveness of bodies which one is near or which one is seeking ("I smelled him out"): smell is a come-or-go signal. Hence "It stinks" expresses maximum rejection or repulsion: do not even go near—the farther away the better—do not even think about it. Taste above all discriminates, distinguishing what is agreeable or disagreeable for intussusception by one's own organism (food) or psyche (aesthetic taste). Touch, including kinesthesia, helps form the concepts of exteriority and interiority. We feel ourselves inside our own bodies, and the world as outside. We can feel free, not "boxed in." We explore tactually the inside of a box, and there are jokes about the drunk feeling his way confusedly around a lamp post and exclaiming in his confusion, "I'm walled in." But to explore an interior, touch must violate the interior, invade it, even break it open. Kinesthesia, it is true, gives me access to my own interior without violation—I feel myself somehow inside my own body and feel my body inside my own skin—but kinesthesia gives me direct access to nothing but myself. Other interiors are inaccessible to it (except through empathy, indirectly).

Sound, on the other hand, reveals the interior without the necessity of physical invasion. Thus we tap a wall to discover where it is hollow inside, or we ring a silver-colored coin to discover whether it is perhaps lead inside. To discover such things by sight, we should have to open what we examine, making the inside an outside, destroying its interiority as such. Sound reveals interiors because its nature is determined by interior relationships. The sound of a violin is determined by the interior structure of its strings, of its bridge, and of the wood in its sound-board, by the shape of the interior cavity in the body of the violin, and other interior conditions. Filled with concrete or water, the violin would sound different.

We should recall here that in dealing with interior and exterior we are not, strictly speaking, dealing with mathematical concepts. Like left and right, or up and down, or the directions north, south, east, and west, the concepts interior and exterior cannot be defined mathematically or distinguished from each other mathematically, although they may be accepted as given and then assigned different mathematical values. These are strictly "existential" terms. Many attempts to define such terms are circular. *Webster's New World Dictionary of the American Language,* College Edition (World Publishing Co., 1954) defines left as "of or designating that side of man's body which is toward the west when one faces north" and then defines "west" as "the direction to the left of a person facing north." This is hopeless, and thus the same dictionary adds to this definition of left, the phrase "usually the side of the less-used hand." This is the better definition. The Merriam *Webster's Seventh New Collegiate Dictionary* (1963), based on *Webster's New International Dictionary,* Third Edition, proposes such a definition first: "left" means "related to or being nearer the weaker hand in most persons" and "west" is "the general direction of sunset." These latter definitions are existential in the sense that they point not to an abstract set of relations but to an existent historical situation or event or series of events: matters have so worked out that most persons do have their weaker hand on the same side; the sun sets regularly in a certain position. The definition can point only to the historical, existential fact and structure itself on this fact.

"Interior" and "exterior" are similarly existential or historically grounded, and dictionary definitions of them tend to be even more relentlessly circular. Interior is referred to "in," which in turn is referred to "within," "inside," and so on—always the "in" or some variant of it, such as "between" or "bounded," eludes definition. The same is true of out and exterior. Ultimately the meaning of in and out or interior and exterior depends on pointing to a historical or existential fact, a fact which appears ultimately to be that of self and other, our experience of ourselves as existing somehow inside our bodies with an exterior world outside. What we mean by in and out comes from our experience of ourselves. We find ourselves situated in insideness and outsideness. Our bodies are a frontier, and the side which is most ourselves is "in."

As material being develops higher forms, interiority increases. This has been spelled out in great detail by

Pierre Teilhard de Chardin. It appears also that, in some
general way, this interiority is involved with the interiorizing economy of sound itself. The lowest forms of
life, such as protozoans, would appear to have no real
voice, although something like it may exist for them in
the form of vibrations. Mollusks, too, appear voiceless.
Crustaceans and arthropods have voice of a sort, but curiously externalized for the most part, produced from the
exoskeleton; however, it thereupon resonates within the
body. Exceptions to this rule among arthropods would be
the death's-head hawk-moth and a few other insects noted
by V. C. Wynne-Edwards in *Animal Dispersion in Relation to Social Behaviour* (p. 43). These have more interior
sources of sound, as do also a few fishes which produce
swim-bladder vibrations. Nevertheless, true voice in the
sense of sound emergent from within is for the most part
a characteristic of the higher animals—amphibians, reptiles, birds, and mammals—and rather more common
among these as one moves up the scale to more advanced
orders. Only some amphibians (frogs and toads but not
salamanders) are highly vocal, reptiles only occasionally
so (as the alligator). Birds as a group are more persistently
vocal than lower forms. Mammals vary in their use of
vocalization but, like birds, they regularly have highly
developed interior sound organs (vocal chords). The
large hammerheaded fruit bat has pharyngeal air sacs
almost a third of the size of its entire body to aid in the
production of sound, and some apes (howler monkeys,
gibbons, gorillas) also have fantastically developed interior resonating structures (Wynne-Edwards, pp. 55–57).
One can thus say that, speaking generally, voice becomes
more operative as we move up the evolutionary scale
and that bodily structure becomes somehow more res-
onant.

The increasing exploitation of voice as one moves up

the evolutionary scale toward greater "interiority" of being parallels the movement toward intelligence, suggesting what will be treated in the next section of this chapter,
"The Affinity of Sound and Thought." Intelligence,
in its subhuman analogue as in its human form, is closely
associated with sound.

Recent studies by Winthrop Kellogg and others, and
not a little semipopular and popular literature, have
called attention to the case of porpoises. It has been
suggested that much of the "intelligence" of these mammals may be due to their extremely high discriminatory
ability regarding sound, made possible by the extraordinarily fine construction of their ear. This much involvement in a world of sound creates the impression of
humanness.

Many differences as well as similarities between porpoises' use of sound and man's can be noted. One of some
significance here is that, while porpoises use sound signals
as do other animals for communication between individuals, their principal use of sound appears to be a type of
sonar. Sound is less porpoise-to-porpoise than it is por-
poise-to-inert-object-and-back; "voice" here is less communication than probe. Porpoises produce sound (by
what means is not yet sure; perhaps through structures in
the blowhole, for they have no vocal cords) largely to
bounce it off objects, as bats do, so as to locate objects
and define them with remarkable accuracy. Insofar as
this sound-probe technique reports surface extent and
shape, it makes hearing into a kind of vision. Because
the objects involved not only reflect sound but also resonate in various ways, sending back variously sounding
echoes according to their constitution, porpoises can also
through sonar distinguish the quality of objects (soft,
hard—fish from wooden models of fish, for example).
Even though it resonates, however, sound thus used is less

interiorized than voice as typically used by man for communication between the deep interior and essentially
private consciousnesses of unique human beings. The
hyperdevelopment of the porpoises's "voice" and hearing
is largely for dealing with objects; man's corresponding
development is interpersonal.

In *The Miraculous Birth of Language,* Richard Albert
Wilson explores the origin of language in terms of the
development of life. He suggests that the animal's resort
to sound in its calls, a kind of "rudi-language," effects a
change in the cosmic totality because "it explicitly an-
ticipates time," since, although sound thus used "is also
no doubt a report of the animal's present or immediate
past state, . . . its chief significance is its reference to the
future and thus its involvement in purposiveness" (p.
160). This suggestion of Wilson's and those which I have
just presented above were developed independently, but
they seem to jibe with one another. One might combine
them in the further suggestion that sound is in certain
ways a preferred field for the movement from inertness
to intelligence, from object-like exteriority to the interiority of living beings and finally of persons. Wilson's
"purposiveness" is a function of intelligence. It is also
by the same token a function of interiority. To act with
purpose is to determine even exterior process and structures from within consciousness itself.

*Sound unites groups of living beings as nothing else
does.* There is some relationship between resort to sound
and socialization of life. The relationship is not absolute;
many animals, such as ants or some fish, have a kind of
group organization which appears quite independent of
the use of sound. Many others use all their senses, or
most of them, for social purposes. Niko Tinbergen has
shown this beautifully and circumstantially in *The Her-*

ring Gull's World. Nevertheless, once production of sound is arrived at in evolutionary development, the fact that sound signals present, ongoing activity gives it immediate value in establishing social relations, particularly flexible ones in variable situations. Sound reciprocates. Sounds which I produce tend to evoke responses from outside me in a way that very few of my visible or tangible activities do. Sound even reciprocates between living and nonliving things, as was shown for porpoises and bats. The response here is from an object, a thing— although, since sound makes the thing to a degree resonate from its interior, the object or thing is less a pure surface than it is to sight. A fortiori, sound is useful for eliciting true responses from other living organisms, and that even at a distance. In *Animal Dispersion in Relation to Social Behaviour* Wynne-Edwards (p. 63) calls attention to the fact that animal sound almost always is a signal to others *within* the species (it operates in a *communal* framework) and that interspecific use of sound is rare to the point of virtual nonexistence. Normally lions roar not to frighten their prey or even other competing carnivores but to signal other lions (this may include occasionally frightening *them*). On the other hand, visual and olfactory as well as tactual signals are regularly used to affect other species; for example, to frighten or discourage predators.

Touch is also a reciprocating sense, but the distance tolerated in sound as against touch is important, for socialization commonly demands a certain distance. Although sometimes it may have tactile aspects, of itself socialization is not physical compactness. This is true even of organisms lower than man. "Individual distance" is enforced in the social life of animals, as Wynne-Edwards details (pp. 133–34). The colonies of sea birds

reported by Tinbergen, by Peter Marler and William
Hamilton, and by many others are true social groups,
but in their nesting colonies they enforce rigid territorial
rules which preclude not only contact but even proximity except between mates and between parents and
their young. The social structures of the colony are maintained by visual signals and in a special way by cries,
which can simultaneously relate individuals to one another and warn each to keep his distance. Physical contact
would destroy this complex social organization. A fortiori, human privacy or dignity imposes severe limits on
reciprocity achieved by touch. Sound provides reciprocity
and communication without collision or friction.

Thus because of the very nature of sound as such, voice
has a kind of primacy in the formation of true communities of men, groups of individuals constituted by shared
awarenesses. A common language is essential for a real
community to form. It binds man not only in pairs or
families but, as nothing else does, in large groups, and as
a consequence it has a kind of primacy in communication
even between individuals. It would appear that precisely
because sound is so interiorizing and thus exploitable by
man at depths unknown to less interiorized creatures, it
implements socialization or even forces it as nothing else
can. True interiority makes it possible to address others:
only insofar as a person has interior resources, insofar as
he experiences his full self, can he also relate to others,
for addressing or relating to them involves him precisely
in interiority, too, since they are interiors. Thus addressing others is not quite "facing" them insofar as facing
is a visually based concept that calls for a turning outward. Communication is more inwardness than outwardness. It is not entirely satisfactory even to say that man is
an interior exteriorizing himself. To exteriorize oneself

without interiorization is to devote oneself to things, which alone are not satisfying. To address or communicate with other persons is to participate in their inwardness as well as in our own.

The word, and particularly the spoken word, is curiously reciprocating not only intentionally, in what it is meant to do (establish relationships with another), but also in the very medium in which it exists. Sound binds interiors to one another as interiors. Even in the physical world this is so; sounds echo and resonate, provided that reciprocating physical interiors are at hand. Sights may reflect, from surfaces. Strumming on a bass viol will make a nearby one sound, by virtue of outside impact of energy but in such a way as to reveal its interior structures.

Because the spoken word moves from interior to interior, encounter between man and man is achieved largely through voice. The modes of encounter are innumerable—a glance, a gesture, a touch, even an odor—but among these the spoken word is paramount. Encounters with others in which no words are ever exchanged are hardly encounters at all. The written word alone will not do, for it is not sufficiently living and refreshing. The scholar, isolated in his den with his books and sheets of writing paper, is plunged into words, but he is still liable to the charge of being "dead"; one thinks again of Browning's poem, *The Grammarian's Funeral*. Despite the nourishment they furnish, books taken alone are killing. Renaissance humanists such as Machiavelli could think of the authors in their libraries as living men: "They receive me with friendship; in their company I feed upon the only nourishment which is truly mine, the nourishment I was born to receive. Without false shame I venture to converse with them." But afterward, Machiavelli also ventured to tell others who were truly living all about it. He gives us this account in a letter of December 10, 1513, to Francesco Vettori, and we can be sure that he conversed with friends such as Vettori about his conversations with his books, so that this letter itself, though a written instrument, was close to the world of real conversation, oral exchange, as humanists' letters commonly were. Man must give meaning and life to his actions, including his study of books, by his encounters with others, which means that in one way or another, explicitly or implicitly, he must relate his other actions to spoken words.

Since pure interiors (persons) do communicate with one another so largely by voice, the silencing of words portends in some way withdrawal into oneself. Such withdrawal need not be antisocial, for the interior into which one withdraws is the ground of all communication. Religious silence, for example, undertaken in union with others and out of regard for God and all mankind, can be fruitful and is, but such silence relates at many points to the spoken word and constitutes itself a kind of communication and encounter. So does writing, of course. And yet, because it consists of silent words, writing introduces a whole new set of structures within the psyche: communication which lacks the normal social aspect of communication, encounter with one who is not present, participation in the thought of others without commitment or involvement. Oral or illiterate peoples are understandably suspicious of literates as "slickers," the noncommitted and disinterested whom one cannot trust.

Although oral–aural cultures certainly differ vastly from one another both in explored and unexplored ways, it appears that at least a great many of them commonly conceive of actuality as united in some kind of harmony rather than in the visualist terms whereby cosmological unity is commonly pictured in modern technological society. Spitzer's *Classical and Christian Ideas of World Harmony* provides massive detail illustrating the more aural bent of the Western mind in its earlier phases by contrast with the present visualist bent in the West and to a growing extent elsewhere. Reviewing psychological and anthropological studies of present-day cultures still relatively illiterate, Carothers describes such culture as encouraging habits of "auditory synthesis" as against the habits of "visual synthesis" enforced by modern science and grounded in literacy.

We should remember, however, that auditory synthesis does not quite entirely describe the earlier or more primitive, residually oral state of mind, for the term synthesis is itself a visualist construct, meaning at root a putting together—that is, an operation conceived of as local motion in a spatial field, a visually (or visually–tactually) conceived operation. It would be more accurate to oppose "visual synthesis" with "(auditory) harmony," conceiving the auditory in auditory terms. However, auditory synthesis has something to recommend it, for all explanation entails some conversion to visual–tactile concepts. To call for explanation (root meaning: unfolding, laying out flat) is to call for analysis, the fragmentation that belongs more properly to vision than to the other senses. While explanation thus helps understanding, it provides of its very nature an extremely limited participation in actuality—knowing more and more about less and less—unless it is accompanied by other modes of understanding.

Habits of dominantly auditory synthesis long survive the introduction of writing, as can be seen for the seventeenth and eighteenth centuries in John Hollander's *The Untuning of the Sky* and for the earlier periods of Western culture in Spitzer's book just mentioned. Spitzer sees the old auditory sense of unity (although he does not use this precise term) encapsulated permanently in the German word *Stimmung* and its cognates (*dass stimmt, Stimme,* etc.), on which his entire book is simply a comment. *Stimmung* is of course untranslatable, but a close English equivalent would be "tunedness"—a sense of unity working out from the world of sound to all actuality. There are of course many other points in other languages and cultures at which the old oral–aural awareness of fullness, completeness, and unity works itself out. And there are movements to strengthen this awareness in new ways today. Milič Čapek's *Philosophical Impact of Contemporary Physics* (pp. 170–71) proposes that modern physics resort to sound-based concepts to supplement (but of course without abandoning) the visually based apparatus in which physics has specialized.

Sound situates man in the middle of actuality and in simultaneity, whereas vision situates man in front of things and in sequentiality. Since technological man is more addicted to sight than to sound, we can start here with sight. Sight presents surfaces, as we have seen; but it does not present all surfaces, only those that are in front of us. We speak of sight as man knows it; what the world looks like to an insect with compound eyes presenting dozens of slightly different views of the same object simultaneously, or to a crustacean with eyes on stalks capable of viewing opposed sides of an object simultaneously is another thing. And yet not entirely another thing for even here we encounter surface as surface: sight is feedback, because all sight registers reflected light.

As a human being, I see only what is ahead, not what I know is behind. To view the world around me, I must turn my eyes, taking in one section after another, establishing a sequence. To view a friend from all sides, I must walk around him or have him turn around. There is no way to view all that is visible around me at once. As Merleau-Ponty has nicely put it in his "L'Oeil et l'esprit," vision is a dissecting sense. Or, to put it another way, one can say that it is sequential. It presents one thing after another. Even though each part of the landscape surrounding me on all sides is contemporaneous with every other part, sight splits it up temporally, gives it a one-piece-after-another quality. Sight, despite the fact that it is seemingly more independent of time than sound (which exists only when it is perishing in time) nevertheless is nonsimultaneous. The actuality around me accessible to sight, although it is all simultaneously on hand, can be caught by vision only in a succession of "fixes."

Sound is quite different. At a given instant I hear not merely what is in front of me or behind me or at either side, but all these things simultaneously, and what is above and below as well. We have just noted that there is no way to view all that is around me at once. By contrast, I not only can but must hear all the sounds around me at once. Sound thus situates me in the midst of a world.

Because it situates me in the midst of a world, sound conveys simultaneity. Although sound itself is fleeting, as we have seen, what it conveys at any instant of its duration is not dissected but caught in the actuality of the present, which is rich, manifold, full of diverse action, the only moment when everything is really going on at once. The ticking of my watch, the ringing of a church bell, a quick step on the floor, and the lowing of a diesel horn merge. One of the special terrors of those addicted chiefly to auditory syntheses is due to the disparity between this world of sound and that of sight: hearing makes me intimately aware of a great many goings-on which it lets me know are simultaneous but which I cannot possibly view simultaneously and thus have difficulty in dissecting or analyzing, and consequently of managing. Auditory syntheses overwhelm me with phenomena beyond all control.

Hearing does not of itself dissect as sight does. It will register all the sounds within its range, which are selected out only by specific acts of attention, and then only if competing sounds are not too loud. Of itself, hearing unites the sounds. It moves toward harmony. When the sounds will not unite, when they are cacophonous, hearing is in agony, for it cannot eliminate selectively—there is no auditory equivalent of averting one's face or eyes—even though with proper stimulus or effort the individual organism can attend to a select band of sound.

Although, as we have seen, sound perishes each instant that it lives, the instant when it does live is rich. Through sound we can become present to a totality which is a fullness, a plenitude. A symphony, produced by an orchestra which is seen as merely in front of us, fills the entire hall and assaults us from all sides. Stereophonic sound is sound in its full normalcy. Of its very nature, the sound world has depth, dimension, fullness such as the visual, despite its own distinctive beauties, can never achieve.

This is to say, too, that sound and hearing have a special relationship to our sense of presence. When we speak of a presence in its fullest sense—the presence which we experience in the case of another human being, which another person exercises on us and which no object or living being less than human can exercise—we speak of something that surrounds us, in which we are situated. "I am *in* his presence," we say, not "in front of his presence." Being in is what we experience in a world of sound.

Specializing in auditory syntheses and specializing in

visual syntheses foster different personality structures and different characteristic anxieties. Personality structure varies in accordance with variations in communications media and consequent variations in the organization of the sensorium. Obviously, these variations will not be the same or equally discernible in all cultures, but they are recognizable at times and analyzable to a degree.

In a world dominated by sound impressions, the individual is enveloped in a certain unpredictability. As has been seen, sound itself signals that action is going on. Something is happening, so you had better be alert. Sounds, moreover, tend to assimilate themselves to voices, whether in primitive cultures where thunder is heard as the voice of God or in our present-day imagination where in the depths of a dark wood the noises which even the most "advanced" technologically educated person hears about him strongly suggest voices, living beings, very likely persons, for intersubjectivity is one of the primary modes by which man's life-world is constituted. A world of sounds thus tends to grow into a world of voices and of persons, those most unpredictable of all creatures. Cultures given to auditory syntheses have this background for anxieties, and for their tendencies to animism.

Whatever the influence of this background, it appears from other evidence that at least a good many oral–aural cultures manifest characteristic anxiety syndromes which are far from typical in societies where the effects of literacy have been assimilated. Research in diverse non-literate cultures of Asia, Oceania, Africa, and the Americas, reported by Marvin K. Opler in *Culture, Psychiatry, and Human Values* (p. 135) has shown in these cultures, by contrast with literate cultures, a "uniformly . . . high incidence of states of confused excitement, with disorganizing amounts of anxiety, fear, and hostility present,

... frequently associated with either indiscriminate homi-
cidal behaviour or self-mutilation, or both, in a setting
of catathymic outbursts of activity." In other words, when
they are under emotional pressure, individuals in these
cultures tend far more than do literates to break out in
frenzied rages which often lead to indiscriminate
slaughter.

Linguistic history appears to confirm these results of
anthropological and psychological studies by attesting to
standard anxiety–hostility syndromes in primitive populations. The terms "to go berserk" or "to run amok"
attest that among the basically illiterate primitive Scan-
dinavians and Southeast Asians respectively this sort of
frenzied behavior was regular enough to generate the
special terms which we have imported into English. Opler
(p. 133) notes additional terms for similar behavior
among other nonliterate peoples. Scandinavian berserkers (bear-shirts), as in the *Ynglingasaga,* could apparently
work themselves into a frenzy more or less at will. In
Birth and Rebirth (p. 81) Mircea Eliade has related the
berserkers to members of the other *Männerbünde* of the
ancient Germanic civilization: one entered these men's
societies by undergoing terrifying ordeals (such as fighting unarmed) during which one had to behave as a beast
of prey. In the perspectives suggested by Carothers one
might say that the candidates for these societies learned
to respond to psychological stress by outbursts of wild
anxiety and hostility.

The riots in the Republic of the Congo at the achievement of independence a few years ago perhaps provide
more recent evidence of oral–aural anxiety syndromes.
I recall in particular the press reports of a Congolese
officer whose comment, when he was asked about the
riots, was quite simply, "What did you expect?" That is

to say, "Don't armies everywhere riot this way from time to time when the pressure builds up?"

One thinks further in this connection of the wrath of epic warriors, recalling that the epic is a form with its roots and its persistent conventions deriving from oral cultures. Achilles' wrath does not occur directly in battle, it is true, but the weight given it, which to speak frankly is quite unconvincing today, may well derive from association between warriors and states of blind frenzy. It is not impossible that the highly conventional (if also erratic) wrath of epic warriors all the way down to Orlando is referable to confused cultural memories of earlier favored frenzied states retained as epic conventions even when they had grown less understandable and more palpably histrionic as social conditions and personality structures changed with the growing effects of literacy. The "fury" of Orlando in Ariosto's *Orlando furioso* would appear to be such a confused and adjusted wrath, partly a takeoff on courtly love madness but given an epic military turn which evokes Ariosto's indulgent irony shot through at times with high comedy showing a basic uneasiness about epic conventions in general.

Whatever the traces which may have appeared in the epic, and survived more or less equivocally as this oral genre adjusted itself to writing and finally was driven to suicide by print, the outburst of confused, violently hostile anxiety is real enough in many oral cultures. (One cannot of course say with surety in all of them.) The psychological studies by Carothers, Seligman, and others, summarized by Opler in the work cited above, suggest that these outbursts, "often self-terminating in natural course" (you actually cure yourself by massacring others) result from a lack of systematized fancy or delusions acting as ego defenses. A great variety of studies shows that illiterates seldom if ever indulge in the schizophrenic delusional systematization which is a regular syndrome of individuals under great stress in literate cultures. That is to say, under psychological pressure, illiterates do not commonly withdraw into themselves to create a little dream-world where everything can be ideally ordered. In the study earlier cited, Carothers notes (p. 307) that among African illiterates "categories described as 'paranoic,' 'paraphrenic,' and 'paranoid' are seldom seen" and that among these illiterates "in general, the clinical picture in schizophrenic patients is marked by confusion." The individual is psychologically faced outward, he is a "tribal" man, and, under duress, he directs his anxieties and hostilities outward toward the material world around him and chiefly to what he is most intimately aware of in that aurally or vocally conceived world, that is, to his fellow man.

The extremely confused anxiety and hostility syndromes reported by Carothers and those he draws on are of course not necessarily the only behavioral manifestations in oral cultures related to schizoid phenomena of the sort found among literates. In *Magic and Schizophrenia* Géza Róheim has shown relationships between magical practices and schizophrenic behavior. There is some sort of connection, it would appear, between magic and anxiety, and it would seem not impossible to correlate Carothers' work and that of Róheim, who traces schizophrenia in general to an oral trauma (p. 221).

With writing, and more intensely with print, the individual first becomes aware of himself as capable of thinking for himself to a degree impossible for relatively overcommunalized tribal man. Without literacy man tends to solve problems in terms of what people do or say—in the tradition of the tribe, without much personal analysis. He lives in what anthropologists call a "shame" culture, which institutionalizes public pressures on individuals to ensure conformity to tribal modes of behavior. With literacy, the individual finds it possible to think through a situation more from within his own mind out of his own personal resources and in terms of an objectively analyzed situation which confronts him. He becomes more original and individual, detribalized.

This withdrawal into the self, however, involves special strains of its own. Carothers has associated literacy with growth in guilt feelings, pointing out that among African illiterates, "depressive syndromes with retardation and ideas of guilt, unworthiness, or remorse are hardly to be found." The guilt is associated, of course, with the sense of responsibility, the responsibility connected with a sense of one's interior as one's own, keener among literates than among illiterates. Where the schizophrenic illiterate is marked by confusion with resulting outbursts of anxiety and hostility, the schizophrenic literate can withdraw within himself to construct his own world, self-consistent but maintained by his own effort.

The literacy with which illiteracy is contrasted in the studies reported by Carothers and Opler is uniformly alphabetic literacy. We do not know what effect learning Chinese character writing or other nonalphabetic scripts would have on personality structures. But one can conjecture how the phonetic alphabet encourages schizophrenic delusional systematization.

First, reading of any sort forces the individual into himself by confronting him with thought in isolation, alone. The book takes the reader out of the tribe. His thought still has a minimal social guise: it is in a book, which comes from another. But the other is not there. The reader follows thought all alone.

Beyond this, script, and particularly the alphabet, provides a heightened experience of order. The world of thought is itself a beautifully intricate world, and the world of words is likewise impressively, if mysteriously, organized. But visual space appears to be, as we have seen, a special symbol of order and control. When the exquisitely organized worlds of thought and speech (with their natural affinity for each other) are further ordered by reduction to segmentation, to spatial surface, the possibility of control and organization of the world represented through thought and word becomes overpowering. Print, because it is still more spatially tidy, is more convincing than even writing: "I saw it in the book." The expression registers the automatic, subconsciously driven reaction. To attack the printed word would be to attack *the* symbol of order.

In his sensitive novel *No Longer at Ease,* concerned with the acculturation of his native Nigeria, Chinua Achebe cogently portrays (pp. 126–27) the awesome impression which knowledge of writing has made on a thoughtful elderly man, who is fascinated by its order and stability and rather given to explaining this order and stability to illiterate kinsmen. He urges them to meditate on Pilate's words (which he quotes in oral fashion, that is thematically, not verbatim, suppressing Pilate's "I"): "What is written is written." The same man is even more impressed by print. He never destroys a piece of printed paper, but in boxes and the corners of his room saves every bit of it he can find. Order so assured as that of printed words deserves to be preserved, whatever the words say. It appears reasonable that such experience of this spectacularly ordered environment for thought, free from interference, simply there, unattended and unsupervised by any discernible person,

would open to the overstrained psyche the new possibility of withdrawal into a world away from the tribe, a
private world of delusional systematization—an escape
not into violence or tribal magic, but into the interior
of one's own consciousness, rendered schizoid but once
and for all consistent with itself.

We can go even further than this. The alphabet, useful
and indispensable as it has certainly proved to be, itself
entails to some extent delusional systematization if not
necessarily schizophrenia properly so called. The alphabet, after all, is a careful pretense. Letters are simply not
sounds, do not have the properties of sounds. As we have
seen, their whole existence and economy of operation is
in a temporally neuter space rather than within the
living stream of time. With alphabetic writing, a kind of
pretense, a remoteness from actuality, becomes institutionalized.

Of course it can be maintained that even spoken words
are pretenses too, in the sense that they are out of contact
with the actuality they represent. Words are symbols,
and all symbolization proceeds by indirection and to this
extent demands a lack of contact with reality. It is of the
nature of symbolization that the symbol stands for something other than itself. Man's knowledge is roundabout,
and he conceives of reality not by dealing with it in the
raw but by removing himself from it through symbolization, thus to achieve a more fruitful union. He re-pre-
sents in symbols, conceptual and verbal, what is present
on other grounds. We shall not enter into the question
of conceptual symbolization here, but consider only the
sensible word. To the extent that he uses symbols to represent actuality to himself, and especially in his use of
perishing vocal symbols, words, to achieve contact with
truth which he knows as extratemporal and permanent,

man, too, resorts to pretense. But the pretense in oral verbalization is less contrived than in alphabetic writing. For reasons which we can suggest later, resort to sound for intelligibility comes about naturally. Reduction of this sound to space is by contrast artificial, contrived.

Even though chirographic and typographic man is less inclined to manifest the frenzied anxiety–hostility syndrome of oral–aural man, he does have special anxieties of his own, for, as was noted earlier in connection with the Freudian psychosexual sequences, chirographic and typographic man must keep order in an artificial spatial world of speech, not only far removed from the real habitat of speech but at root not entirely compatible with it. Though serviceable and enriching beyond all measure, nevertheless, by comparison with the oral medium, writing and print are permanently decadent. However vaguely, they entail some special threat of death. "The letter kills, but the spirit gives life" (II Cor. 3:6). The spirit (Latin, *spiritus*), we remember, meant the breath, the vehicle of the living word in time.

THE AFFINITY OF SOUND AND THOUGHT

In all human cultures the spoken word appears as the closest sensory equivalent of fully developed interior thought. Thought is nested in speech. In considering the relationship of the word and sound, we must raise the question whether this has to be so. In its external expression, need man's thought make for the auditory world so directly as it in fact does? Instead of expressing truth through sound for the ear, could thought express and communicate itself with equal urgency and effectiveness through touch or taste or smell or vision? It makes use of these senses to a degree, of course. But could it do so more radically, so that instead of a lecture in spoken words about something, one could have a tactile object or a series of tastes or smells or pictures which, with no assistance from any oral verbalization at all, would explain, let us say, the theory of relativity? Or could one work out the theory of relativity without resort, direct or indirect, to verbalization, using instead of words (sounds) operations in the other sensory fields?

We can perhaps dismiss the fields of touch and taste and smell as being too "proximate" (to use the Freudian term) to us, not abstract enough, not removed enough from our bodies or from sensory objects themselves to enable us to control the field sufficiently or adequately to represent otherness. Sight appears more plausible, however, as a possible substitute for sound. Could we have visual words—not visual representations of sounds as with the alphabet, but visual constructs which independently of all sounds and all oral words would serve as words do? We must insist on "independently of all sounds and all oral words," for there are indeed ways of "thinking" with symbols which at the time are not verbalized, except that such symbols at one point or another are explained, given their meaning, through words, and thus are virtually verbal in the sense that they are cued into the oral.

Or, recasting the question, since script, and particularly the alphabet, substitutes for the spoken word so well (although, as we have seen, not perfectly nor without permanent strain), might not the "word" have originated in the visual field in the first place? Could not thought have started by attaching itself to written marks unrelated to sounds and performing the same function that words as sounds perform, that is, forming the matrix and the expression for internal, intellectual concepts and judgments? Vision is, after all, highly informative. In the *Summa Theologica* (I, 84, 2c) Aquinas, following a line of thought well developed before his time and since, styles vision the *sensus magis cognoscitivus,* a sense more informative than the other senses, as it is also more abstract, spiritual, perfect, and generalized (*communior*) than the other senses (I, 78, 3c); this shows how far scholastic thought had moved into full objectification. Why could thought as such and communication not have been linked initially with vision, so that one might start with a spatial sign instead of a vocal word? Or why could not conceptualization have been linked directly with one of the other senses—touch or smell or taste? Do words, which are the very web of thought, have to be sounds?

The historical fact is that the world of sound (which, as we have seen is of course associated to some degree with the tactile and especially the kinesthetic) has proved in all cultures the most immediate sensory coefficient of thought. Sight may provide a great deal of the material to think *about,* but the terms *in* which all men do their thinking correspond to words, that is, to sounds. One can readily discern several reasons why this is so, and probably necessarily so: connections between sound, thought, and communication; connections between sound, thought, truth, and time; connections between the structure of predication itself and vocalization. These reasons can be taken up here in order.

Connections between sound, thought, and communication. From the earliest individual experience, thought in any developed form and the spoken word are not quite the same thing and are not always tied together in the same way, and yet, basically, they are united, as Gilbert Ryle, for example, has shown in *The Concept of Mind.* We have no instances of conceptualized thought arising in complete independence of words. Even deaf children learn from those who themselves are vocalizers. They participate indirectly in a world held together by voice.

Neither do we have any instances of languages which are not in one way or another constituted in sound. In *A Study of Glossematics,* Bertha Siertsema has gone at length (pp. 109–27, etc.) into the question of the primacy of sound in language, examining the various theories or simple assertions (for example, Bertrand Russell's) which contest the primacy of sound and maintain that it would be possible to have a language entirely independent of sound phenomena. As a result of her survey, the primacy of sound emerges as quite incontestable. "Languages" making no acknowledged or overt use of sound always depend (often in elaborately veiled ways) upon languages which are built in sound.

We have only to look at the way in which a child begins to speak and think in order to see the actual state of affairs here. A great deal of work has been done on this subject, but the basic patterns of development are accessible in standard studies such as Otto Jespersen's book, *Language: Its Nature, Origin, and Development,* which will provide ample background for the present discussion, although this discussion itself draws very little on Jespersen directly.

Jespersen and others make explicit what we all know from experience and daily observation: children do not achieve thinking by themselves. They learn to think as they are introduced into the use of words which are far older than they themselves and far older than their teachers, and which belong not to them but to everybody. This fact is strikingly underlined by the plight of congenitally deaf children. Although the congenitally deaf are not entirely out of contact with the world of sound, because they can at least see the visible concomitants or results of verbal activity—lip movements, changes in posture related to verbal communication, as when individuals face each other or whisper into each other's ears, and so on—nevertheless such contacts with sound are for them desperately indirect and confusing. Until the pedagogical techniques for introducing deaf-mutes more thoroughly, if always indirectly, into the oral–aural world were perfected in the past few generations, deaf-mutes always grew up intellectually subnormal. Left unattended, the congenitally deaf are far more intellectually retarded than the congenitally blind.

A child has a potential of his own for thinking, but he needs oral–aural contact with others to actuate it. A lalling stage is typical of human infants, and apparently of human infants alone, for it does not appear even among the higher anthropoids. In *The Ape in Our House,* Cathy Hayes reports about the young chimpanzee which was raised by her and her husband as though it were a human infant. She notes (pp. 60–67, 101, 127, 136) that, although they were watching for something like the lalling stage in the chimpanzee, they found none. Like other chimpanzees, Viki had standard reflex instinctive signal sounds, and she would make sounds if someone was around making sounds at her, as a dog will reply to another's barking. The few spontaneous sounds she for a while gave vent to ceased suddenly at four months for good. Later she learned to produce an "ahhh" sound on purpose, that is, not simply as a reflex. The three words she was finally taught to say (mama, papa, cup) were taught to her by *manipulating her lips* while rewarding her (emotionally at least) for saying her "ahhh" —she was this far from the human child's spontaneous projection of a persistent effluvium of sound around himself in which he lives.

A human infant is a strikingly different being from the little ape. During the lalling stage he surrounds himself with a float of sound, which involves, of course, kinesthetic sensations, since words are "mouthed" sounds. He burbles and gurgles and crows and often plays with his lips at the same time. Parents and others are intrigued by the activity. When the child chances on a sound approximating "mama," for example, they often become ecstatic. The child finds that from here on his world blooms in a most wonderful way. He is made over, fondled, caressed (Skinnerian psychologists, who tend to cast explanations in visual–tactile terms, would say he is "reinforced"), and he soon learns that saying mama is a highly rewarding diversion, especially given a certain state of affairs in the world around him, this "big, blooming, buzzing confusion" that William James identifies as the product of the relatively undeveloped, undifferentiated sensorium of the child. Soon associations begin to form under repeated and even frantic encouragement from adults. Between this sound which he makes and that persistent portion of this big, blooming, buzzing confusion which adults recognize as the child's mother, an association is established, as a result of the work of the others around the infant. The child's own mental activities are in some mysterious way engaged in and activated by this process, and before long he gradually forms the budding concept of mama or mother which goes with the spoken sound and he applies this concept to the someone he has been coached into separating from the confusion and identifying as some sort of unified being.

Which did the child learn first? Did he learn first to isolate "mama" from the confusion of his sensory world and thereby to think mama first or did he learn the word mama first? The question appears quite impossible to

answer. If anything, the word came first and the concept
after. Only the word was not really a word until the concept accompanied it. Previously it was just a sound. Of
course in this process, as we have indicated, other senses
were active—touch, kinesthesia, and sight, as well as
smell and even taste. But the process terminates in an intimate association between thought and hearing. Why?
We can postpone dealing with this question for a moment until we note some further details about the social
character of man's thought.

Language gives the infant access to hundreds of thousands of years of human experience—millions of man-
hours previously spent in developing the concepts with
which language furnishes him. It is at least questionable
whether anyone would have an effective incentive to
think in the absence of a going language, access to the
world of sound, and older persons eager to initiate him
into the linguistic world. Even if he did have an incentive, he might well never really get his thinking drives
off the ground. Instead of forming the concept of mama
or man as he is in fact so urgently coached into doing,
he might waste his time forming fruitless and relatively
unreal categories. He might group together, for example,
all upright, brown, smoothish things—chair legs, tree
trunks, brown painted oars leaning against houses, and
so on. Or he might form a concept grouping all small
fuzzy, yellow things: dandelions, certain caterpillars (but
only certain ones), pieces of fluff from two of his mother's
dresses, and other miscellanea. Even when they are being
inducted actively into the use of thought and language,
as Jespersen has noted (pp. 113, 127, etc.), children do
temporarily construct such categories, which they later
discard as inoperable in the linguistic economy around
them (some languages and economies of thought work

with categories which others do not use, but there are countless categories which in any economy of language or thought are useless and disabling). Later on, when the child grows up and becomes a basic research scientist or a philosopher, he can experiment again in novel and unusual concepts more knowingly and with better hope of productivity.

The origins of thought and language in the individual's history make evident the radically social nature of thought itself. As we know it, thought appears only in a linguistic setting. There is a limitless variety of non-verbal activity connected with thinking, but when our thought is fully developed, it manifests itself as verbalized, although the thought may be interior and the word not spoken. To be verbalized, it must become part of a going language—although if it is truly original thought, it may alter the language somewhat—and the fact that it is part of a going language means that it is communicable. In this sense, human thought can never be strictly private at all.

Such considerations show the unreality of the question whether on one or another occasion wordless thoughts are possible, at least insofar as the present problems are concerned. Such wordless thoughts would come into being in an individual who in one way or another knew at least some words. They would thus be framed or bound, if not in words, at least in a universe of consciousness actualized through verbal activity and experience. For a thought to be purely wordless it would have to originate in an individual who had never known any words. Whether such a human being, completely unaffected directly or indirectly by speech in himself or others, could mature to the point of actually thinking at all appears at best unlikely. We need a social setting, not incidentally because it is pleasant and congenial, but absolutely, to get our own private potential under way, to induct us into the awareness of self and others which, since our thinking is budded onto communication, sets the thinking itself in operation.

Needing the social setting to get thinking under way means, in effect, to need sound. As has been earlier suggested, a spoken language unites communities as nothing else does. The psychological reasons for this are by no means all understood. But one reason is certainly the interiorizing quality of sound and thus of voice. Voice, as has been explained, manifests interiors as interiors and unites them. Since thought arises in a human community and since a human community is essentially a union of interior consciousnesses, each self-driven and completely open only to itself (no one else knows what I experience when I say "I"), and yet consciously and reflectively conjoined with others (that is, joined in terms of its own interiority), it appears understandable that that particular sense world which is of its nature most directly interior would be the most readily exploitable in direct connection with thought.

Such a world is the world of sound. Vision, as stated earlier, of itself manifests only surfaces, superficies, outsides; to see the inside of anything, one has to make it somehow an outside, cutting the object open or entering it (as a room) to see its interior as a surface. Exploring an interior by touch violates the interior, invades it, as we have likewise seen. The tactile sense which gives us impressions of insideness or interiority without entailing violation or invasion is kinesthesia, which provides us with the feel of ourselves inside our own bodies. But kinesthesia does not give us an experience of interiority in others: we have no experience of kinesthesia outside our own selves. Smell and taste are, as we have seen, essentially come-or-go senses and, like touch, proximity senses as well, too close to bodily reactions and too specialized and uncontrollable to serve as flexible communications media.

Sound is not only interior-manifesting, but highly flexible—that is, variable with little or no bodily effort (once the organism has had practice in producing sound). It is also, as has been seen, noninterfering: one can use the voice while doing things with the muscles of the hands, legs, and other parts of the body. This gives it a social advantage; it interferes minimally or not at all with bodily activity often needed for social involvement.

Of the other modes of communication, that most like sound is gesture, with which Père Marcel Jousse has so intimately and accurately connected the use of voice. Gesture is apprehended visually, with a large admixture of tactile and kinesthetic awarenesses. Chiefly these latter make it like sound. In *The Barbarian Within* (pp. 51–53) I have discussed the way we apprehend the meaning of words by imagining ourselves making them. We gather the meaning of gestures in similar fashion. Gestures in a way come from the interior, too, as sounds do; they are external projections of the interior economy of the human body. They are like sound, too, in that they progress through time. The meaning of a bow is in its progression from uprightness to the inclined position. Even frozen gestures have their meaning in terms of the progression which, imaginatively at least, preceded them. The upraised arm of the Statue of Liberty has its meaning because it is up*raised:* one senses that it was not always thus, that the figure moved its arm from a lower plane to this high elevation and holds it there with effort. And yet gesture is not like sound in at least two important ways.

First, it can be frozen or stopped: it is not so irretrievably bound to time as sound is, for, when stopped, sound leaves behind not a permanent something but only its opposite, silence. Moreover, gesture is "interfering." It demands the cessation of a great many physical activities which can be carried on easily while one is talking. Further, it is not so directly interiorizing as sound by the very fact that it is visually apprehended. Gesture has surface, although it does not consist simply of surface. Finally, it is not so socializing as sound, nor so reciprocating, nor so versatile. The intertribal sign language of the Plains Indians of the United States did not unite the Indians so intimately as did the spoken languages of the individual tribes.

In his work on the peoples of the Middle East whom he so aptly styles "verbomotor" (*verbomoteur*), Jousse made much of the connection between gesture or visible bodily movement and the spoken word, and rightly so. It may be that human communication began with gesture and proceeded from there to sound (voice). Gesture would be a beautiful beginning, for gesture is a beautiful and supple thing. But, if this was a development which really took place, the shift from gesture to sound was, on the whole, unmistakably an advance in communications and in human relations.

Connections between sound, thought, truth, and time. Sound belongs with thought not only because of its interiorizing and socializing powers but also because of its relationship to time. As has been earlier explained, sound is time-bound: it exists by moving through time. Sound can never be sensed other than as something *going on.* Joined to the forces of life, sound has a peculiar fecundity. Richard Albert Wilson has called attention in *The Miraculous Birth of Language* (pp. 160, 234–43), as noted earlier, to the way in which even the animal's voice as sound is future-oriented and hence pitched toward purposiveness. When we consider the relationship of sound to human intelligence itself, we notice certain other connections. Human knowledge, in the sense of formal intellectual cognition, is time-bound. It exists in its full intensity only when the knower is doing something; in a certain sense, human knowledge, too, is something going on, an activity which, not only when it is moving toward its goal, but also when it has achieved its goal, is truly an event rather than a permanent condition.

In treating of the relationship between thought and linguistic articulation, I do not wish to imply either that everything we do when we think is verbal or that there are no ways of possessing truth other than verbalized concepts. What we do when we are thinking certainly no one has completely and adequately described. The subject has hardly been a neglected one, as can be seen by examining, for example, George Humphrey's *Thinking,* but the potpourri of impressions, images, words formed and half-formed, snatches of dialogue, imaginative constructs, "insights" (this term says everything and nothing, and, of course, assimilates intellectual knowledge only to sight), floods of feeling, moments of seeming stultification of all faculties, distractions fought off or welcomed or sought for—all this and all the other innumerable goings-on in the consciousness when we are "thinking" probably will forever elude total itemization. Thought is connected with words, but it is not a chain of verbalization in all or even most instances.

Moreover, if we take thought in its reference to the achievement of truth, we must also acknowledge that there are many ways of possessing truth other than through verbalized thought. It is evident enough that there is a possession of truth which consists in a kind of authenticity of one's whole being and which is not directly a matter of having correctly formed concepts placed in the correct enunciable propositions. Truth can come into man's possession in ways other than direct conceptualization. It can be known in the proper attunement of man to actuality. One can sense the truth in a situation or simply in being itself without formalizing this truth in concepts which are fully developed and thus admit of verbalization.

Yet, for all this, the possession of truth does call for conceptualization and thus verbalization. The truths which man possesses or thinks he possesses through "attunedness" or in other inarticulate ways demand testing, and the only way they can formally be tested is by being conceptualized (and thus articulated, at least in the imagination). Whatever man knows, he is driven inexorably to conceptualize as definitively as possible and to articulate. The history of mankind is the history of greater and greater conceptualization and verbalization of truth, at least some of which was held in infraconceptual form, unverbalized, from the beginning. Post-Hegelian man is well aware of this movement whereby as man moves through history everything becomes more and more explicit. In its addiction to spelling out everything, even the hitherto most guarded areas of personal consciousness, our age makes this movement toward the explicit, the fully conceptualized, the totally articulate, more spectacularly evident than ever before.

To see the relationship of sound with thought, truth, and time, it is necessary to look into the various activities involved in formal, conceptualized knowledge in their relationship to formal truth. The question of truth does not apply directly to all the activities involved in conceptualized knowing. This is a philosophical common-place. Concepts themselves are used in knowing and are critical in our grasp of truth, and yet a concept as such is strictly speaking neither true nor false. It makes no sense to ask, "Is this true or false: 'Overcoat'?" or "Is this true or false: 'Six o'clock'?" or "Is this true or false: 'Idiosyncrasy'?" There is no way to answer such questions. They make no sense. Overcoat is of itself neither true nor false, nor is six o'clock or idiosyncrasy. Isolated concepts express neither truth nor falsehood. They can be adequate or inadequate, but as adequate concepts can serve in a false statement, so even an inadequate concept can serve in a true statement: "The common concept of race is inadequate" is a true statement.

Moreover, the various reasoning processes, which are also used in knowing, as such are strictly speaking neither true nor false. They are only correct or incorrect. A false syllogism, for example, might be made up of three perfectly true statements: "All trees perish after a certain time; tree is a sound; therefore all sounds perish after a certain time." Each of the members of this supposed syllogism is true: there is nothing strictly untrue or false about it. It is defective as a reasoning process simply because it is incorrect, wrongly structured: the parts, though true, do not hang together, are not effectively related.

There is only one place in the intellective or knowledge processes where the question of truth or falsity directly applies: this is the point at which we form a judgment, at which we predicate something of something, join a subject and a predicate. We may know truth in various ways, but only in predication can truth and falsity be formally tested. To any direct juncture of subject-member with predicate-member the question,

Is this true? applies (although it may not always be possible to answer the question). Thus although it is mean-
ingless to ask, "Is this true or false: 'Overcoat' or 'Six
o'clock' or 'Idiosyncrasy'?" it is quite meaningful to ask,
"Is this true: 'This is an overcoat' or 'It is not yet six
o'clock' or 'Emily Dickinson writes of idiosyncrasy in
her poems'?" That is to say, the plenary act of intellection, of knowing in full formal attire, is the judgment,
the statement, the union of subject and predicate. It is
when one says, "A is B," or "A is not B," that the basic
question regarding knowledge can be applied, the question of truth or falsehood.

The origins and structure of the subject–predicate relationship are buried in the origins of language itself.
There is some evidence that in the earlier stages of languages nouns and verbs are not so completely disjoined
from each other as they are in later stages of linguistic
development, as Heinz Werner and Bernard Kaplan
have explained in *Symbol Formation* (pp. 474–503).
"Young" languages often employ holophrastic symbolization, unitary forms referring to a single complex state of
affairs. Even a language developed as far as classical Latin
regularly uses forms such as *cogitavisset,* which would
break down in an "older" or later-stage language such as
modern English into separate elements, "he would have
thought." The Latin he (or she or it) is not simply understood in *cogitavisset:* it is expressed by the "-t," although
this is not a clear-cut distinct subject form but part of the
verb or predicate. Nevertheless, it appears clear that the
differentiation maximized in languages such as Modern
English, which regularly uses quite distinct words for
subjects and predicates, is germinally present in all utterance which actually affirms or denies something. In an
article, "Noun and Verb in Universal Grammar," R. H.

Robins has pointed out that "Grammatical analysis in terms of a basic distinction of nominal and verbal categories succeeds in new fields and stands critical examination in the older areas of language study where so much else of traditional grammar has had to be abandoned." This does not mean that we know all there is to know about subject and predicate relationships, but it does indicate that the statements which we have adduced for examination here may be considered true universal paradigms.

The judgment, or juncture of subject-member and predicate-member, expressed or implied, is necessary for knowledge to be fully present even to my own mind. Only when I "say" a truth to myself can I be sure that I really know it. My memory may be stored with all sorts of potential from study and reflection, but I must activate this store of knowledge, bring it into consciousness, in order actually to possess it or see it fully as knowledge. Only when I thus maneuver my knowledge in subject–predicate relationships can I explicitly and fully experience it to test and taste its truth. This means in effect that I must say it to myself interiorly, effecting in my consciousness the juncture of subject and predicate, and to this extent moving from subject to predicate in a certain expanse of time.

Like the external verbal statement which is its co-efficient, the judgment thus exists in a sense while it is passing out of existence. I can, of course, revive the judgment or the statement over and over again, savoring its truth each time: "This is an overcoat," "This is an overcoat," and so on. Or I can keep at the focus of my attention the imaginative construct on which the knowledge bears, a geometrical figure or the image of this gray overcoat, so that the judgment can be revived instantaneously any time I want. But only in some such sense is my knowledge enduring. Often when we say we know something—Euclidean geometry or American geography—we of course mean this, that our imaginations are in such condition that we can revive knowledge in these fields on demand. But in the strict sense we actually know to the full what we are actually "judging" here and now for its truth or falsity. We know in the strict sense, that is, by a kind of transit through time.

In a certain way it is of course true that our actual intellectual knowing seems in a way to escape time or transcend it. What we have called the taste of truth appears to have no real duration. I possess the truth, savor it, test it, know it as truth and not falsity, in the judgment "This is an overcoat," not simply when the concepts represented by these words pass through my consciousness but more properly at the instant, the "moment of truth," when I *experience* the juncture of subject and predicate, the moment when (after sensing the meaning of the judgment, if you want, in advance), I actually taste its meaning, when the statement comes alive and flashes into consciousness so that I sense that it signifies, that it says something, so that I can "tell" it is true or false. This moment of truth is hard to pin down exactly. It is after I say "This" and probably before I quite finish "overcoat," for inner awareness is perhaps to a degree psychologically ahead of its verbalization.

The moment of truth, moreover, probably is not exactly the same every time I utter the statement, and if I utter it often enough will disappear altogether—the perceptual field disintegrates and the words become mere sounds, no longer significant. Nevertheless, it appears that the experience of truth, the moment of truth, does occur as a kind of instantaneous realization. It is not something felt as protracted, drawn out in time. "This is a watch." For how long does the living juncture of sub-ject-member (this) and predicate-member (is a watch) actually endure? The juncture as such, effected when subject and predicate are in a sense·felt as one, certainly has some kind of quasi-instantaneous, timeless air. To this extent, the moment of truth is psychological, not a movement through time. It escapes time. But it does so in its own special way. A landscape is independent of time, too, but in a different fashion. A landscape lies relatively unchanged as the stream of time moves on. The moment of truth does not at all lie unchanged as the stream of time moves on. It comes as a flash, only more instantaneously than a flash. It does not outlast a certain expanse of time. Functioning in a statement, where its relation to truth can be tested, the word thus rises out of and above time.

Nevertheless, the moment of truth is also very ob-viously surrounded by time, bounded by duration. The way to it, its milieu, its surrounding, its environment and ground, the words themselves and the succession of concepts (subject before predicate, or sometimes in some languages predicate before subject), the progression from "this" to "watch" is all very definitely in time. "Only through time time is conquered," writes T. S. Eliot with great wisdom in *Burnt Norton*. He is echoing a vast tradi-tion which in various ways would incorporate the kind of awareness I have tried to recreate here. The word is both in time and beyond time. The tiniest truth is eternal.

The moment of truth rises above time by a movement through time. The movement through time allies our realization of truth immediately with sound, which, as we have seen, has a built-in relationship to the passage of time which the objects of senses other than hearing do not have. Our knowing is time-bound as sound is time-bound. Hence it appears natural enough that thought be more intimately linked with sound and hearing than with any other field of sense perception.

To this account of the connections of sound, thought, and time one might object that the causality might well work in the opposite direction. We have said that human thought allies itself with words because it is time-bound. Could it not be that it is time-bound because it allies itself with words? Indeed it could. Since we learn to talk and to think simultaneously, one activity structures the other. Man's thought is the kind of thought it is because it takes form in a matrix of sound. It takes form in a matrix of sound because it is the kind of thought it is. We can speculate if we wish about what other thought unconnected to time and sound would be. In the *Summa Theologica* (I, 58, 4; etc.) Aquinas, at least, though he was far less attentive to sound as such than we have been here, was quite sure that such thought would entail no juncture of subject and predicate and also such thought is quite unthinkable directly by man and unimaginable (it would involve no imagination because it would be without images). Until we can produce some such thought for inspection, however, we shall have to restrict our descriptive analyses to the only kind of thought of which we do have experience, that directly or indirectly in a matrix of sound.

Connections between predication and vocalization. There is a final reason for the alliance of sound and thought which shows itself in descriptions of the judgment or the statement, that is, of the process of predication. For it would appear impossible to state fully what is meant by the so-called juncture of subject and predicate without some reference to an act of utterance, to

the production of sound. Predication, the so-called joining of subject and predicate, making a judgment, seemingly cannot be conceived of simply by analogy with an
operation in a visual or other sensory field: at one point
or another descriptions of predication resort to thinking
of it as a saying, a production of sound.

It would appear otherwise from the fact that we do
speak of a copula, such as "is," which "joins" terms to
form a judgment: *The man is tall.* Is not the notion of
coupling or juncture a spatially conceived notion, rep-
resentable on a visual or visual–tactile field? Surely it is.
But how useful is this notion here? It is too general to
be definitive. Terms such as "and" or "also" couple or
join other terms without constituting predication. What
makes a judgment or statement is not that it involves a
juncture but that in it precisely a *predicate* term is
joined to a subject, that is, related to the subject in the
way in which predicates relate to subjects.

The key word in the definition is not "joined" but
"predicate." Predicate means something said, and quite
literally so. *Praedicatum* (something said before an auditory, a proclamation, declaration) is the Latin equivalent, part for part (*prae+dicare*), of the Greek term
katēgoría (*katá+agorá*), which means an accusation,
charge, something cried out against someone in the
marketplace (the *agorá*). When we refer to joining a
predicate to a subject, we thus are in effect referring to
bringing an *accusation* to bear against a subject.

The relationship is that of a visual (or visual–tactile)
spatial field (subject) to an oral–aural field (predicate).
The subject (Latin *subjectum*, something thrown under;
matching the Greek *hypokeimenon*, something lying
under, placed under), is conceived of as in a spatial field.
The predicate or *katēgoría* is conceived of as an oral–

aural phenomenon, a saying. The Latin language registers the state of affairs here in another way: *verbum*, the
general Latin term for word, is used also to designate the
predicate rather than the subject (it gives us our term,
verb). The verb is a word—that is, it is something spoken
—in a more intense fashion than is a subject. It is significant that when one points at an object to give it a
name (*nomen*, the Latin for name, means also noun, and
gives us our English word, noun) the pointing gesture
(a spatial operation) normally stands for the subject and
the word uttered belongs to the predicate member of the
utterance. Thus when a child points to a tree and utters
the word tree, he ordinarily means, "[This]/[is a] tree."

This account of knowledge of course raises an obvious
difficulty concerning the permanence of knowledge. If
knowledge comes to man basically as an event, how can
it refer to what is permanent? This difficulty is rather a
shallow one. The fact that the act of knowing is for us an
event does not incapacitate it for relating to and registering truths that are not mere events but permanent and
invariable, relatively or absolutely. The act of knowing
is not a dramatization of its object. Thought does not
have to reproduce duration or permanence in order to
represent it. It takes no longer to think of a millennium
than of a minute. And the fact that a statement about you
is a fleeting thing does not mean that the person who
makes the statement is unaware that you are relatively
permanent, that you have been on hand for twenty or
thirty or seventy years. By the same token, a fleeting
statement can refer to a quite timeless truth, cognized in
time. As we have seen, a judgment or statement has its
own way of transcending the temporal, from within the
temporal itself.

A second difficulty perhaps warrants more attention.

If intellectual knowledge is an event for man, how does it in any sense abide in him? For we do think of knowledge as abiding, as something permanently possessed. What does it mean to say that I have known a theorem of Euclid's twenty years when I have not actually thought of it except at rare intervals during this period? It means quite obviously that during this period I have been able to call the knowledge of the theorem into my consciousness at will, and it means no more. The shopworn distinction between "habitual" and "actual" knowledge is meaningful here. I have the knowledge as a kind of possession, a *habitus,* even when I am not thinking about it. But unless I am actually conscious of something, it can hardly be said that I know it in the full sense of the term. As an actuality, my habitual knowledge can come into being only by passing into and out of time.

These are rather commonplace matters, but they can be disquieting. Many, perhaps most, persons in our culture are driven to think of intellectual knowledge in terms of space and vision. As has been seen, vision is at its optimum when its object is quiescent. To deny quiescence in any way to intellectual knowledge appears to such persons, as it appeared to their progenitor Plato, somehow destructive, for it leaves them no way to conceive of knowledge at all. It has never occurred to them how far knowing is not just a "gaze," an inspection, but more radically an act like an utterance. Only derivatively and at second hand can our formal access to truth be endowed with spatial qualities, quiescence, quasipermanence. Knowledge as had by man belongs in the first instance with the living word in time. This is its habitat, its home. Truth, permanent though it is, is formally accessible to man primarily in terms of an intellectual event, not in terms of a diagram. The diagram is only a prop to knowledge. Like other quantifications associated with knowledge, diagrams belong with the hardware that can be put on computers. They are the paraphernalia of knowledge which are often necessarily massive but which themselves are not knowledge. Knowledge is actual in the judgment, statement, assertion—that is, in an event in time through which radical intelligibility is realized. Insofar as it escapes time, and, as has been seen, there is a sense in which it does do this, the intellect does not come to rest in the kind of permanence represented by motionless objects in space. Rather, if we may resort to a spatial metaphor while protesting the metaphor's inadequacy, it leaps out of time into a living instant, a luminous present. Here it lives its truth. Awareness of the irreducibly nonspatial elements in thought is crucial if we are to grasp the meaning and the sacredness of the word.

The permanence associated with spatial representations is, after all, deceptive. In fact, everything in space moves and, even if it did not, local quiescence is not permanence. All that is mortal decays. A picture may be centuries old but it has been and is still changing, slowly, so that by contrast with the living word, moving through this present instant of time, it appears unchanging. But the permanence is, in the last analysis, relative, and the living word used in an utterance, as we have seen, achieves a kind of timelessness or rather supratemporal existence which spatial quiescence can never achieve. Only God is unchanging, and if we think of his changelessness in terms of immobility in space—as, in one way or another, we are pretty well doomed to do—we must always remind ourselves that while divine constancy is in one way like such spatial changelessness it is in another way not like it at all, for God lives, and to comprehend life we must somehow think of motion, too.

At this point the analogy between the word of God and the word of man breaks down. For the world of sound, while it has life, does lack permanence, whereas "the word of our God stands forever" (Isa. 40:8). In Christian teaching the word of God is permanent, however, not with the quasipermanence of space but with the more real permanence of silence. Silence refers to the sound world again, but negatively. It is that enduring condition of which sound is only the interruption. Encounter with God can be realized in the spoken human word, but because human words do not endure and silence does, encounter with God is even more encounter with silence. In the Hebreo-Christian tradition this silence is known to be living and active, a communication between persons, more like a word than anything else. Is not what we have called the moment of truth, the instant when we savor the truth or falsity of an utterance, a kind of silence? If it is, it in some way endures.

SOUND AND THE SACRAL: ACOUSTIC SPACE

The desacralization of man's life-world has been the object of a great deal of recent study, not much of which had had to do with the word as sound or with developments within the sensorium as such. Gerardus van der Leeuw in *Religion in Essence and Manifestation* and Mircea Eliade in *The Sacred and the Profane* and *Patterns in Comparative Religion* have pulled together great masses of material to show the historical roots of religion in a sense of sacred time and space, marked by hierophanies. In *The Sacred and the Profane* Eliade has pointed out that desacralization of the world has been a quite modern phenomenon, and this recentness of desacralization has been much commented on by others. Professor Eliade does not undertake to detail in these

works how or why this desacralization or secularization
has occurred, although he suggests that it has been a
correlative of a new sense of homogeneous time and
space unmarked by any special sacred occurrences. It is
a commonplace that the development of modern science
and technology has favored such a sense of time and
space and thus has furthered secularization.

The growth of desacralized areas in man's life-world—
a growth which is by no means always displeasing to those
religiously committed persons who know that the cause
of religion is not served by denying all relevance to the
secular—is due certainly to a complex of causes, often
confusingly interrelated. Not a few of these appear definitely connected with our concern about the word as
sound and about its presence as word among men and
thus warrant some attention here.

The desacralization of culture, first of all, is certainly
influenced by the sequence of development in the verbal
media. Migration of the word from the world of sound
into the space world via the alphabet lies at the base of
modern technology, which is unthinkable without written records and which cannot make productive use of
pictographic writing as it does of the alphabet. But more
than this, the shift of focus from the spoken word and
habits of auditory synthesis to the alphabetized written
word and visual synthesis (actuality is measured by picturability) devitalizes the universe, weakens the sense of
presence in man's life-world, and in doing so tends to
render this world profane, to make it an agglomeration
of things.

From what has been said here earlier regarding the
nature of the word as sound, it should be obvious that the
habits of auditory synthesis common in cultures which
are purely or residually oral–aural contribute to the

primitive sacral sense. Sound of itself generates a sense of mystery. Unlike time and space, which may or may not suggest activity, sound of itself, as an outgoing phenomenon, registers the actual use of power. Moreover, sound (in conjunction with the kinesthetic and tactile elements which its perception normally involves) is a manifestation of an interior. Voice, for man the paradigm of all sound, manifests the actual use of power by the most interior of interiors, a person. In a universe conceived in terms of auditory synthesis, the sense of personal activity is overwhelming. This fact is critical in the Hebreo-Christian tradition, where God himself is personal, but it is operative in all religions insofar as any manifestation of the sacred, willy-nilly, suggests personal presence. It is impossible to be reverent to a thing as simply a thing.

Habits of auditory synthesis give rise to a special sense of space itself. For besides visual–tactile space there is also acoustic space (which, through voice and hearing, has its own associations with the kinesthetic and tactual not quite the same as the kinesthetic and tactual associations of sight). We can apprehend space in terms of sound and echoes (abetted by tactile associations). Space thus apprehended has qualities of its own. It is not spread out in front of us as a field of vision but diffused around us. Sound, as has been seen, can be apprehended from any direction, so that the hearer is situated in a center of an acoustic field, not in front of it (so that it is indeed hardly a field).

This fact may perhaps be connected with the primitive tendency to associate religious ceremonial with being in the middle of things, at the center of the world, the *omphalos* or *umbilicus* or navel of the universe, which Mircea Eliade discusses in *Patterns in Comparative Re-*

ligion (pp. 231–35, etc.). Being in the midst of reality is curiously personalizing in implication, since acoustic space is in a way a vast interior in the center of which the listener finds himself together with his interlocutors. The oral–aural individual thus does not find himself simply situated somewhere in neutral, visual–tactile, Copernican space. Rather, he finds himself in a kind of vast interiority.

Because of its association with sound, acoustic space implies presence far more than does visual space. As has been seen, noises one hears, for example in a woods at night, register in the imagination as presences—person-like manifestations—far more than do movements which one merely sees. In this sense acoustic space is precisely not "pure" space. It is essentially inhabited space. This is the sort of space in which early man typically lives and which he must abandon to enter into the pure space conceived of primarily in a field of vision (and touch). Pure space comes rather late into man's ken as his sensorium is reorganized, in some cultures at least, to minimize the ear and maximize the eye.

In the pre-Copernican world, what we may presume to be this pure space is often likely not to be such, or likely not to be entirely such. Thus, for example, in the case mentioned earlier from Ivins' *Art and Geometry* (pp. 1–13), the ancient Greek sense of geometric space, while highly visual, was also more tactile than is our modern sense of geometric space.

Heightening the tactile element in spatial awareness can ally space indirectly with sound. Touch is a kind of bridge between sight and sound, since it tends to annex itself to them both. The association of touch with vision is obvious enough from the fact that we apprehend texture visually. We can look at pictures of rough-planed

wood or freshly sliced bread or tooled stone or a cobble-
stone street and sense their texture simply from what our
retina tells us. James J. Gibson has shown this in detail
in *The Perception of the Visual World* (pp. 80–81, etc.).
Gibson has not, however, gone into the fact that makes
these findings of particular interest here, namely, that
the concept of texture itself derives not from sight but
from touch (including kinesthesia). When we say we
know the texture of something we mean we know what
it would *feel* like. The fact that we may know this from
vision without any here and now tactual experience of the
object (though not without memory of such experience)
shows how touch locks itself into sight. Sight does not
convey sound or smell or taste with any of the directness
with which it thus conveys touch (texture).

In a comparable, but different, way touch is associated
with sound. The apprehension of rhythm in music or
speech readily sets our foot or hand tapping, eliciting a
kinesthetic response—and that far more readily than
rhythmic flashes of color or of figures on a visual field
will do. The throbbing of deep notes on a bass viol or
drum can be felt by the sense of touch as well as heard.
As has been seen in chapter 1, muscular tension required
for pronouncing a particular sound is often interpreted
as greater sound volume.

With what precise areas of touch or "feeling" sight
and sound variously associate is matter for study; in *The
Human Senses* (p. 158) Geldard, citing Boring, mentions
twenty-seven such areas or subsenses. A good many of
these, including muscular pressure, tendinous strain, and
vibration, appear clearly associated both with visually
apprehended texture and with hearing. Given the ways
in which touch perceptions thus annex themselves to
both sight and sound, it becomes credible that when the

tactile element in the apprehension of space is heightened, the suggestion of sound, with its own tactile associations, is correspondingly heightened. For the Greeks,
even geometric space (which Ivins has shown the Greeks
apprehended in a highly tactile fashion, as has been
seen) thus had vague acoustic associations. Since ancient
times, however, space had tended to lose not only its
acoustic qualities but its tactile as well, at least in the
sense that if modern technological man has not entirely
forgotten acoustic and tactile–visual space (as he of course
has not), he has readier access to the more purely visual,
neutral space of modern geometry and post-Newtonian
physics.

The depersonalization of space has been due not
merely to its dissociation from sound but also to its
association with vision. For vision of itself, employed
in isolation from the other senses, depersonalizes relations. This fact can be ascertained quite readily. In any
culture it is a risky business to look at another person
for any length of time except under one certain condition. Children must be taught this early: "Don't stare!"
The steady stare is worse than physical insult. Looking
fixedly at another person has normally the effect of reducing him to a surface, a non-interior, and thus to the
status of a thing, a mere object. One can, however, look
at another without limit of time so long as a conversation
is going on. Speech establishes the specifically human
relation that takes the edge off the cruelty of vision.

One can also look intently at another without limit
of time so long as the one being looked at is demonstrating an action or process—showing how he repairs a watch
or how he and four others can outplay another five on a
basketball court. In such a situation, the demonstration
is deliberate communication, a kind of word; indeed, it is

often accompanied by words to make plain what it is intended to be. If the demonstrator does not intend his action as communication, visual inspection of what he is doing becomes objectionable again. Thus it is dangerous to stare at a man working out his income tax report, even though at a distance that renders the figures indecipherable. The person being watched must, at least by tacit consent, present his actions as communication, and the observer must receive them as such. Otherwise the person being watched is downgraded to the level of a thing. The paradigm of communication is dialogue, a two-way transaction in a world of sound, which is a world of response, of echo. Vision by contrast is of itself a one-way operation.

Personal relations demand interchange of personal interiors, and, while vision can support and abet such interchange, it cannot of itself alone maintain the interchange. As Eugen Rosenstock-Huessy has put it in *Die Vollzahl der Zeiten* (my translation): "Experiences of the first order, of the first rank, are never realized through the eye" (p. 33). It is virtually intolerable for two persons, even persons deeply in love, to look steadily into one another's faces without doing anything else for longer than a few brief moments. Embarrassment immediately sets in, acute discomfort, and the drive to say something or to do something normally becomes irresistible. The cold, cutting, silent stare has its effect because of the power of vision to reduce its object to a thing-status when vision is not mollified by speech.

All this is far from saying that visual space as such is totally depersonalized, dehumanized, and thereby necessarily object-like and profane. Visually perceived space, too, is felt to be, at decent intervals, inhabited by presence. A vista through space over the crest of a mountain range can be awe-inspiring, suggesting the presence or

presences which are of the substance of romantic awareness and which can readily tinge this awareness with
pantheism. The sight of a neighborhood where one has
spent one's youth can suggest presences. But the presence
is something added to the space as visually perceived. It is
visual space plus. Without memories (or the ability to
fabricate imaginary memories of what may have happened in the neighborhood) the space is empty. It is
otherwise with sound. Manifestation of personal presence
is not something added to voice. Voice is not *peopled*
with presences. It itself is the manifestation of presence,
and as such has permanent religious possibilities. Only,
unlike space, sound does not endure. It can only be protracted.

The other senses, too, besides hearing and sight can
have to do with presence. All of them can thus convey a
feeling of religious awe. It is a commonplace that mystics
resort to them to describe the nature of mystical experience. Smell, closely linked to memory, can readily plunge
us into the past and evoke a sense of other persons. Even
taste, which is closely tied to smell, has root enough in
memory to do the same—I can recall how the taste of a
soup suddenly called up a whole forgotten boyhood world
—although the discriminatory power of taste can make it
disastrously self-centered.

Still, smell and taste hardly have to do with any sense
of space. Touch does. We can apprehend space by run-
ning our hand over a surface—kinesthesia, the sense of
the position of our own bodily parts enters into our apprehension here. And tactile apprehensions of spatial
extent can be personal, as when contact conveys affection.
In this sense touch can certainly mediate presence, but
at the risk of loss of reverence. "Do not touch me, for
I have not yet ascended to my Father" (John 20:17).
Touch is the most intimate of senses, but also the most

threatening, since it can so easily degenerate into object-like control (manipulation) of another. It is the most familiar sense, and familiarity can breed contempt, the reduction of person to object. Thus tactile space does not have the same personalizing implications as acoustic space. Only the sense of hearing gives us a space which is by direct suggestion peopled and by the same token endowed with sacral qualities.

SOUND, SIGHT, AND "REALITY"

To a culture so visualist as ours (despite the recent build-up of the auditory), the world of early oral–aural man and the sense of presence it enjoys can appear curiously unreal. It seems too little objective, too much given to illusion, too threatened by subjective forces. For us, not hearing but seeing is believing. We feel truly at home only in a world of sight and "objective reality."

Our sense of objective reality, however, is on closer inspection less directly connected with sight than it would seem to be. Its roots are in touch. Dr. Johnson made this clear when he undertook to refute Berkeley tactilely—once one felt contact with a stone one kicked with one's foot, idealism, Johnson thought or pretended, was doomed. His state of mind persists and no doubt will always persist. "Real as this stone," we say, feeling ourselves clutching it with our fist, in actuality or in imagination. By touch we assure ourselves that the stone is there, is objective, for, more than other senses, touch indeed attests to existence which is objective in the sense of real-but-not-me.

And yet, by the very fact that it attests the not-me more than any other sense, touch involves my own subjectivity more than any other sense. When I feel this objective

something "out there," beyond the bounds of my body,
I also at the same instant experience my own self. I feel
other and self simultaneously. This is how I can dif-
ferentiate them. Each time I feel something, I also feel
myself feeling what I feel. Something like this double
perception is true in virtually all, or even probably in
absolutely all of the twenty-seven subsenses which
Geldard in *The Human Senses* (p. 158) notes as commonly grouped under touch or feeling—for example, the
subsenses of pressure, contact, prick pain, quick pain,
deep pain, warmth, muscular pressure, nausea, and so
on. Kinesthesia, the sense of one's own bodily movements
and position, of course frequently enters into touch and
helps convey the feel of self (though less clearly perhaps
in thermal sensations than in other touch sensations).

This sense of oneself in the act of perceiving is less obvious in senses other than touch. When I see something,
I do not directly see myself seeing or in any other way
sense myself as immediately involved the way I am involved in touch. Nor when I hear something do I hear
myself hearing—although as the kinesthetic (touch) element in hearing becomes more assertive (for example,
with the heavy throbbing of bass instruments in music),
I do begin to experience myself, but in a tactile more
directly than in an auditory way: my body begins to
participate in the rhythms muscularly. In smell, there is
little of the self involved, although there may be a strong
suggestion of another self. Taste, unmistakably a proximity sense, is close to touch, and to a degree I do experience myself tasting. Thus it is natural for Gerard Manley
Hopkins, in the opening paragraph of his comments on
the Spiritual Exercises of St. Ignatius Loyola, to write of
"my consciousness and feeling of myself, that taste of
myself . . . more distinctive than the taste of ale or alum."

He says taste rather than merely feeling of self because he is concerned here not merely with the sense of self-possession but, more specifically, with discrimination of sense of self from sense of other, and taste is eminently the discriminatory sense.

In the relationship of feeling to our sense of reality we thus encounter a paradox. When I say real, something existing outside my own consciousness of it, something out there and in this sense objective, I do not actually mean existing with no relationship to me. Because my concept of reality is tied up with the sense of touch, it is also tied up with my sense of my own being. "Real" means, in this way, not just something out there but something that I am involved in and that is involved in me (or, by extension, something that I could be involved in or that could be involved in me). The objective reality of something is in this way measured by one's own subjective awareness (as caught in the sense of touch), not merely by something out there but rather by something out there interacting with something in here.

Touch thus gives us an intimate sense of ourselves and of otherness simultaneously. For in addition to being the sense in which we most sense ourselves sensing, it is also the one in which what is perceived can be perceived most as an obstacle, a resistance, an *opposed* other. When we are physically overpowered, it is the sense of touch which is most involved. In a way it might appear that vision gives us the sense of otherness more than touch insofar as the object of vision is far distant, or can be. Sight registers the stars, billions of light-years away. What could be less myself, more "other"? Or hearing, in registering an active use of power over which I have no control, registers a source other than I. But touch registers an otherness which is somehow struggling against us, and which is thus maximally other. Touch involves resistance apprehended definitely as resistance (again, less clearly in the thermal group of sensations). Here is the heart of the paradox: the sense which involves me most intimately also involves what is not me most inescapably. Moreover, the borderline between subject and object here is curiously reciprocating, and to that extent vague. To sense an object as truly hard, I must tense my muscles to hardness in order to test its resistance: I sense it to a degree by assimilating myself to it. Correspondingly, to sense softness, I relax my muscles, become soft myself. In order to sense red, the eye does not "become" red in any so crass a way.

Because the meaning of reality is so specifically and tortuously involved with the sense of touch, one could advocate using in English the term actuality instead of reality wherever possible. There is much to say for this usage. If often keeps discussion on a surer footing. The only difficulty is that "actual" does not seem quite so real or perhaps even so actual as "real" does, precisely because real is grounded so patently in touch.

If our sense of reality is thus tactilely based more directly than it is visually based, it does in fact have close connections with the visual, too. Touch registers extension in space, and sight also gives immediate access to extension. Extension is thus a kind of bridge between touch and sight, between the lowest, most concrete sense (the sense that demands closest approximation of the sensor to its object) and the highest, least concrete, most abstract sense, the sense tolerating the greatest distance from its object, and indeed demanding a certain distance in order to function at all. As a field shared by the two senses, extension can associate vision with the tactile feel for "reality." Once this association is effected and touch and sight have joined forces to define the real, the other senses have a hard time of it. Sound, for example, is likely to be considered not so real when it is heard as when it is measured in wavelengths: wavelengths can be displayed visually on an extended surface. This then, wavelengths, is what sound really "is." Apart from the wavelengths, the rest of sound, including the noise it makes, is subjective, a projection of some sort from inside ourselves.

Yet the depersonalized, objective world which extension has engendered, the quantified world of modern technology, is likewise involved with the subjective, in a comparable if by no means identical way. First, insofar as this world is grounded in touch, it is, as has just been seen, tied in with one's sense of one*self* as sensing. But secondly, more than this, the depersonalized objective world is involved with the subjective in that it turns up later in human history, after an elaborate psychological evolution extending over centuries and millennia, which it has been the business of the present work to suggest in some sketchy fashion. Only after a long psychological evolution do we find the massive psychological constructs through which we interpret the physical world today. Certainly nothing is more a fabrication of the human mind (however warranted a fabrication, for the mind is an instrument for building knowledge) than the immensely complicated psychological structures which we call science and through which we have learned to view the objective world.

It is true, of course, that the primary quality of extension, which is registered so directly by touch and sight, is more permanent or abiding than other sense qualities, and in this sense more real. Yet if we define reality in these terms, we become largely incapacitated for dealing with persons. Persons are potentialities, sources of power, and, although they may be extended in space, this is not what gives us our sense of them as persons, for extension in space is essentially passive. Persons, moreover, precisely as persons are eminently real. The most elementary psychological data make clear that our relations with other persons are powerful determinants of our actions if they are not indeed the most powerful of all determinants. Since voice manifests the person at a kind of maximum, hearing puts us in contact with the personal grounds of actuality of reality in a specially intense way.

Verbomotor man is on this score in fact better attuned to reality or actuality than is visualist man. He is also more attuned to the reality or actuality of process. Sound, as has been seen, always indicates that a source of power is in active operation. Verbomotor man's specialization in sound thus gives him an experience of living within events more intense than the experience of visualist man. This does not mean that verbomotor primitives would be better able to manage a modern industrial complex than the technologists who actually do manage it. Other factors are involved in management of complicated processes than just verbomotor structure. It may mean, however, that today's actual managers could do better if they were more verbomotor in personality organization or that in fact they are more verbomotor than is commonly thought. They certainly attend more conferences, engage in more brainstorming, are more sensitive to the word in many of its public aspects than nineteenth-century industrialists commonly were. The recent step-up of the auditory in our culture, as we have seen, has given managers, like others in our technological society, a sense of greater participation in actuality than man had before the advent of telephone, radio, and television. Tensions exist in our awareness of the state of affairs here because in this world of aural activity our speculative frames of reference remain so largely visual–tactile.

We return then to the question of whose sense of reality is more of a projection, that of primitive, auditory man or that of the visualist? Which is more real? In fact, neither the auditory nor the visual–tactile world-view is a "projection." The concept of projection (a concept with a visualist–tactile base) is itself inadequate here. The senses are part of the individual's own being, but they interact, each sense in its own way, with certain components of actuality outside (and to a degree at the same time inside) the individual. The world is both personalist and objective. Our intellectual understanding of it is at its optimum not only like sight but also like hearing as well as like smell and taste and touch. The sensorial organization specific to any given time and culture may bring us to overspecialize in certain features of actuality and to neglect others. Each organization of the sensorium will likewise predispose us for errors typical of such an organization: verbomotor man can overplay the personal as visualist man can underplay it. As in all activities caught in human limitations and human fallibility, the remedy here will be reflection. When we cannot do away with our limitations, we can at least neutralize them to the extent that we can assess them as limitations and thus keep ourselves from being taken in.

4

The Word as History: Sacred and Profane

This brief survey of transformations of the spoken word and of some of the consequences of the transformations should make it evident that the history of what was originally the spoken word cannot be considered merely as a chain of events, a series of phenomena strung out in a neutral field of time, but rather must be taken as a succession of difficult, and often traumatic, reorientations of the human psyche. As the word moves from sound into space (without ever fully departing from sound) and then restructures itself electronically into sound in a new way, the sensorium is reorganized and man's relationship to the physical world around him, to his fellow men, to his own thought, and to himself radically changes.

The transformations of the word affect the total situation of man in the world to such a degree as to suggest new kinds of answers, although still only partial ones, to the old questions that lie at the root of history— What is going on in the world? What is the succession of events in human existence about? Answers to such questions provided by historians of the past have tended to focus on successions of external events. From antiquity through the eighteenth century, secular history, insofar as it was distinguished from religious history, tended to be thought of chiefly as political history, the story of external events in externally constituted realms. Even among religiously oriented historians, when Christian salvation history was either distinguished from secular history (as in Augustine's *City of God*) or amalgamated with it (as in Joachim de Floris), secular history was taken to be constituted largely of widely known external happenings. But by the time of Giambattista Vico (1688–1744), the historical mind has taken a noteworthy Cartesian-like interiorizing turn. In *The New Science* Vico starts with his own "truth beyond question," namely that "this world of civil society has certainly been made by men, and that its principles can and must therefore be found within the modifications of our own human mind." History here somehow comes out of man: to this extent, as Löwith has suggested in *Meaning in History* (p. 119), attention is focused on the human interior. Hegel (1770–1831) goes farther. For him the history of external events merges with the development of an absolute (interior) Spirit, and for Auguste Comte (1789–1857), history has become the history of civilization and of knowledge. From Hegel on, political and other external history has been more and more overlaid, or underpinned, by what might be called psychological history with the work of Löwith and that of H. Stuart Hughes in *Consciousness and Society* and comparable work by others.

A further step in the same direction is taken by Freud, who in *Civilization and Its Discontents* and elsewhere relates the existence and operation of historical institutions to the structure and restructurings of the psyche itself. The story of social and even political institutions is now told (in part) in terms of what individuals do to survive: they repress the "pleasure principle," followed initially by the id, in favor of the "reality principle," which is sponsored by the ego. The reality principle calls for postponement of immediate gratification in order to secure subsequent real gratification and demands for its operation a sense of guilt developed under a third sector of the psyche, the superego. At this point, external and public institutions such as kingship and democracy and war can be at least partly accounted for in terms of the individuals'. interior reactions to their own fathers and mothers and to themselves. External institutions can be seen to depend upon complicated interior restructurings of the psyche (and vice versa). Not just "ways of looking at things" but the entire personality structure, from abstract heights to uttermost subconscious depths, is quite different in men coming from different civilizations. Monarchy and democracy both arise from and create differently organized interior personality structures. Insistent awareness of the interaction of interior consciousness and external institutions inspires some of the best historical work of today, such as that of H. Stuart Hughes or that of Löwith in the books just mentioned. The absence or feebleness of this awareness is probably Toynbee's most central weakness.

In *Eros and Civilization* Herbert Marcuse develops these ideas further and suggests (p. 57) that each individual's "autonomous personality appears as the *frozen manifestation of the general repression of mankind.*" In less specialized perspectives, we could say that history is deposited in all of us as personality structure. The framework of awareness out of which I face actuality is the past of mankind, which I acquire as structure in my consciousness of myself and of my life-world by growing into consciousness in the culture that has bred me.

The work of the phenomenologists, from Husserl on, is of a piece with the development of historiography and with the work of Freud insofar as it intensifies man's sense of interiorized history by making more accessible to descriptive treatment the inner world of consciousness in its "intentionality" or other-directedness. And in an even more sweeping fashion, Pierre Teilhard de Chardin has undertaken in *The Phenomenon of Man* and elsewhere to relate the interior consciousness of individual human beings to the external history of the cosmos. This he does by showing how human consciousness itself, as "interiority," is not an entirely isolated phenomenon but rather constitutes the definitive breakthrough following on a series of preparatory breakthroughs into interiority achieved as inorganic matter, and then organic matter, have become more and more "interiorized" or organized from within through the stages of cosmic and biological evolution.

Our present concern with the history of the word and of the media of communication, verbal and other, is patently part of man's larger present concern with history as an interior as well as an exterior reality. The word itself is both interior and exterior: it is, as we have seen, a partial exteriorization of an interior seeking another interior. The primary physical medium of the word— sound—is itself an exteriorization of a physical interior, setting up reverberations in other physical interiors.

WORD OF GOD IN HEBREW AND CHRISTIAN TRADITION

Hebrew and Christian theology has to a degree felt the effects of what we have here called the interiorization

of history. It has registered these effects chiefly through
existentialist and phenomenological concerns. Thus far,
however, it has done little to understand the word of
God in terms of the relationship of word to sound. The
patristic age and even the scholastic age were far more
oral than our own is, and yet neither reflected on the oral
to the degree that it reflected on the visual, as in the well-
known and indubitably valuable exploitation of light
imagery in treating of the generation of the Son or Word
by the Father.

There is, of course, a vast and rich literature of the
Word. Literature about preaching will obviously be concerned with the spoken word as such. But it is informative to note how much of the literature concerned with
the Word as the Person of Jesus, from patristic times on,
has veered away from considering the Word in terms of
sound to consider the Word in terms of knowledge-by-
vision—the Word (or Son) as the "image" of the Father
is interpreted all but inevitably as some kind of visual
image. What might be a complementary treatment, and
a more direct one, of the Word in terms of voice and
sound has been rather thoroughly neglected.

An oral–aural theology of revelation through the Word
of God would entail an oral–aural theology of the Trinity, which could explicate the "intersubjectivity" of the
three Persons in terms of communication conceived of
as focused (analogously) in a world of sound rather than
in a world of space and light. Such a theology is still so
underdeveloped as to be virtually nonexistent. In the
Catholic tradition certainly, instead of a theology of
shared consciousness and personal presence, as examination of theological manuals such as Tanqueray's makes
clear, we have thus far principally a theology of "rela-

tions" (a concept visually based: *referre, relatus,* to carry back, carried back). The communication of the Persons with one another is typically treated in terms of *circumincessio,* a "walking-around-in" (one another). This latter is patently a concept based on a visual analogy with strong tactile and kinesthetic components. These concepts, with others like them, have profoundly aided understanding and should certainly be respected, but their awkwardness shows the strain under which visual analogies must operate when one is speaking of conscious awareness or of presence as such.

A theology of the Word of God as word will not of course explicate everything, if only because the history of the word of God among men is not identical with the history of the human word. For the history of the human word is not the history of salvation, as the history of God's word is. But because the human word is uttered at the juncture where interior awareness and external event meet and where, moreover, encounter between person and person occurs at its most human depths, the history of the word and thus of verbal media has rather more immediate religious relevance than the history of kingdoms and principalities. Study of man in terms of the changes in the verbal media establishes new grounds for the relation of sacred and secular history.

The Christian should, however, be under no illusion that the history of the word will enable him to explain profane history in terms of salvation history (as Bossuet and others have attempted to do) or the history of salvation—the Incarnation and its consequences as known to the man of faith—in terms of secular history (as Voltaire and others have undertaken to do). But the Christian will consider that, while sacred and profane history are neither the same nor varieties of each other, they are mysteriously related, casting on each other reciprocating, if mysterious, light.

Any understanding of the word of God as word must of course take cognizance of the fact that word of God is used in a number of senses within the Hebrew and the Christian tradition, senses not any the less bewildering because of the fact that all of them are related to one another. It would be impossible here to explicate all the details of the various senses, but we can survey some main centers of meaning for the term as found in the Scriptures and basic Church documents from antiquity to the present, such as are collected in Denziger's *Enchiridion symbolorum* and in Leith's handy *Creeds of the Churches*. Details of the various meanings are further discussed by the Catholic theologian Hans Urs von Balthasar in his *Word and Revelation* and by the Protestant theologian Gerhard Ebeling in his *Word and Faith,* to cite only two recent sources.

In the Bible, as in some other religious traditions, the word of God often refers to an exercise of divine power. God's word is efficacious. "By the word of the Lord the heavens were made," reads Psalm 32 (33), which continues, "He spoke, and it was made; he commanded, and it stood forth." In Isaiah 55:10–11, the word implements God's will: "For just as from the heavens the rain and snow come down and do not return there till they have watered the earth, making it fertile and fruitful, giving seed to him who sows and bread to him who eats, so shall my word be that goes forth from my mouth; it shall not return to me void, but shall do my will, achieving the end for which I sent it." More particularly, the word of God refers to communication from God to man. Such communication can range from something private and humanly inexpressible within the quiet of the individual soul out to the communication implied by the mere existence of the universe itself as either created or controlled by God. With the propensity for auditory models common to highly oral cultures, the Bible often refers to the universe as "speaking" of God or as speaking God. "The heavens declare the glory of God," proclaims Psalm 18 (19).

The word of God can also mean God's communication to the Prophets or others who are to speak out for him (a prophet is first an utterer of God's word, only secondarily a seer). From this sense another readily derives, that of the utterance of the prophets or others speaking what God has given them to speak as from him. The prophet would ordinarily know that his message came from God, but in biblical accounts he also might not. Balaam (Num. 23:7–24:25) and Caiphas (John 12:49–52) prophesied in spite of themselves, and Caiphas without knowing that he was prophesying. Further extended, the word of God is what is heard by Christians in sermons. Speaking for a group of Reformers in 1566, the Second Helvetic Confession (Leith, *Creeds of the Churches,* p. 133) makes explicit and strategic use of this meaning to advertise the high value Protestants generally put on preaching: the Confession states that the preaching of the word of God *is* the word of God.

God's word can also mean his communication to the inspired writers of the Bible. These writers of God's word were not necessarily the utterers of God's word, for the prophets who received and spoke God's word or those who composed songs such as the Psalms were not necessarily the ones who wrote the prophetic books or the Psalter. Catholic theology, which is probably the most elaborately detailed in its theoretical treatment of inspiration (see Lohfink's survey, "The Inerrancy and the Unity of Scripture"), does not commonly consider it necessary that the writer of Sacred Scripture even be aware that what he is writing is God's inspired word. Inspiration is not necessarily conscious. It is recognized by its acceptance in the Church, not by its writer's assertion, gratuitous or even accompanied by proofs, that he writes under divine inspiration.

The word of God can also mean what was actually written down in the original texts of the Bible and, by indefinite extension, in copies of these texts and in translations and copies of translations and translations of translations, and so on. This is one of the commonest meanings of the word of God in actual popular usage. "It is in the Bible"—"it" being the translated written utterance. The history of the biblical text is intricate beyond belief, since the Bible often incorporates into itself lengthy passages previously pretty well shaped up elsewhere either by formalized oral tradition or in writing. At what point such preexisting portions become the word of God is not easy for the most adept theologians to say. Catholic theology, which here again has probably developed its theoretical structures most elaborately, is in a state of active evolution at this point, especially since modern scholarship has uncovered not only the complications of the textual history of the Bible but also the intricate and frequently very sophisticated oral substratum, often a formal catechesis, passed on from generation to generation. Some theologians, as Dennis J. McCarthy in a study on "Personality, Society, and Inspiration," speak of parts even of this oral substratum also as the word of God in the sense that they would accord to it some sort of divine inspiration.

Finally, there is the Word of God Who is Jesus Christ.

Once Christ comes, this sense of the Word of God becomes for the Christian more central than any other sense. In classic trinitarian theology, developed by reflection on the Scriptures in the light of both biblical and extrabiblical knowledge and forming the permanent core of Catholic thought and liturgy, the Word or Son, the Second Person of the Trinity, is the primary "utterance" of the Father, equally eternal. "In the beginning was the word, and the Word was with God, and the Word was God" (John 1:1). The Father's Word, which God the Father "speaks," is a substantial Word, a Person, God like the Father, but a different Person from the Father—another "I" Who even to the Father is "Thou," to put it in present-day personalist terminology (a terminology which makes rather more accessible than formerly the meaning of much in trinitarian theology). Although human concepts can never apply adequately to God, but only imperfectly, no matter how they are refined, nevertheless the human terms "Word" and "Son" apply to the Second Person with a directness enjoyed by no other terms. The Second Person is the Word, although he is so in a trans-human sense, a fuller sense, a sense of which the most penetrating human concept of "word" is only a poor echo. Thus it is true to say that the Second Person is the Word, although doing so strains the human concept beyond its normal limits. The assertion has its full meaning only in faith, as is the case with other assertions regarding Jesus—"No one can say 'Jesus is Lord' except by the Holy Spirit" (I Cor. 12:3). The Word, the Son, himself God, is, in classic trinitarian theology, the one who takes to his person a human nature so that thenceforward the "Thou" which is addressed to the man Jesus Christ is addressed necessarily to God himself, in the Second Person, for there is only one "Thou" here, a single "Thou" with a divine and a human mode of existence or nature, a divine and human actuality and "resonance" (one might also say a divine and a human "face," but this visually based concept necessarily suggests superficiality if not indeed two individuals).

Jesus Christ was of course visible during his life on earth, but to say he was "visible" or "manifest" or that he "showed himself" does not restrict his sensible presence to the field of vision, but rather takes vision as the surrogate or paradigm for all the senses. Thus "visible" does for "sensible." Nevertheless, despite this assertiveness of vision in descriptions of the Word Incarnate, his incarnation maintains for the believer a special rapport with sound, for he who is manifest is the Word. One of Jesus' disciples can say that what he has seen with his eyes and touched with his hands (as well as heard), what has "appeared" to man, is the Word of Life (I John 1:1). The Christian hierophany is in this sense oral–aural. Indeed, as applied to the *Word* of God the very concept of "hiero*phany*" bogs down insofar as the concept is rooted exclusively in visual apprehension: the second part of the term "hierophany" echoes the meaning of the Greek *phainein,* to bring to light, to show, make clear (with primary reference to vision). For if God manifests or shows himself here in the Word (as there is of course ample scriptural warrant for the believer to say he does), he more fundamentally *communicates* himself. Communication peaks in sound.

At this point, the "word of God" becomes more than ever a kaleidoscope of interwoven meanings, for the Word of God, Jesus Christ, himself actually speaks, using human words, but manifesting through these words more than they usually manifest precisely because he is *the* Word. We are faced further with the fact that the Word of God in his sensible human nature is at first, like other men, an infant, who does not speak (*in-fans* is Latin for nonspeaker). A long-standing heritage of profound meditation on this theme of the "unspeaking Word," the *Verbum infans,* runs from Augustine and other patristic sources through the medieval theologians and a nativity sermon by Lancelot Andrewes in the year 1611 to T. S. Eliot's lines in *Gerontion,* "The word within a word, unable to speak a word,/Swaddled with darkness." When the Word does speak, the words of the Word, the sayings of Jesus, themselves become the core of the good news, the Gospel, part of the Bible—which is as a whole the word of God already. Acceptance of God's kingdom, which these sayings of Jesus announce, is dependent upon hearing, directly or indirectly: *"Fides ex auditu"*—Faith comes through hearing—Paul declares (Rom. 10:17).

God's word, in all its senses, is for the believer of course not entirely like man's word. For it is also like the opposite of man's word, silence. Man's word is fleeting precisely because of the way it not only flows through time but depends on time, vanishing successively with each instance in which it comes into existence. But "the word of our God stands forever" (Isa. 40:8). It occupies time without disappearing with time. It is also like silence, for silence endures; and silence, moreover, in a real way is for man even more communicative than words. It is, as has been seen, of a piece with sound, for it is sound's polar opposite: sound and silence define each other. Words must be interspersed with pauses, silences, to be understood. Indeed, the deepest understanding, especially as between persons, comes often in the silence that follows an utterance, as the effects of the words reverberate without sound in the auditor's (and the speaker's) mind. For sound itself is defective in accomplishing its own aims. Silence makes up for what sound lacks. There has perhaps never been an asceticism, and certainly never a Christian asceticism, which has not made much of silence as a way of life and a mode of communication and presence.

The term "word of God" can be explored endlessly, and a halt must be called here. Through the entire web of meaning, it will be noted, the sense of the spoken word is everywhere utterly basic. To this sense is tied, as has been seen, the feeling for the word as effective, real, powerful, eventful. For truly conceived as sound, the word, like all sound, signals the present use of power. When the Son is conceived of as the Word of God, he is certainly not conceived of as a written word, either in the Father's thought or in our own. The Father "utters" the Word. And the Third Person of the Trinity, significantly, is thought of in the Scriptures and subsequently in classical Christian theology as breath (Latin, *spiritus*), the Holy Spirit—connection with oral utterance is patent here. The spoken word is inseparable from the breath, though it is not the breath. Even in the Scriptures as written documents, indeed especially in the Scriptures, the word of God is the work of the Spirit: the biblical writers are "inspired," that is, "breathed into by the Holy Spirit" (II Pet. 1–21). Without the Spirit, the "breath" of life, the written letter itself is a threat: "For the letter kills, but the spirit gives life" (II Cor. 3:6).

The centrality of the spoken word as a point of reference for the various senses of the word of God is due not only to the fact that the spoken word is always primary (writing and print always refer directly or remotely to the word as sound) but also to the fact that the Bible, from Genesis through the entire New Testament including its epistolary parts, registers the oral culture still so dominant when the Bible came into being. Typographic man, unreflective until recently concerning the oral structures of all early human culture, has tended to interpret the oral state of mind as simply "oriental." Thus in *La Parole et l'écriture* (p. 94), Louis Lavelle echoes a tradition widespread even among scholars when he writes that "all Orientals think that in addition to physical forces there is a magic force which is that of language." We have seen earlier how the attribution of "force" to language derives not from some unaccountable geographico-cultural situation but from the habit of thinking of language in auditory terms (as M. Lavelle's own culture had also once done) rather than in visualist–typographic terms, and how there is as much truth as magic in the persuasion that language has real force. The oral state of mind and psychological structures so evident in the Bible are strange to us, as we now know, not because we are "Western" but because we are typographic folk, more intensely alphabetized than were the ancient Hebrews.

At the same time, however, despite this firm oral–aural grounding of the various scriptural and traditional meanings of word of God, God's word in all its senses within the Hebrew and Christian traditions was definitively conveyed to man through a chirographic culture—indeed through one of the first alphabetized cultures. The word of God centered in the Hebrew and Christian heritage thus came to man at a strategic point in history, which is to say, as we have seen, at a strategic point in the development of the human psyche, when the oral–aural world was being reshaped toward visualism by the force of alphabetic writing.

For the unbeliever, this is an invitation to explain the

Hebrew and Christian revelation as no more than a projection of the human psyche at one of its stages of development. The notion of the word of God fits the psychological structures of the milieu in which it acquires its biblical currency. Such association of the word of God, of course, is hardly an embarrassment to the believer unless he is unconscionably naive. All man's concepts always fit the psychological structures of the milieu in which they develop, today just as well as in the past. This does not disqualify them from representing truth but rather orients them historically and helps validate them. The thinking that constitutes our highly quantified modern physical science fits our visualist psychological structures today. True though it is, such science could come into being only in a sensorium organized as ours is, relating itself to man's life-world (of which science is now a part) as ours does, and such science will doubtless be altered (which is not to say disqualified) as the sensorium changes in generations to come. Primitive man could not have known modern science without restructuring his personality in the process—something in his own day quite impossible for him. The question is thus not whether one's views or beliefs or knowledge reflect one's psychological structures or even psychological needs (if they do not, they are useless for representing objective truth) but whether they do so in the right way or not—whether in doing so they relate to actuality. Believers have found that their notions of the word of God do so relate.

Indeed, the fact that the focal point of Hebrew and, even more, of Christian belief is found in a culture which for historical reasons makes so much of the word should be thoroughly reassuring for the believer: God entered into human history in a special fashion at the precise time when psychological structures assured that his entrance would have greatest opportunity to endure and flower. To assure maximum presence through history, the Word came in the ripeness of time, when a sense of the oral was still dominant and when at the same time the alphabet could give divine revelation among men a new kind of endurance and stability. The believer finds it providential that divine revelation let down its roots into human culture and consciousness after the alphabet was devised but before print had overgrown major oral structures and before our electronic culture further obscured the basic nature of the word.

5

The Word and the Quest for Peace

POLEMIC AND THE WORD

Central to the history of the word, both secular and religious, is a vexing group of phenomena and questions involving the relationship of the word and peace. In some of the perspectives earlier suggested here, it would appear that the word is an assault or a threatened assault on another person and, to that extent at least, a warlike manifestation. And in the following pages it will be seen that oral cultures in certain ways do in fact foster a polemic world view. This is all the more puzzling because of the way in which the word is ordered essentially, if somewhat mysteriously, to peace.

The word moves toward peace because the word mediates between person and person. No matter how much it gets caught up in currents of hostility, the word can never be turned into a totally warlike instrument. So long as two persons keep talking, despite themselves they are not totally hostile. This is one of the things that makes hateful talk hurt so much: you are punishing someone with whom you are somehow still at one by reason of the fact that you are maintaining verbal contact with an individual who is obviously to a degree at one with you if he replies. Hostile talk is hate in the midst of love *manqué,* or perhaps of wounded love.

All verbal abuse attests some attraction between interlocutors as well as their hostility. Even in the formalized
all-out verbal hostility of standard epic fliting, as in
Homer or *Beowulf* or the medieval *Disputisoun between
the Body and the Soul* or *The Owl and the Nightingale,*
through all their contention the disputants manifest
simultaneously some reluctant or wry attraction, even
admiration, and thereby attest to a strange pacific undertow in their streams of verbal abuse. In these instances
the contestants are distanced from each other not only by
contention but also by nature or status or profession or
culture, and the irenic pull in speech can be relatively
unnoticed. Verbal abuse carried on between those more
closely attached to each other produces greater tension
still. Hence the nerve-racking effects of the domestic fliting in Edward Albee's *Who's Afraid of Virginia Woolf?*
By making the contestants husband and wife, Albee maximizes the attraction of his hostile characters for each
other and thereby the love–hostility tension which the
fliting itself suggests and which the title of the play, whatever its actual immediate source, clearly sets forth: Virginia (young girl, innocent, lovable, winsome) Woolf
(savage beast, malevolent, hateful, repulsive), plus the
attraction–repulsion stance of "Who's afraid?"

When hostility becomes total, the most vicious name-
calling is inadequate: speech is simply broken off entirely.
One assaults another physically or at least "cuts" him by
passing him in total silence. Or one goes to court, where,
significantly, the parties do not speak directly to each
other but only to the judge, whose decision, if accepted
as just by both parties, at least in theory and intent brings
them to resume normal conversation with each other
once more. The use of advocates or lawyers as intermediaries shows further how the courtroom situation registers

the breakdown of ordinary verbal exchange. Mediation is here three-deep: between the parties there intervene the accuser's lawyer, the judge, and the defendant's lawyer. In a similar way, the breakdown to total hostility in international relations is commonly signaled by withdrawal of diplomatic representatives. The hostile nations cease talking directly. For a while, they may resort to intermediaries for diplomatic business. Should matters worsen, the next step is physical attack, war. If noncommunication persists without physical attack, we have a "cold war," which is indeed war, for without communication there is no peace.

But granted all this, that speech as such in some way both signals and fosters accord, the fact is that the history of the word, at least in the West, is intimately tied up with the history of certain kinds of polemic. Indeed, the main line in the history of verbal communication can be significantly plotted by studying changes in the uses of hostility. Changes here relate directly to the movement from primitive oral culture to our present communications situation. The changes have simultaneously secular relevance and, especially in the Hebreo-Christian tradition, religious relevance as well. In brief, the movement from oral through typographic culture, as we shall see, corresponds in great part in a shift from a more polemically textured culture to a less polemically textured one, from a culture in which personality structures are expressly organized quite typically for combat, real or imaginary, to one in which hostilities are less publicly exploited and personality structures become expressly organized for greater "objectivity" and, ultimately, for decision making under maximally quantified, neutralized control (decision making based on massive command of data such as computers implement).

The Polemic Texture of Verbomotor Culture

Any student of earlier periods of Western culture from classical antiquity through the Middle Ages and the Renaissance soon becomes aware that he is dealing with cultures in which overt personal hostilities are exhibited and even flaunted far more than in the ordinary technological style of existence. It may sound quaint to say this in a society so unfortunately given to wars as our technological society still is, but, despite the potential for mass destruction in an atomic age, the evidence is overpowering that earlier man commonly accepted hostility as part of the manifest fabric of life to a degree beyond that typical of technological man.

The point here has to do not with hostilities connected with out-and-out wars, or even with cold wars, but rather with the way in which the individual experienced himself in his environment, human and natural. It is not that individuals in technologized cultures necessarily feel fewer hostilities than did earlier man, but only that earlier cultures on the whole (for these cultures differed much among themselves) displayed hostilities more overtly as an expected response to the environment. In *Man and the Sacred,* Roger Caillois contrasts primitive society, where war commonly (though of course not in every instance) constitutes "a permanent state that forms the fabric of basic existence," with modern society, which takes peace to be the permanent or normally expected state, at least psychologically (p. 177). In primitive society even festivals are often defined by their relationship to war. They are allied to war in that both "inaugurate a period of vigorous socialization and share instruments, resources, and powers in common" (p. 166). The festival, however, interrupts the normal flow of hostilities, "temporarily reconciles the worst enemies, causing them to fraternize," but "in the same effervescence" characterizing the state of war, as when the Olympic Games suspended Greek quarrels. In modern society, Caillois goes on to explain, "the opposite occurs," for it is not festivals but wars which stop everything. The football game is not the interruption that the Olympic Games were; it is rather more of the regular cloth of life. Modern man's festivals are less urgent than primitive man's because modern man, even when he wars, does not regard war as being necessarily of the fabric of basic existence.

All primitive societies are not of course equally warlike, but there are or have been enough that are or were of the cast Caillois describes to give his generalization real substance. One thinks not only of the ancient Greeks or Romans but also of the world of the Old Testament Hebrews, where individuals took for granted that their surroundings were swarming with active, enterprising foes. "Behold my enemies are many, and they hate me violently" (Psalm 24[25]:19) is a constant Old Testament theme, recurring not only in the many Psalms of malediction but elsewhere, too, from Genesis through Maccabees. Play, which in the past, as today, could work off aggressiveness in harmless and even constructive fashion, was more likely to be itself martial play; and grimmer contests, such as dueling, publicly advertised hostilities in the fabric of real life, as of course did also the common custom of bearing arms.

The nonhuman environment, too, was often felt as the object of combat. Disease, which technological man has learned to view and work against objectively, easily became a "foe." A work, for example, such as *Bulleins Bulwarke of Defence against All Sicknes, Sornes, and*

Woundes (London, 1562) perpetuates a long-standing outlook, of which technological man is not entirely free when he describes his "battles" against disease. The sea and the mountains and the weather were equally hostile —until the Romantic era, which, as will shortly be seen, marks the end of the old oral polemic culture on other scores, too. The awful brutality of punishment in earlier ages—again up to Romanticism—is widely known.

It is a common complaint today that literature is filled with violence, but much earlier literature, as the oral performance which lay behind it, not only was filled with violence but institutionalized it. The great verbal art form coming out of the heroic age, the epic, took the martial as its central theme. It celebrated verbal as well as physical combat. Epic poetry formalizes verbal polemic in fliting, the systematic exchange of savage recriminations between opposed characters.

The reasons for the overt hostilities of early man's life-world were of course complex. One evident reason was the lack of mastery over environment. An economy of scarcity prevailed everywhere, as it still prevails over much of our globe. With a limited supply even of necessities, abundance for one automatically spelled scarcity for others or—what came to the same thing—was thought to do so. Life was physically more of a struggle than it is for those living in a technologized economy of abundance under the auspices of modern medicine. Death struck often far earlier than today and more unexpectedly, unless one concedes that it was actually expected all the time. Infant and child mortality was high, as Philippe Ariès circumstantially reports in *Centuries of Childhood* (pp. 38–41). "All mine die in infancy," wrote Montaigne of his children with a resignation that strikes us as distressingly offhand and impersonal.

The individual in such cultures rightly felt himself physically beset by his environment, and his hostilities were understandably more likely to show. Part of this environment was his fellow men. As we know from urban conditions today, overcrowding and the resulting lack of privacy can develop hostilities to the point of explosion. Earlier societies lacked privacy almost everywhere, as Ariès has documented in detail. Even in Europe of the sixteenth century and later, the most privileged classes lived in houses swarming with as many as sixty or eighty occupants, houses where even bedrooms formed regular avenues for traffic from one part of the house to the other, day and night (the curtains on the four-poster beds were not merely for decoration; there were besides the itinerants, often several beds in one room). Lower classes lived in even more exacerbating proximity to their fellows. Privacy is pretty well a modern invention. In earlier tribal societies, the individual found life a texture of inescapable personal contacts, many of which are a torture sure to nourish hostilities.

In such societies, the individual is, it is true, protected and given a sense of identity by the in-group or in-groups with which he is associated. But it is a commonplace that in tribal societies, as for example among early American Indians, in-group identity is achieved all too often by feeding on hostilities toward out-groups. Murder, intolerable within the clan, is negligible or even admirable if the victim is an outsider. Tribal structures generated feuding on a large scale, extramural and intramural, from that in King David's family in the Books of Kings through that in Homer and on down to the Hatfields and the McCoys celebrated in the ballads of the hill country in the eastern and central United States.

Little wonder that social institutions were interpreted in polemic or quasipolemic terms with an insistence that strikes us as bizarre. Renaissance treatises for educating the courtier, for example, such as Castiglione's *Il Cortegiano* or Sir Thomas Elyot's *The Book Named the Governor,* are likely to trace governmental failures deriving as we now know, from complex economic, social, political, and psychological "forces," to enemies among the king's advisors—"bad guys." Book prefaces and dedications, curiously enough, provide an excellent sampling of how man felt his life-world as late as the age immediately following the development of print. Hostility here manifests itself not merely in the excoriation of various persons (often enough including the printer) but also in praising patrons or other dedicatees, for the writer of dedications commonly pictures the dedicatee as surrounded by hosts of enemies from whom the author and his friends gallantly propose to defend him. Of the one hundred and twenty pieces in Clara Gebert's *Anthology of Elizabethan Dedications and Prefaces,* I find only twenty which do not mention or clearly deal with enmity, hostility, protest, or fear, and all but two of these twenty are so fulsome in their praise as to suggest that their dedicatees are actually under threat from others. In *The Professional Writer in Elizabethan England* (p. 44), Edwin Haviland Miller has noted similar quarrelsomeness or sycophancy in writers' relations to readers. This polemic is all highly conventional, to be sure, but one wonders about the texture of the soil on which such conventions could ever have been made to stand in such massive and bizarre array.

The polemic stance which came so naturally to earlier man of course manifests itself in many ways in close association with his use of the word. Education in ancient Greece and Rome was predominantly rhetorical, for combat in the law courts or legislative bodies or elsewhere— even when rhetoric took a purely epideictic turn and became the showy use of words, it never lost its combative cast entirely. The medieval universities erected dialectical jousting into the sole and prescribed way of intellectual life, unable to find a way to truth except by cutting through whole phalanxes of adversaries, real or imaginary.

Explanations of the overt hostilities of earlier cultures based on economic conditions and social structures are certainly valid enough so far as they go, and nothing that we have found here would minimize them. The history of the word, however, suggests that there are still further dimensions to the situation beyond those which the socioeconomic explanations account for. Not merely external conditions but also interior psychological structures (themselves both cause and effect of the external conditions) were at work to produce the polemic bias in early society. Habits of auditory synthesis charged man's life-world with dynamism and threat which visual syntheses would later minimize. The spoken word itself is dynamic in implication, as has been seen, and, moreover, the modes of information storage demanded by oral culture and persisting long after writing and print, as has also been seen, encouraged a world view in which even nonhuman actuality was assimilated to a struggle polarized around good and evil, virtue and vice. In such a view, polemic becomes a major constituent of actuality, an accepted element of existence of a magnitude no longer appealing to modern technological man.

Here lies much of the explanation for an overwhelmingly assertive phenomenon which is massively present, thoroughly researched in some of its details, and yet so little accounted for as a whole: the extraordinary quantity of literature welling out of antiquity through the Middle Ages and well past the Renaissance which is self-consciously and explicitly concerned with praise and blame, virtue and vice. Superficially, preoccupation with virtue and vice can be interpreted as an index of the religiosity of a culture, and it is frequently so interpreted, particularly in studies of the European Middle Ages. But from what we have seen it should be apparent that the tendency to reduce all of human existence, including patently nonmoral areas such as the incidence of disease or of physical cataclysm to strongly outlined virtue–vice or praise–blame categories can be due in great part to the tendency in oral or residually oral cultures to cast up accounts of actuality in terms of contests between individuals. Virtue and vice polarities thus enter deeply into knowledge-storing systems, as Frances A. Yates makes clear in *The Art of Memory* (pp. 84, etc.). This is not to say that virtue and vice are not themselves actualities, for they certainly are. But the reality of virtues and vices does not of itself justify the abandon with which early nontechnological societies have tended to polarize in virtue–vice categories not merely moral matters as such but also a great deal of essentially nonmoral actuality, seeing, for example, the operation of what we know today to be economic or social or political or even purely physical forces as essentially naked struggles between moral good and evil.

We have enough scholarly studies of virtue–vice polarity in early literature to make it evident how widespread and weighty a cultural phenomenon we are dealing with here. Much of the study has been focused on the Middle Ages, where the preoccupation with virtue and vice reaches one of its peaks. Johan Huizinga provides a good deal of material in *The Waning of the Middle Ages* and we have many special studies such as Morton Bloomfield's on *The Seven Deadly Sins,* or other studies on the tradition of the four "cardinal" virtues of prudence, justice, temperance, and fortitude, on the twelve moral virtues (which furnished Spenser with the schema for his epic), on the dance of death, the morality plays exemplified by *Everyman* which erect virtues and vices into dramatic personifications, and the incalculably numerous and massive collections of *exempla,* stories about men or beasts, including bestiaries proper, ranged often under headings of various virtues or vices. These last well illustrate the moral torque given to much nonmoral material. For example, as Florence McCulloch reports in *Medieval Latin and French Bestiaries* (pp. 91–92), in the bestiaries the whale's habit of sounding makes him a symbol of deceit, for he thereby drowns the innocent picnickers or shipwrecked sailors who, with surprising regularity, mistake his back for an island, beach a boat there, and, predictably, light a fire. (To a less moralizing age the ignited whale would appear to be practicing not the vice of deceit but simply the virtue of self-preservation.) This reduction of irrelevant material to virtue–vice polarities is well known in medieval scholarship, although it is not ordinarily viewed in the perspectives suggested here as residual oralism. In *The Enduring Monument,* O. B. Hardison has shown how strongly the virtue–vice preoccupation persisted through the sixteenth and seventeenth centuries. The way in which the commonplace tradition, itself a product and later a persistent relic of oral culture, drifted into almost exclusive concern with virtue and vice has been discussed in chapter 2 above.

The deeper roots of this preoccupation with virtue and vice trace in part to a polemic spirit connected with the oral cultural institutions tied in so intimately with what has long been called the "heroic age." In chapter 2 we

drew on Eric Havelock's *Preface to Plato* to show how
the processing of knowledge for retention, recall, and
use in an oral culture tends to develop characters which
are more or less types. Here we can turn again to Havelock's analysis of the oral culture of Homeric Greece to
show further how the economy of knowledge demanded
by oral society readily generates a quite overtly hostile
context for human life.

In an oral culture knowledge cannot be stored in abstract, categorized forms. This is not because oral–aural
peoples for some inscrutable or even perverse reasons
elect to be "imaginative" or "concrete" or "oriental"
rather than abstract or scientific. The large-scale accumulation of exact knowledge which makes possible elaborate
and dispassionate causal analyses and sharp abstract cat-
egorization depends absolutely on writing. Astronomy,
mathematics, physics, grammar, logic, metaphysics, and
all other abstract knowledges remain mere potentials of
the human mind until some use can be made of script.
Without script, knowledge is best stored not in abstract
categories but in terms of events, happenings, *res gestae*—
things done or goings-on. Such events are preserved in
the minds of men not by being classified and listed but by
being clustered into the stories told about a relatively
small number of heroic figures. This economy of storage
determines what sort of knowledge is stored. "The psychology of oral memorization and oral record," writes
Havelock (p. 171), "required the content of what is
memorized to be a set of doings." An oral culture has
great difficulty in formulating abstractions, because they
are not the kind of knowledge it can readily recall.

Doings imply actors or agents. In the oral conceptual
economy, all phenomena, even nonhuman ones, must in
some manner be translated into the doings of such agents

or made to cluster around their doings. Otherwise they are lost. Thus Homer's famous catalogue of ships in the second book of the *Iliad,* which interests us today largely as a kind of list conveying demographic information of the sort one finds in a gazetteer, is in Homer made a part of the panoply of epic battle.

In oral cultures virtually all conceptualization, including what will later be reshaped into abstract sciences, is thus kept close to the human life-world. Moreover, since public law and custom are of major importance for social survival but cannot be put on record, they must constantly be talked about or sung about, else they vanish from consciousness. Hence the figures around whom knowledge is made to cluster, those about whom stories are told or sung, must be made into conspicuous personages, foci of common attention, individuals embodying open public concerns, as written laws would later be matters of open public concern. In other words, the figures around whom knowledge is made to cluster must be heroes, culturally "large" or "heavy" figures like Odysseus or Achilles or Oedipus. Such figures are absolutely essential for oral culture in order to anchor the float of detail which literate cultures fix in script. These figures, moreover, cannot be too numerous or attention will be dissipated and focus blurred. The familiar practice sets in of attributing actions which historically were accomplished by various individuals to a limited number of major figures (Rome's complex early history is seen as the biography of Aeneas or as the story of Romulus and Remus); only with writing and print could the number of characters in a modern history book or in fiction such as *Finnegans Wake* be possible at all.

Thus the epic hero, from one point of view, appears as an answer to the problem of knowledge storage and communication in oral–aural cultures (where indeed storage and communication are virtually the same thing). Homer, it will be remembered from what was said in chapter 2 above, was not merely a verbal entertainer, but concurrently a knowledge storer and repeater, the best his oral culture could produce. His heroes were not only entertaining but also highly serviceable. With writing and print, heroic figures decline on both these scores. The decline is observable in literature, but it is equally observable in political life. Bureaucracy is based on written storage of records, as its name hints (*bureau,* desk), and as bureaucracy becomes a more and more effective way to successful government (Machiavelli was a clerk), the heroic figure of the king is no longer needed as a rallying point for political organization. Loyalties can be otherwise mobilized.

When manuscript and print cultures gradually replace the old oral institutions, the hero operates less and less effectively and convincingly as the oral residue in such cultures shrinks more and more. By the beginning of our present electronic age, when the possibility of storing detailed verbalized knowledge becomes virtually infinite, the hero has almost vanished as a major conservator of culture. He is replaced by his opposite, the antihero who, instead of storing knowledge, comes ultimately to reflect wryly on the vast quantities of it which are stored and on the storage media themselves, as do Samuel Beckett's typical technological-age antiheroes Murphy or Malone or, more particularly, Krapp, mulling over the hopeless electronic reproduction of his own earlier voice in *Krapp's Last Tape.*

The older method of knowledge storage, in terms of actions attributed to heroes, establishes a world view in which even the physical forces at work are seen in terms

of interactions involving men and/or highly anthropo-
morphized gods. Such a world view automatically generates a high quotient of hostility. Events are typically
seen as resulting not from natural forces but from personal decisions. When something undesirable happens,
one surmises that it is the work of an enemy, a malevolent
will. Disaster, of which there is always a surfeit, implies
the existence of a foe. Habits of auditory synthesis support this polemic outlook by representing the world not
as a float of objects strung out before one's eyes but rather
as a happening or event, something going on.

Unable to control or even to assemble massive causal
detail, oral–aural man thus tends to believe or to make
out that matters stand the way they do because some*body*
has *done* something, made some sort of decision, perhaps
out of caprice, ill will, or perversity. It is often said that
proximate physical causes do not interest oral–aural man.
This of course is nonsense. Proximate physical causes
interest him intensely, but he has limited access to their
operations, which he can conceptualize only with difficulty if at all. Human motivation and decision, on the
other hand, are familiar to him, and he is prone to design
his explanations so that he can ascribe to personal action
what otherwise eludes his understanding. Unable, for
example, to identify the physical causes for meteorologi-
cal phenomena, he tends to account for them in terms
of motivation and resulting decisions in the lives of living
beings, ordinarily the gods: Zeus has a bad day and shows
it by making thunder. As convenient sources of explanation, gods are multiplied. Havelock (pp. 169–70) points
out how an oral culture thus favors polytheism and
animism. A pantheon should not be too large, just as an
epic cast of characters must not be so large as to over-
burden oral storage devices (the inflated pantheons of late

Greece and Rome are known to be synthetic developments of fairly literate cultures). But a decently populous
pantheon, like a decently full cast of epic characters, provides the set of personal tensions, hostilities, and hence ac-
ceptable motivations for what is going on in heaven and
on earth. In striking contrast to the plausible motivations
of such a pantheon, the will of a single omnipotent God
remains essentially inscrutable. Monotheism goes not
so much with myth as with science.

Havelock thus indirectly suggests the importance of
literacy in the economy of Hebrew revelation. It should
be a bit easier for literates to stay on a monotheistic track.
Nevertheless, since the ancient Hebrews were so oral
and unscientific despite the alphabet, it is strange that
they could maintain the monotheistic tradition so effectively as they did. More thoroughly alphabetized
cultures like that of the Greeks have normally a far
worse record of entrenched polytheism.

FLITING, RHETORIC, DIALECTIC, AND OBJECTIVITY

One of the characteristic verbal institutions of an oral
culture, polarized as this is around personal tensions, is
that of fliting, already mentioned above, the concerted
exchange of personal abuse, combined often with boast
and challenge, which forms a staple of oral performance
especially but not exclusively in the epic from the *Iliad*
through *Beowulf* and beyond. The scurrilous and witty
verse in medieval debates, such as one finds in *The Owl
and the Nightingale,* perpetuate this old oral tradition.
In *The Untuning of the Sky,* John Hollander has traced
a whole minor genre of contentious bird literature (pp.
226–27). The relationship of the musical concerto form

to this rhetorical tradition one can guess at. In literature, exchange of abuse continues to Rabelais and the Renaissance generally, contributing massively to the inflammatory language of religious and scholarly quarrels of the period. Fliting lingers to a degree even today when oral elements in verbalization are high—as, for example, in the political oration (which has become less excoriating, however, since technologized by television) and not infrequently in the drama, as for example in Albee's play mentioned earlier, *Who's Afraid of Virginia Woolf?* The strong oral tradition in Ireland has always favored varieties of verbal combat, which Irish writers like James Joyce and Brendan Behan have known how to put to good use.

The state of mind signaled by a taste for fliting and characteristic of heroic, oral–aural cultures persisted with surprising strength in the West much longer than might have been expected. It is understandable that old oral sets of mind would disappear only slowly despite the development of writing and even of print, since vast pockets of illiteracy remained through Western culture as a whole into modern times, and indeed in some countries still remain. What is more surprising is that the old oral sets of mind were actually enforced by literacy itself. Paradoxically, the Latin language, around which writing and literary education were focused in the West from antiquity through the nineteenth century, had been formed in a highly oral age and enshrined profoundly oral institutions. Because the educational system which was bequeathed to the West by ancient Greece and Rome, maintained with some modifications in the Middle Ages and revitalized by the Renaissance, was based on assimilation of ancient Latin cultural ideals, it institutionalized the oral and helped preserve it far beyond what might otherwise have been normal expectation. The system which had this effect was that based on the *artes sermocinales,* the arts of discussion (*sermocinari,* to discuss, converse) or of conceptionalization and communication, that is, grammar, rhetoric, and dialectic or logic, often referred to as the trivium.

Of these three arts it was the latter two which most directly preserved the polemic state of mind of heroic or oral culture. As has been seen, grammar was concerned in a special way with writing. *Grammatikos* in Greek meant one who studied *grammata* or letters of the alphabet. The term was rendered in early Latin *litteratus,* a "lettered" man; later Latin dropped the native *litteratus* and appropriated the Greek term as *grammaticus.* As one concerned with the totality of what was written, the *grammaticus* or lettered man soon was understood to be the learned or scholarly man, the savant. But when Latin became a chirographically controlled language into which one was initiated always through writing, grammar was gradually reduced for the most part to the first and most elementary art of the trivium. One's first contact with Latin was normally not in speaking it before one could write, but in writing it. Not oral use (as is the case with a mother tongue) but the written alphabet was the point of ingress. Grammar governed writing. Thus it tended to become not the sum total of learning, but the beginning of learning, an elementary subject—indeed, the most elementary school subject. The older idea of the grammarian as a totally learned man was preserved to a degree; it is curiously enshrined today in our word "glamor," a Scottish by-form of "grammar," meaning originally vast learning, deep or mysterious lore, and thus the power to enchant or cast a spell and hence to "charm" us. But this aggrandized meaning did not always and everywhere persist. By and large, from the time Latin ceased to be a vernacular, grammar meant more and more not comprehensive learning but the first subject one encountered in formal education. This is why we still today call an elementary school a grammar school (that is, originally, a place to study Latin grammar, the most elementary of all school subjects).

The other two more advanced *artes sermocinales* were patently oral in cast. Rhetoric was the art governing oral delivery, *rhētorikē* being the Greek term for the art of oratory. Even when the term was applied to writing (as it was at times even in antiquity), so long as the ancient Greek and Roman understanding of the term remained operative, which is to say roughly until the triumph of Romanticism, the oral grounding of rhetoric was always in evidence. Insofar as rhetoric governed pre-Romantic expression, oratory notably governed this expression. Over the teaching of writing in Renaissance schools, for example, there hangs a feeling that the paradigm of all expression is the oration, for writing itself was taught through the teaching of rhetoric. The term rhetoric could not escape the pull of its own history, which aligned it with oral performance, however vaguely. When Reniassance humanists restored or reinforced the cult of classical rhetoric, they by that very fact willy-nilly rehabilitated and reinforced the old oral and polemic institutions.

Dialectic or logic (the terms were often synonymous, although at times distinguished) was basically an oral art, too. For Cicero, *dialectica* was the *ars disserendi*, or art of discourse, for one studied the structure of thought in connection with the use of these structures in speech, in argumentation. The Middle Ages was much given also to the study of formal logic, which has to do with "pure" thought structure, purportedly independent of back-and-forth argumentative use and purportedly distinct as a logic of "necessity" or logic of science from all such logics of probability as can be used in argumentation and debate. But the art and use of argumentation or disputation was so deep-grained in medieval culture that, in practice, interest in formal logic and interest in disputing with other persons often came to much the same thing. One fostered the other. In *Les Structures anthropologiques de l'imaginaire* (pp. 165, 187, 191–99, 472–73), Gilbert Durand has shown some of the fascinating psychological relationships between the diagrammatic and diaeretic preoccupations of formal logic and the antithetical procedures of dialectic, which cast no small light on the medieval propensity to merge interest in pure logic with a polemic cast of mind. The quest for symmetry, the "diurnal regime" of the mind, the drive for analytic clarity, is essentially polemic and, carried to its extreme, becomes schizophrenic, when the individual interprets his life-world totally in terms of controlled diagrammatic structures and pushes the distinction between self and world to its extreme limits (pp. 453 ff.).

The standard medieval logical treatise, the *Summulae logicales* of Peter of Spain (1210/20–1277), a contemporary of Aquinas, mingles the two viewpoints, one presenting logic as purely abstract structure and the other as the art of disputation. Formal logic was studied largely for dispute, and disputation served to settle and brace the thought structures provided by formal logic. When formal logic atrophied through the fifteenth and sixteenth centuries, so did the scholastic disputation. The age of Descartes (1596–1650) saw the displacement of the logic of disputation by a logic of private inquiry, which was the art not of discourse but the art of "thinking," presumably, all along, in the privacy of one's own skull. Strangely but significantly, the Cartesian interest in a private logic of inquiry fostered not the study of formal logic but rather of a psychologized logic, leading to associationist philosophy and Kantian preoccupations.

The balance between rhetoric and logic varied from age to age. In antiquity, rhetoric was dominant, cultivated and described by the Sophists and even by Aristotle himself, who sought to disinfect rhetoric from "sophistry" (which, as Croll shows in *Style, Rhetoric, and Rhythm,* p. 58, meant that Aristotle oriented rhetoric toward writing more than toward oratory). Cicero, Quintilian, the Church Fathers, and thousands of lesser practitioners continued the study and teaching of rhetoric. Rhetoric furnished the ancient world, as we have seen, with its educational ideal: the rhetorician or public speaker was the perfectly educated man for pagan Greek and Roman culture, and provided the fundamental humanistic material which Christian education sought to form in Christ. Rhetoric was of immense importance in the Christian liturgy. Unlike many or most other religions, the Hebreo-Christian tradition taught belief in a personal God who was deeply concerned about man and who, though utterly transcendent, could be approached by man argumentatively, as in the Psalms and the Book of Job. The Roman and Greek liturgies made classical rhetoric a tremendously effective vehicle for biblical teaching.

In the Middle Ages, however, with the coming of the universities and a more speculative, "scientific" mind, dialectic rose in importance and to a degree eclipsed rhetoric in the school curriculum, where rhetoric tended to be understood as an intermediate course in Latin expression following upon the elementary course, grammar. With the Renaissance, rhetoric was again accorded more honor, although the Renaissance humanists never succeeded in doing away with the dialectical heritage of scholasticism.

The range of the twin subjects through their long and involved history was incredibly wide, as can be seen through the studies collected by Schwartz and Rycenga. Between them, rhetoric and dialectic controlled virtually all verbalized, formalized knowledge from antiquity through the seventeenth century. Rhetoric entered into the very fabric of philosophy, theology, medicine, law, courtly behavior and manners generally, poetry (commonly thought of as simply a special kind of rhetoric) and prose both secular and religious, painting and sculpture (iconography has intimate associations with rhetoric, as can be seen in L'Orange's *Studies in the Iconography of Cosmic Kingship*), linguistic behavior in Latin and the vernaculars, politics, architecture, and the teaching of mathematics. Through the Middle Ages, dialectic also affected most or all of these, for all formal teaching was cast in a dialectical framework. Thomas Aquinas wrote his *Summa Theologica* in a kind of inside-out dialectical form (objections, statement of his own position, and finally answers to objections) simply because it seemed the thing to do. Matching Aristotle with Thomas, Dante in the *Convivio* (II.27) portrays the Stagirite as fighting with the opponents of truth before he himself stated what the truth was. In academia, strife was de rigueur. One secured even the degree of doctor of medicine by demonstrating ability to argue down one's opponents.

It is patent how dialectic fostered a polemic view of life. As the art of disputation, dialectic is contentious and partisan by definition, polarizing issues, even the most scientific issues, in terms of yes and no, your side and my side, forming schools or sects in the learned world. But rhetoric is even more contentious, if not always obviously so. Our tendency to think of rhetoric as mere ornamentation or verbal pyrotechnics obscures this fact. Understood more basically as the art of public speaking (Aristotle at the opening of his *Rhetoric* had seen it as the art of finding the means of persuasion for any subject matter whatsoever), rhetoric implies and engenders commitment. The public speaker is never an impartial investigator. He has taken a stand. He wishes to persuade, to win others to his side. In his *Institutio oratoria (Training in Oratory)*, Quintilian insists that orators are armed for real strife (X.i.28–29).

The sides which rhetoric forms, moreover, are more real and meaningful than those which dialectic typically brings into being. For rhetoric has to do with the human life-world, whereas dialectic typically has to do with more abstract or objective matters. Dialectic is often presented as a way of truth, in the sense of scientific truth, through the clash of opinions. But abstract truth, whatever its ultimate consequences, is often quite remote from going human interests. Losing a speculative debate on the physical constitution of the earth's core is unlikely to have immediate repercussions on the life of the loser or anyone around him. The issues are abstract, and defeat generally means loss of face and no more. For the orator, on the other hand, issues are often agonizingly concrete. If he is counsel for the defense and is defeated, not merely has he lost face but his client may also very well lose his head. If an argument about the constitution of the earth's core happens to be practical and thus rhetorical rather than purely speculative—a sum of money should be invested in a certain sort of research because the core is in a certain semifluid state—the issues can become much more urgent.

The implications of the rhetorical situation are clear. Even more than dialectic, rhetoric tends to polarize life in partisan terms rooted not in abstract issues to which one may or may not be committed but rooted rather in concrete life situations. The formal cultivation of rhetoric thus quite as much as the formal cultivation of dialectic perpetuated the polemic institutions of the old oral–aural culture, keeping the exaggerated virtue–vice polarity of such cultures alive long past the time when the advance of writing and typography and the waning of feudalism had spelled the doom of the old partisan, oral–aural outlook.

The effects of the academic cultivation of rhetoric and dialectic upon the psychological structures of pretechnological man have never been fully described and seldom even adverted to. Sweeping as it may sound, and even brash, to say so, the fact is that from antiquity until well through the eighteenth century the formal educational system that trained the Western mind at no point undertook to train a student to be "objective." Objectivity could be achieved and certainly was achieved, but its achievement was more or less a matter of individual enterprise. What we today style objectivity was not, indeed, positively downgraded. But in the academic world, where the modes of expression taught were all rhetorical (persuasive) or dialectical (disputatious), it was simply not provided for at all.

Academic training taught a student only how to take a stand and defend it and how to attack the defenses of others who were taking stands. Besides the forms of argumentation used for dialectic, the dominant, and in-

deed virtually the only form of verbal organization
taught in schools from antiquity until, roughly, the beginnings of Romanticism was that of the oration, whose
parts were enumerated variously, from two to seven, but
always centered on the proof of one's position seen as
under attack by adversaries. Poetry was normally a part
or adjunct of rhetoric, typically concerned with virtue
and vice. Treatises were organized as orations: Sir Philip
Sidney's *Defense of Poesy* is a typical and well-known example. Letters were often similarly organized. Angel
Day's *The English Secretorie* (1635) treats of epistles
laudatory, vituperative, reprehensory, accusatory, excusa-
tory, purgatory, defensory, invective and comminatory,
among others. History itself was a kind of oratory, featuring long speeches, often of opponents. Visual observation
might be reported, and was notably from Aristotle and
Thucydides on. But nowhere was the student taught such
procedure, nowhere called on in the course of formal
academic training to observe something and report verbally on his observation. There was a rhetorical figure
known as description, but such description was learned
by studying and imitating the descriptions of others, not
by looking at things. One mastered modes of description
known to be or presumed to be satisfactory for argumentative purposes. Textbooks such as the *Officina* of
Joannes Ravisius Textor in the sixteenth century en-
shrine the age-old tradition, with their descriptions,
ready-made, of a dark night or a long time. This kind of
commonplace approach is not to be scorned. It produced
Shakespeare and most of the literature of Western Europe at least until the Romantic movement. But, like
most dramatic effectiveness, Shakespeare's effectiveness
is highly polemic, not "objective" or scientific.

Polemic characterized not only literature but learning

itself. The polemic state of learning is well epitomized in the tremendously influential French savant Peter Ramus (1515–72), who, as I have reported in *Ramus, Method, and the Decay of Dialogue* (pp. 32–34, 197), conceived of his lectures on grammar and mathematics, supplementing his textbooks on these subjects, as refutations of his adversaries. If there was no adversary, real or imagined, there was seemingly nothing to say.

Human knowledge always involves countless questions to which, at least for the moment, only probable answers can be advanced. In the past, from antiquity through the Renaissance, each of the probable answers was championed by a school of followers, attached to their intellectual leader by a kind of tribal loyalty, so that, to a degree which is seldom if ever realized today in fully technologized societies, learning was caught up in personal commitments. "Plato is my friend, Aristotle is my friend, but truth is still more my friend" (*Amicus Plato, amicus Aristoteles, sed magis amicus veritas*) the Cambridge Puritan William Ames inscribes on the title page of his *Philosophemeta* (1643) or *Introduction to Philosophy*. Such declarations of independence strike us today as normal, but they might at the time have been interpreted as intellectual cowardice. Thus in his *Systema Physicum* (Book VI, chapter v, col. 1680) the German polymath Bartholomaeus Keckermann (1571–1609) scolds Jean Bodin for "taking refuge in ignorance" (*ad asylum ignorantiae confugere*) because Bodin had declared that he simply did not know the nature of the comets. Keckermann protested that he should rather have fought his way like a man through the opinions of embattled philosophers in the hope of achieving truth. It is easy to see how this disputatious, often precociously committed mentality aligns itself with the feudal world of personal attachments and loyalties, and thus how feudal-ism itself had deep oral roots and was doomed in a world of print, with all such a totally literate and objective world implied.

The fact that the polemic stance appears associated with the state of the word in oral culture makes it par-ticularly intriguing that the culture of the Middle Ages, a manuscript culture with strong oral undertow, where the state of the word in the media was unsettled, should have centered so much of its disputation around the na-ture of terms themselves and their role in the "location" of concepts—Were universals in things or in the words only? Nominalists or Terminists developed a philosophy around the study of names (*nomina*) or terms, and the ways of "being-in" discussed by Aristotle. A manuscript culture had made urgent the problem of locating terms or concepts in their correct "place."

Through the Renaissance and much later, polemic flourishes around further discussions of language itself. A typical production is Andreas Guarna's Latin work published at Strasbourg in 1512 and translated into English in 1569 by William Hayward as *Bellum Gram-maticale: A Discourse of Great War and Dissention be-tween Two Worthy Princes, the Noune and the Verbe.* Probably the greatest show of hostility in the titles and substance of the sixteenth- and seventeenth-century books is provided by writers on linguistic matters, as can be seen throughout Richard Foster Jones' account, *The Triumph of the English Language.* And even today the contest between grammarians (chirographically oriented) and linguistics specialists (orally oriented) continues the old tradition of virulent dispute concerning words. Dic-tionaries, from that of Dr. Johnson to *Webster's New In-ternational Dictionary,* Third Edition, are foci of active polemic. As I have suggested in a recent book, *In the Human Grain* (pp. 53–58) the adjustment of oral speech to writing calls for a great investment of energy. Consequently, to the oral polemic tendencies there accrue anxieties about the state of the word in its artificial medium of space.

The fact that dialectic and rhetoric, with all the contentiousness they entailed, dominated the intellectual and academic world from classical antiquity with gradual diminution through the Enlightenment has long been known. Indeed, it is a commonplace. But the sweeping implications of this fact have seldom been attended to. The shift from the old science to the new in the sixteenth and especially the seventeenth century has often been pictured as a substitution of inductive for deductive methods. Recent scholarship has become increasingly aware of the inadequacy of such a picture to account for what was really going on. For one thing, no one was ever against induction: learned men simply assumed it had been performed by ordinary rule-of-thumb observation verifiable anytime in everyone's life, not only under special laboratory controls. Everybody saw stones and feathers fall and thus observed that heavy bodies fall faster than light bodies. Moreover, deduction has never been discarded in science: modern scientific procedures carry it farther than ever before (as they also carry induction farther).

A reason for the development of modern science much more profound and real than the displacement of deduction by induction was the shift from the old oral–aural, conversational, disputatious, semianimistic, personalized feeling for knowledge, entailing a proclivity for auditory syntheses, to a feeling for knowledge as aligned with vision much more unequivocally than it had been in the past. This feeling had been already strong in ancient Greece, but it was inhibited there by vigorously competing oral drives. It came into its own only after print. The term "observation," which finally became the shibboleth of the new science, it should be noted, refers directly to vision and only to vision. Presumably the new science was interested in studying everything, even nonvisual sensory phenomena, by observation. There is, of course, a fallacy here, for observation refers primarily to ocular perception: there is no way to register sound as such by observation, strictly speaking, although sound is as much a fact as shape is, if not so stable a one. Sound cannot be directly observed—it can only be listened to, heard—though it can be treated indirectly, and quite productively, as though it were observable. The problem here is by no means semantic; it is an existential problem. The new science in fact made very little of sound as sound, as we have seen. Basically, it depended on an apotheosis of vision and of visually conceived, neutral mathematical space.

Scholars have long known that the new science was at many points opposed to the disputatious world of scholastic philosophy as well as to the rhetorical world of Renaissance humanists. But because we have been generally unaware of the historical and psychological importance of the media and the concomitant shifts in the sensorium, we have not known what to make of this opposition or of the passing of the scholastic disputation and all it stood for. What it stood for, in common cause with rhetoric, we can now see, was a residual oralism, an oralism codified by writing, an approach to knowledge perpetuating, really but quite unreflectively, the old oral–aural world with this world's devotion to the spoken word. This is not to say that medieval man did not down-

grade the spoken word by comparison with antiquity.
He did, as has been seen. Far more than had the ancient
Greeks, he heightened the visualist, quantified quotients
of awareness. But he did so with minimal reflectiveness.
The Middle Ages lived through a great reorganization
of the sensorium without knowing it was doing so.

The struggle, in which the disputatious oral approach
to existence and knowledge lost much of its hold, was a
struggle between hearing and seeing. Seeing won. With
the shift in the sensorium by print, the large-scale campaign for the "clear and distinct" soon began, led by
Ramus and focused by Descartes—a campaign for visually conceived cognitive enterprise. Ramist charts and
Cartesian vortices replaced the ancient cosmic harmonies.
The Muses, with their song, disappeared. Knowledge, in
the sense of intellectual knowledge, was henceforth, more
than ever before, to be conceived of almost solely by
analogy with vision. And the implications of the purely
visual world, where instead of communication between
man and man there can be only "contact" between object and object, were to be enforced. Henceforth, thought
was to be considered as taking place in private, within
one's own isolated head, and thus presumably without
language and without history, since language is not private but communal, and history testifies to the fact that
my thought does not start on its own but is always a
response to someone else's, a modified echo or an echo
with something added. Rhetoric underwent a similar
transformation. In *The History of Signboards* (pp. 30–
31) Larwood and Hotten have shown how by the eighteenth century in place of the old emblematic symbols (an
ivy bush for a tavern, three balls for a pawnbroker, and so
on) lettered signs began to appear on the streets of the
Western world, and modern display advertising was born

—a rhetoric of the visualized word. This was a step beyond typography, which had merely fixed the word in space. The word was exhibited more and more as a picture might be, finally producing present-day newspaper, magazine, and billboard display advertising, in which illustrations of things and configurations of words combine on an equal footing in a new kind of rhetorical space to exercise a kind of persuasion which would have been not merely ineffective but quite unintelligible to a Moses, Aristotle, Cicero, Aquinas, John Milton, and probably even to an Alexander Pope.

OBJECTIVITY AND SUBJECTIVITY

To say that a culture dominated by rhetoric and dialectic based its academic program on polemic exercises is not to say that in such a culture or in earlier preliterate culture all objectivity was impossible. There are various kinds of objectivity. One consists in fairness or impartiality in giving each man his due. Fairness or impartiality, the dispassionate judging of an individual's merit without regard to his impact on one's own world is encountered frequently in oral–aural cultures. In Homer, for example, there is a good deal of fairness regarding Hector's worth, although Hector was on the wrong side. The Old Testament attributes utter fairness to God who has no "respect of persons nor desire of gifts" (Paralipomenon or II Chron. 19:7), and similar fairness to human rulers.

It is not unreasonable to think that the practice of this fairness or impartiality reaches back into the preliterate stages of the cultures which put Homer and the Old Testament into writing. Nevertheless this kind of objectivity or impartiality is evaluative and personal, belonging to a world where the reporter and his material (another person or quasiperson), really do interact rather discernibly. Homer's "objective" treatment of Hector is response to human appeal. It is really praise, a rhetorical form for which rhetoric had a standard name, encomium. There is nothing uncommitted about an encomium. It takes sides not against but with its object. Impartiality here is achieved by the way in which encomia and blame are distributed, as when an encomium is uttered not only concerning one's friends but also concerning the deserving adversary, or when an individual is praised for some things and blamed for others. Ancient biographers such as Suetonius and Plutarch already evaluate the subjects of their writing with a certain amount of this impartiality or objectivity. In a world so taken up with the human or quasihuman as an oral–aural world necessarily is, impartiality will be the chief form of objectivity. In this world, man's relation even to inanimate nature is imbued with quasihuman relations.

Another kind of objectivity does not get involved in human values as such. This objectivity, essential for scientific explanation, becomes possible when one envisions the world as set off from oneself as essentially neuter, uncommitted, and indifferent to the viewer. Study of such a world is felt to be not a response to the world but an operation upon it. Knowledge in its optimum or typical condition regards not persons or quasipersons but neutral objects. Whether such objectivity can be achieved and verbalized in a preliterate culture is at least questionable, for, as we have seen, in such cultures spoken words, the only words such cultures know, ordinarily are closely tied to living interactions of man with man. They are dynamic and charged with the emotion involved necessarily in interpersonal relations, since all words occur in "existential" situations between man and man.

Thought, inextricably bound up with words, is associated in a preliterate culture not with a world where observation works dispassionately but with the dynamic, the interpersonal. The physical milieu itself is not felt as indifferent to the writer and to the observer and thinker.

By the time writing has the hold it achieved among the ancient Greeks, something like a vision of a neutral world is largely arrived at, even though the universe is still shot through with animism, as in Aristotle's living celestial spheres. Philosophical treatises even from very ancient times are capital examples of such a vision of a neutral world. Still, their kind of objectivity is typically speculative rather than descriptive (except of human behavior, as in the Socratic dialogues, or of mathematical abstractions). The neutral stance is taken toward the world of ideas rather than toward the physical world as such. Moreover, even speculatively objective works commonly approach their subject matter through a polemic network of argumentation and answers to real and conjectural objections. This can be seen not only in Socrates' dialogues (that is, in Plato's written recreation of them, which is all we have), but also in much of Aristotle's work on natural history, which is not dialogic in form but remains highly argumentative in its speculation.

Descriptive objectivity is met with also in ancient historians, as when Thucydides in chapter 7 of *The Peloponnesian War,* gives his account of the plague at Athens, and it is found to some extent in what today we would call biological works, such as Aristotle's book *On the Parts of Animals* or in Pliny's *Natural History,* although here objectivity is inextricably fouled with legend (reports slanted toward what men say rather than what men see) and disabled by the absence of exactly repeatable pictorial statements, which would become current only

toward the end of the fifteenth century with the introduction of engraved illustrations.

Such works attest both a movement toward neutral
description of an indifferent external world and persistent vagaries of the movement. So long as culture was
dominantly oral–aural, attempts at neutral objectivity
would be under constant danger of distortion due to the
often unwitting but inevitable tendency to cast thought
and expression in the approved polemic mold which was
part of the standard equipment provided by formal education for man's confrontation of the world. It was not
simply that the writer had an audience in mind—every
writer, including the present-day scientific writer, must
have an audience in mind. It was rather that the writer's
formal training gave him the orator's stance, passionate
involvement in his material, and a feeling that there was
an adversary at large. Opponents, real or conventional,
took his eye off the object.

The history of "objective" and "subjective," with their
cognates and synonyms in various languages, is itself illuminating here. The terms object and subject have had
a long career, but the tendency to set them off against
each other in the objective–subjective dyad with which
we are so familiar today is relatively new. The meanings
of object and subject have in fact virtually reversed themselves in the course of their development, as the *Oxford
English Dictionary* and other lexicographical works circumstantially report. In the tradition of ancient and
medieval Aristotelianism, earlier users of the term "subject" (*subjectum*) think of a subject chiefly or typically as
that in which attributes inhere—as, for example, the
attribute of whiteness might "inhere" in a dog, its subject
(the concept of inhering has, it is evident, largely a tactile
base). Since subjective means "pertaining to the subject

as that in which attributes inhere," it thus means "existing in itself" or paramountly real and stable. By the same token, the subject is that to which something is done: it receives action in this Aristotelian setting, whereas today we are more likely to think of the object as receiving action (in a somewhat different sense, to be sure). In the Aristotelian tradition attributes were "predicated" of the subject. In the assertion "The dog is white," the subjectively constituted dog is thus more real, more substantial, more stable than its attribute, white. (The concept substance, *substantia* in Latin, *hypokeimenon* in Greek, both based on the notion of standing underneath or lying underneath, has a strong tactile base, mingled with some visual elements.) Moreover, it receives action in that it is "subjected" to predicates (*praedicamenta*, *catēgoriae*), that is, literally, accusations, as was seen in chapter 2. The term "dog" thus *undergoes* or submits to predication, has white imposed on it in this assertion.

Coexistent with this older meaning of subject and subjective was the older meaning of objective, that is, "existing as an object of consciousness as distinct from having a real existence" or "considered only as presented to the mind," as an object of knowledge. It will be noted that, although the terms subject and object and their cognates thus coexisted in early times, they are not at first paired, not set against each other as they commonly are now.

The senses of the terms as opposed to each other today are almost the opposites of the earlier senses, and some of their implications are directly the opposites of the earlier implications. Today it is the objective that is real, stable, as well as receptive of action. The subjective is something only in the consciousness without any necessary extra-mental real existence. It is less stable, less reliable, more likely to vacillate, than the objective is.

Moreover, despite all this, the subjective from another point of view is very active: when things are perceived, it does the perceiving, sometimes even imposing its own subjective forms on other things or objects. The reversal here was historically possible of course because of the neutral quality of the spatial imagery which underlies both concepts. *Subjectum* (*sub+iacere, under+to lie*) means something laid under, and *objectum* (*ob+iacere, against+to lie*) means something laid against, laid in the way of. These are diagrammatic models that can be used to plot a great number of things in a great number of ways.

At the risk of oversimplification, the transit from the older oral–aural sense of a universe felt as somehow vaguely alive to the subjective–objective frame can be stated as follows. For earlier man, under the influence of oral–aural or preliterate communications media, the world tended to be vaguely animistic, as we have seen. Economies of thought built around the study of nature are thus vaguely animistic, for *natura* means at root birth, just as does the Greek word for which it is the equivalent, *physis* (the source of our word physics and its cognates). Studying the nature of a stone or of water was thus, sometimes clearly and more often vaguely, equivalent to studying how it was "born"—studying its origins in terms which relate all origins to origins of life. The living celestial spheres essential to Aristotelian physics and favorable to the concept of the harmony of the spheres, together with the countless related concepts studied by Leo Spitzer in his *Classical and Christian Ideas of World Harmony,* bear testimony, direct or indirect, to the propensity for animism in even a highly sophisticated residually oral culture. The Newtonian revolution, and its accompanying exaltation of the sense of sight at the

expense of hearing, spelled the end of the feeling for a
vitalized universe, assimilated, at least vaguely, to man
and to other more or less anthropologized beings. From
now on the universe was something sighted and measured. Sight registers surfaces, which means that of itself
it encourages one to consider even persons not as interiors
but from the outside. Thus persons, too, tend to be
thought of somehow as objects, though an embarrassing
kind of objects. The entire universe consists essentially
or basically of objects—things. Persons and the consciousness they exhibit are unaccountable intrusions,
foreign to objective reality, which is voiceless and normally passive. The old more or less auditory syntheses had
presented the universe as being, which was here and
now acting, filled with events. For the new, more visual
synthesis, the universe was simply there, a mass of things,
quite uneventful.

The shift from a universe where activity welled up
from within to a universe of objects relatively devoid of
internal resources can of course be detected in many
developments within intellectual history. One development is of particular relevance to a history of the word,
that reported by Edgar Zilzel in his study, "The Genesis
of the Concept of Physical Law."

This concept was activated, Zilzel reports, only from
the early seventeenth century on. In the earlier view of
the universe, beings acted physically as they did not because of "physical laws" but rather because of their
"natures" (something inside them, hence something like
a principle of life, something like consciousness). A stone
fell not because a law of gravity governed it and thus
provided that it should, but because to do so belonged to
the nature of the stone, which was thus powered somehow from within. In the quite different view developed

from the seventeenth century on, things acted as they did typically because of physical laws which somehow "governed" them. A lawgiver other than the stone itself decreed that it should fall. It was "ruled" from the outside.

Zilzel convincingly traces the seventeenth-century activation of the physical law concept to the disappearance of feudal rule-by-tradition and the rise of legislatures and rule by written law. In the light of what we have earlier seen about the differences between the written and the spoken word, some implications of this written-law concept and its application to the physical world become clear. Writing, and particularly alphabetic writing (which lodges sound itself in space), externalizes words themselves, giving them a curious thing-like permanence as marks on a surface, a permanence which does not properly belong to them as sounds. In their native sound habitat, words retain a permanent inwardness, since sound manifests interiors and indeed disappears in the very act of emerging from an interior as sound. Law expressed in words taken as sounds has some of this same personal inwardness, which supports and is supported by the feudal cast of mind. Conceived of, consciously or subconsciously, as something written, law itself thus acquires a somewhat different, relatively objective quality. If it "applies" to someone or something, it applies from the outside.

Of course, one can conceive of law as being somehow inside the persons or things it governs. Indeed, philosophy is filled with explanations how and in what sense a law—for example, the natural law—is inward in this way. It would be interesting to study whether such explanations multiply after the advent of print, which makes so much more compelling the externalizing implications of script. A common way of conceiving of law as within those it governs is to think of it as "written in the heart," a way of thinking which at the same time advertises some kind of external origin, for the implication is that someone else wrote it: one is born with a nature (*natura*, like its Greek equivalent, *physis*, we have seen, at root means birth), but one is hardly born with the ability to write. In any event, the existence of a literature explaining that law is somehow within what it governs only underlines the tendency to think of it as being not in what it governs but as coming from outside. The physical laws are no exception: by contrast with nature as a determinant of physical behavior, they tend to be conceived of as external and to imply that what they govern is relatively passive, as the earlier semianimistic or quasianimistic universe of pre-Newtonian physics had not so clearly been.

But the physical-law concept has another implication, too. For laws, even when considered as somehow externally objective things, are at the same time always to some degree personal: they come from the most personal, the most interior of all acts, the act of decision. The concept of law seemingly always embodies a tension between some kind of objectivity (intensified by writing and print) and personal decision or commitment. Insofar as they, too, carry a personalist implication, the physical laws simply relocate the life-like principle of action (the nature) which earlier philosophies had tended to situate within things before the universe was so drastically "objectified." They situate the personal principle somewhere outside, in the lawgiver. In this frame of thought, the post-typographical concept of physical law appears as a kind of corrective or compensation for the depersonalization of the objective universe. Life or its equivalent has not been really done away with but simply deported. The physical laws provide for the inert, devitalized, silent Newtonian world a source of personalized power lying just outside its bounds. Instead of vaguely life-like natures working inside things, one now has externally operative life, the lawgiver, conceived of as somehow more removed from the real world than "natures" had been. The thing-like objectivity of the devocalized, depersonalized universe is thus protected from too obvious interference.

AUTHORITY AND ORAL–AURAL STRUCTURES

In terms of the oral–aural structures discussed here, the sixteenth-century crises regarding authority both in the religious and in the scientific worlds can be seen in a new and striking way as crises of the word. An oral–aural economy of knowledge is necessarily authoritarian to an extent intolerable in a more visualist culture. This is not simply because someone at the top is peremptorily imposing his views on those below. Such will be the later caricature of authority when it is under attack. The actuality is more complex. A personality structure built up in an oral society, feeling knowledge as essentially something communicated, will be relatively more concerned that this knowledge tie in with what others say and relatively less concerned with its relationship to observation.

In such a society, knowledge is a tribal possession, not a matter of individual speculation; one recalls the studies reported by Carothers and Havelock and discussed at length in chapter 3 above, which show how an oral culture inhibits solitary original speculation. Oral culture does not produce a Descartes or Newton or Einstein. Before literacy, the thought of the entire culture must advance as a unit, with individual contributions, of course, but contributions which are infinitesimal by comparison with today's possibilities. Even the most intellectually venturesome individual simply cannot detach himself from the tribal thought, from what "people say," to the extent we take for granted for virtually everyone today.

This state of affairs changed only slowly with the advent of literacy. Aristotle was still caught up in it, as can be seen in a fascinating work of his so little read that it has no accepted English title. The Latin title retained by Aristotle's translator W. D. Ross in Volume 6 of the *Works* is *De mirabilibus auscultationibus,* which might be translated *On Remarkable Things One Hears Of.* This work consists entirely of statements beginning "Men say that . . . ," or "It is said that . . . ," or "People say . . . ." "It is said that in the island of Gyaros the mice eat iron" (832a). "On the altar of the Orthosian Artemis, it is said that a golden bull stands which bellows when hunters enter the temple" (847b). Or again, rubbing shoulders with this kind of report, another as true as it is marvelous: "Men say that in Egypt the sandpipers fly into the mouths of crocodiles and cleanse their teeth" (831a). The text of Aristotle's works generally, as we have seen, is less firmly anchored in writing than would be the case of most comparable works today. But the existence of such a work as *On Remarkable Things One Hears Of* and its attribution to Aristotle goes still farther in reminding us how dependent thought could still be in some of its reaches on a float of oral reports which were "known" simply because they were said to be so.

In a society where knowledge is kept accessible only by being uttered or largely by being uttered, observation is of course not eliminated, but it is minimized. It is not so much sycophantic as socialized. One feels knowledge as *our* possession rather than as *my* possession; this is the knowledge which Havelock has shown forms the backbone of the Homeric encyclopedia. Under these circumstances there is very little feeling for new, individual, proprietary discovery, but a strong feeling for conserving what threatens to perish at any minute if it is not *said* over and over again. Hence, in great part, the penchant for quoting authorities: these show contact with the sources of the communal heritage, the proficient or professional sayer, who is not an imposition but a necessity.

The oral–aural mind is thus structured to turn by preference away from mere things to the richness of traditional discourse in which true lore about things mingles them with lore about man and thereby accommodates them to the human life-world. This drift of attention can be seen even today as, for example, in a situation described to me not long ago by a friend who was engaged in training engineers from one of the still functionally oral–aural Arab cultures. Literate though the typical young Arab student might be, he was still in the deepest recesses of his being the product of a verbomotor society, an oral–aural personality. When he was faced with the problem of building a bridge, every fiber of his being made him want to respond to the situation by verbalization—he wanted to speak of what so-and-so had said in the past about building a bridge, of great battles fought on or over bridges, of the usefulness of bridges to men, and so on. A bridge, like everything else, had its most glorious existence in the universe of discourse. The idea of withdrawing into himself and starting out with surveying and drilling equipment and sets of mathematical tables to make detailed, mechanical analyses on his own of places where he could set footings or sink cofferdams struck the typical Arab student as antisocial, a prostitution of intellect, infrahuman and bestial.

One of the reasons why an oral–aural culture approaches what we today call the objective world largely by indirection, through what has been said about this world, which is to say through authoritarian structures, is that the objective world is still in such cultures relatively inaccessible to the word. Until quite recent times knowledge concerned with objects was so defectively verbalized that it could not be treated with great respect.

The entire world of objects, things, the artisan's world, the *banausia,* existed largely apart from the word itself. Through classical antiquity, as has been seen in chapter 2, writings concerned with practical activities such as farming tended to be reflective and aphoristic rather than directly descriptive and operational. As a recent study by Sister Marina Gibbons shows, how-to-do-it manuals begin to proliferate only in the first half of the sixteenth century, after the invention of typography. Trades were learned by apprenticeship. A master craftsman could show how to do something, but like almost all craftsmen even today, was quite incapable of explaining in elaborate verbal detail the processes he knew so well. Those who were not craftsmen were not expertly informed about the crafts or were not interested. Moreover, the terms and expressions required for explanation often did not exist except piecemeal and in dialect forms which were not current beyond the limit of a few miles. The rare manuals which were written, such as that of Frontinus earlier discussed, tended to wander off from technical description of things to human-interest stories and reflections on virtues and vices. Verbalization engendered moralizing.

Hostility and disdain for the world of physical objects is not unknown in the intellectual world today—Nietzsche manifested it—but it was far more assertive in the intellectual world of earlier times. In the sixteenth century, as appears from the disputes between Peter Ramus and Jacques Charpentier, detailed in the present author's *Ramus, Method, and the Decay of Dialogue* and *Ramus and Talon Inventory,* mathematics in the sense of calculation having to do with practical problems relating to objective actuality was still generally regarded as beneath the educated man's dignity, although philosophical speculation about mathematics commanded a high degree of respect. Almost two hundred years later, in the third book of *Gulliver's Travels* Jonathan Swift expresses the misgivings still commonly shared in the eighteenth century regarding all "projectors," men devoted to technical novelties ("research and development" today). Swift lived still very much in the old oral–aural world where the objectively considered physical universe was not entirely assimilated.

Examined in terms of the restructuring of the sensorium from its original strongly oral–aural form to a more visualist or visualist–tactile form, the authority crisis thus appears in a new light. Basically here it is not a struggle between members of society but a struggle within the individual soul. The tyrant whom man in the sixteenth and subsequent centuries is trying to free himself from is in great part himself. This has long been evident on other scores. Erik H. Erikson's *Young Man Luther* has made the point that Luther's fixation on the Pope as an image of all that is execrable was due to Luther's personality organization. The Pope became a needed symbol upon whom Luther could project his own problems concerning authority—the problems which, as

Erikson has so masterfully shown, were those of Luther's whole age, giving Luther the tremendous relevance he has for all men, then and now. The most telling battles man fights are of this sort. We hope to have made clear here that involved in the battle as a major factor, although by no means the only one, was the residue of oral–aural attitudes which made necessary the reorganization of the sensorium with a consequent revaluation of both the word and things in their relationship to human life, a revaluation which cost Luther and so many others unconscionable agony.

The End of Orally
Institutionalized Hostilities

In the perspectives which we have here been making use of, the academic tradition in the West is revealed as a massive device for institutionalizing the polemic stances originally fostered in oral culture because of its problems of information storage and its consequent overspecialization in heroic figures and interpersonal struggle as means of interpreting actuality. The modern world dawned with the development of alphabetic printing against a background of hostilities deriving from old oral cultures and formalized by two thousand years of academic tradition in the West. The very structure of knowledge had been largely polemic, for the old oral–aural anxieties of a world polarized around persons had been institutionalized by the centering of formal education around dialectic and rhetoric, both arts of verbal strife.

It is difficult to assess the tremendous reorganizations enforced on a total culture when such widespread polemicized attitudes were relatively neutralized by the shifts to habits of visual synthesis inculcated by print and its sequel, the new science whose spokesmen were Copernicus and Galileo and Newton. The first effects were ambiguous enough, even amusingly so, for the initial movement away from the polemic of academic life itself turned out to be highly polemic: the old system of disputation became an object of dispute between the humanists, who would have no more of it, and the scholastics, for whom it was synonymous with the life of the mind. Even when efforts at reform were not themselves disputatious attacks on the previous systems, new approaches to knowledge were likely to be shot through with oral–aural modes of thought, as was the program of Francis Bacon. Bacon's great work *The Advancement of Learning* (1605) is organized as a classical oration, "proved" by examples, and divides the human understanding into the five parts of Ciceronian rhetoric—invention, judgment, memory, and elocution or tradition (this fourth part including Cicero's remaining part, style), as has been shown by Maurice B. McNamee. In his attack on the old order of things, Bacon inadvertently asserts the old order more preposterously than ever: understanding and rhetoric (oral–aural performance) are in effect one and the same thing! Bacon denies this elsewhere, and yet he cannot escape his oral–aural heritage.

The approach to learning which succeeded the old polemic approach was of course only relatively neutral and has remained so even to our own day, for a certain amount of rivalry or emulation is apparently necessary for achievement in the intellectual world as elsewhere. But our teaching methodology has been depolemicized enough to make the earlier stress on polemic somewhat weird, even to historians. Thus in his recent historical study, *Jesuit Education,* John W. Donohue finds rather incomprehensible the stress on *aemulatio* or rivalry surviving in the schools of the Society of Jesus even through the eighteenth century. In the perspectives here sketched, this is simply the central stress of the whole Western tradition from antiquity until the Romantic age. The early Jesuit schools were, as Father Donohue shows, the first educational system, deliberately pooling the experience of thousands of teachers to devise standard curricula and procedures. Their institutionalizing of the older rule of life (though not without major adjustments) calls special attention to this older rule, especially in a culture moving inexorably into more visualist states of mind.

The older oral polemic institutions in fact at first even profited from the new medium of print, which later was to neutralize the same institutions. No one has yet provided us with a hostility index to assess with exactitude the relative vigor of the polemic spirit in various ages, and yet it seems not imprudent to say that probably no culture has been more riotously polemic in its verbal production than that of Europe in the two centuries after Gutenberg. This was the Europe of Rabelais, Martin Luther, Ulrich von Hutten, Simon Fish, John ("Bilious") Bale, William Tindale, Thomas More, Bellarmine and King James I, John Donne (whose virulently polemic prose is less known than his subtly polemic poetry), of Ben Jonson and John Marston, of Peter Ramus and the phalanxes of disputants from every nation in Europe whom his anti-Aristotelianism and his later anti-anti-Aristotelianism called to typographic arms, of Gabriel Harvey and Thomas Nashe, of Martin Marprelate and his opponents, of the five Presbyterians known collectively as "Smectymnuus" and their respondent Joseph Hall, whose work elicited John Milton's *Apology against a Pamphlet . . . against Smectymnuus* as a sequel to Milton's earlier *Animadversions upon the Remonstrant's De-*

fense against Smectymnuus. The layers of invective are even thicker in John Gother's anonymous tract, *An Amicable Accommodation of the Difference between the Representer and the Answerer in Return to the Last Reply against the Papist Protesting against Protestant Popery* (London, 1686). By this time even the disputants have their tongues in their cheeks.

Not infrequently this age is identified as simply an age of religious controversy. It was, in fact, an age of all sorts of heated controversy, some of which happened to be religious. Arguments about language, for example, as R. F. Jones has shown abundantly in *The Triumph of the English Language,* could be as virulent as those over the Bible. The roots of this polemic are in antiquity and even more in the Middle Ages, but the flower is certainly in the early typographic era. There was nothing quite like it before and there has been nothing quite like it since. Guides through some of the polemic are available in works such as Herschel Baker's *The Wars of Truth* and the present author's *Ramus and Talon Inventory.* But anyone who has worked in the period knows that the polemic in print is too vast for any complete or even adequate guide.

If print was to eliminate or at least reduce in virulence the polemic state of mind, how can this post-Gutenberg outburst of verbal violence be explained? The principal explanation derives from the fact that the phenomenon was a transitory one. This is not the only point in communications history where a new development at first only exaggerates a condition which it will later eliminate. In antiquity, writing had made possible the development of rhetoric and dialectic as formal disciplines, which they could not be in a completely oral culture, and thereby gave a new life temporarily to the oral institutions and states of mind which rhetoric and dialectic nourished themselves on and fed—acceptance of oratory as the paradigm of verbalization, exploitation of dispute to clarify issues, cultivation of the commonplaces, analytic and cumulative, and of formulaic modes of thought and expression, and so on. Print further encouraged exploitation of language as then understood with its still oral polemic structures.

The newer devices were at first thought of as improvements of the old rather than as competing but different inventions with economies of their own. The situation was much like that with the invention of the automobile, thought of initially as a horseless carriage and for years made to look like one. Just as the internal combustion engine at first gave to an already relatively fast vehicle greater velocity than its original source of power could supply, and only later forced the designing of a chassis really adapted to its own potential, so the new medium of print at first gave the old oral–aural contentiousness a sense of increased power before a wider audience, until it became apparent that the new medium was in fact fostering a new "objective" approach even more than it was aiding polemic, and that it was thereby making contentiousness rather outmoded. (Man being what he is, contentiousness is of course always with us to a degree, and always to a degree quite productive, as the polemic or game element in the race to the moon today makes evident.)

Undoubtedly, if we consider in these perspectives the work of an earlier Terry Lecturer, John Dewey, we will find that one facet of his many-faceted significance is that he climaxed the large-scale movement away from polemic in favor of an irenic approach to learning. Of course knowledge has not been depolemicized equally in all quarters even today. The classic Marxist mentality is basically polemic still, nonobjective, essentially feudal, tending to see problems not in terms of purely objective issues, but in terms of heroes and villains, not only internationally but domestically as well. Stalinization and de-Stalinization are strange relicts in a technological culture. Although its polemic is pitched differently from that of the old dialectical–rhetorical tradition, Marxist thought, through Hegel, connects quite directly with that tradition, as the prominence of the term "dialectic" indicates. The term has shifted its direction of growth but its roots are unmistakable.

COMMERCE, VERNACULARS, AND EDUCATION FOR WOMEN

The residual polemic framework for verbal communication inherited through the schools was notably weakened from the sixteenth century on by a curious alliance of forces: those of commerce and technology, those of the vernaculars, and those favoring education for women. The link connecting these seemingly disparate phenomena is their common tendency to eat away at the Latin base for training in verbal expression and in thinking which connected the old dialectico-rhetorical academic tradition directly with the highly oral culture of antiquity.

One would naturally think that the development of science after Galileo and Newton would have depolemicized the oral–aural component in man's life-world by helping situate man in a physical world conceived of as a thing, passive and silent. And it is certainly true that in significant ways it did. The visualization of the new science, with its stress on quantification (mathematics) and observation, minimized the oral–aural component in existence to the advantage of the visual components, helping set up, as we have seen, the new objectivity as a correlative of a new subjectivity. Still, the first effects of the new science were not unequivocally antipolemic. Scientists necessarily moved over the old argumentative academic routes. This was largely true even where the new science grew out of such extra-academic institutions as the Royal Academy in England. A scientific discovery which might be utterly factual and verifiable had to be launched into the academic maelstrom of discussion where polemic currents still held sway. The seventeenth-century disputes touched off by William Harvey's discovery of the circulation of the blood provide well-known evidence in point. Galileo, too, was caught up in one after another whirlpool of disputation.

By contrast with the scientific, intellectual, academic world, the manufacturing, technological, and commercial world is verbally quite peaceful. In *Imperialism and Social Classes* (pp. 90–130) and in *Capitalism, Socialism, and Democracy* (p. 128) Joseph Schumpeter has discussed the antiheroic, politically irenic bias of industrial capitalism, but without attention to communications media. Certainly polemic existed and still exists in industry. Competition is keen, and it is certain that commerce has helped generate wars and that technology has implemented them. But commercial antagonisms are likely to remain at the operational, nonverbal level. Argument does not pay. It is nonproductive. Typically, even today, a commercial firm which may be involved in murderous competition with its rivals is not likely to engage in public vilification. This was true from the early beginnings of modern industrialization. In *The Shocking History of Advertising*, E. S. Turner finds (pp. 33, 267–68) expressions of hostility only on rare occasions between the earliest modern advertisers in the late sixteenth century. Verbally, commerce is all at peace. When wars come about for commercial reasons or partly for commercial reasons, the stated reasons tend to be not commercially but politically framed, although, as Schumpeter makes clear, without the positive enthusiasm for war found in the heroic tradition (that is, in oral culture).

The manufacturing, technological, commercial world can never live far from cold fact. It tends to use words for reportorial purposes, a fact itself which suggests that the development of manufacturing, technology, and commerce both induced and depended upon attitudes toward the word which are little developed in oral cultures. One has only to compare Renaissance Latin humanists' epistolary procedure as prescribed in letter-writing manuals with the vernacular Fugger News Letters to see the difference between the polemic of academia and the businessman's request for simple hard fact which would enable him to conclude a profitable venture. The humanist manuals, as has been seen earlier, often prescribed that letters be cast in the form of an oration, even going so far as to include a refutation of "adversaries." William Fullwood's 1568 *Enimie of Idlenesse* wants letters to be marshaled for argumentative purposes like syllogisms, with a major, minor, and conclusion, and suggests the use in letters of commonplaces in the sense of formulary purple patches on a set subject. Fact was subordinate to a committed stand. Argumentative procedure, however, is of little if any value to the manufacturer or merchant. The uncomplimentary way to put it is to say that the manufacturing and commercial or bourgeois world is morally irresponsible in refusing to take a stand; the complimentary, that it is objective or detached.

Insofar as the commercial world wrote letters at all, it was of course in touch with the academic tradition controlling the use of words, for any letter writing has an academic cast. Script of its nature fosters the academic: one point at which formal schooling began in antiquity was with groups of men who wanted to learn how to write letters, that is, with professional scribes. Businessmen of the Gutenberg era could and did write academically colored letters and even the crudely commercial letter well after print had some alliance with the old rhetorico-dialectical academic milieu.

This can be seen in *The Merchants Avizo* (1607, but entered in the Stationers' Register in 1589), the first general manual for factors or commercial agents in the English-speaking world, written by "their hartie welwisher in Christ, I[ohn] B[rowne], Merchant" of Bristol. Although it is concerned with conveyance of facts, this letter-writing manual preserves, if in a moribund state, the formulaic approaches of the old rhetorical tradition. In the sample letters which Browne provides for commercial agents, each letter begins with the strict formula, "After my duty remembered, I pray for your good health and prosperitie, &c." News is always introduced with a protest of affected modesty or minimization, one of the standard rhetorical "topics of the exordium," cast by Browne invariably in the same words: "Little newes I hear worth the writing: only I understand that there is . . ."—"Here," Browne owlishly directs, "write your news if you have any." The state of the local market is assigned a formula: it is always to be described initially as bad or indifferent, thus, "Touching Sales of Implements, I do understand that it will not fall out to well as I had wished or hoped it would: but . . . ." What followed could as well contradict the preceding formulaic statement as support it. It is obvious that such relicts of the old rhetorical tradition had little fight left in them. They are crutches, and shaky ones, giving shabby academic respectability to litanies of sheer fact, the accounts of goods sold or not sold, bought or not bought, which form the body of the factors' letters as designed by Browne and his colleagues. The commitment of the commercial world to neutrally verbalized fact of itself undermined the Latin polemic tradition.

So did competition from the more and more versatile vernaculars, which were moving into the academic world and into the arts of verbal expression. Cultivation of the vernaculars for scientific or quasiscientific purposes was encouraged more by manufacturing, technology, and commerce than by science as such, which in great part continued to use Latin even into the early nineteenth century, when we find many medical works still published in the Latin tongue. Sponsored by the practical bourgeois world, the vernaculars became more fact-oriented than Latin had ever been. As can be gathered from standard histories of education, the vernacular schools, established in England and France and elsewhere for more or less commercial training, neglected rhetoric in favor of "business" styles of expression. These schools, described by John William Adamson, Ellwood P. Cubberley, Frederick Eby, Hugh M. Pollard, J. W. Ashley Smith, and others, brought in calculation, "arithmetic," and a certain amount of geometry to complement what little they retained of the old arts of communication. The opposition between the Latin-centered, academic, disputatious education and the vernacular, commercial, fact-centered education could still be caught clearly as late as the beginnings of the present century in catalogues of high schools and colleges in the United

States and elsewhere, with their clean distinction between an "academic" (Latin-centered, disputatious, intellectualized, speculatively scientific) course of studies and a "commercial" (vernacular, fact-centered, practical) course.

In the new nondisputatious, fact-centered educational view, which was also a world-view, knowledge itself came to be considered less and less something to parry with, less a weapon and more a commodity, something like merchandise. This view of knowledge both influenced and was favored by Ramist philosophy, as I have undertaken to show in "Ramist Method and the Commercial Mind." In the sixteenth century, one of the great promoters of "practicality" in education, John Amos Comenius (Komensky), in his *Gateway to Languages (Janua linguarum)* could say (p. 128) that "a school is a means of transfusing learning out of books into men." Between the marks on a printed page and knowledge possessed by a human being, the distinction was increasingly blurred in the practical, commercially oriented educational camp. Significantly, the education which typically produced diplomats (as that at Oxford and Cambridge in Great Britain) was not a practical or factual education. It was the old Latin-oriented classical education. On the face of it, Latin has no particular value in training a diplomat. But the tradition symbolized by Latin was essentially a tradition of polemic and dispute, tailor-made for the maturing and implementing of diplomatic instincts.

It is true, of course, that the vernaculars were not unequivocally antirhetorical and antipolemic. In the first place, they remained for over a thousand years more directly oral than Latin was in that they were not so subject to chirographic and typographic control (this control over the vernaculars would become truly effective only in the eighteenth century with the maturing of vernacular dictionaries). Secondly, as used by academically trained or academically influenced speakers and writers, the vernaculars reproduced much of the classical Latin tradition and brandished its warlike equipment. Shakespeare's appropriation into English of dialectic and rhetoric which he studied in Latin has by now been massively documented. Some of his finest effects are achieved by following the Latin rhetorical recipes which he had made his own so intimately that their structures are no longer discernible to the twentieth-century naked eye unaided by such special instruments as Professor T. W. Baldwin's *William Shakspere's Small Latine and Lesse Greeke*. Shakespeare's characters interact polemically in classic dialectical and rhetorical oppositions.

Shakespeare's case is representative. In other vernaculars the situation is roughly the equivalent of that in English, as Curtius' *European Literature and the Latin Middle Ages* makes clear. Among the most spectacularly rhetorical vernacular works on the Continent one might cite, for example, the late fifteenth-century Spanish *La Celestina*, which for rhetorical fireworks, serious and mock-serious, probably outclasses even the works of the sixteenth-century Englishman Thomas Nashe. And of course Rabelais, for the sheer mass of his classically nurtured rhetorical (and dialectical) outpourings and burlesques in the vernacular probably tops all other writers in any of the modern tongues. The Latin-based rhetorico-polemic mechanisms remain highly active in the vernacular long past his day and well into the beginnings of Romanticism. Pope's *Essay on Criticism* and *Essay on Man* as well as Gray's *Elegy Written in a Coun-*

try Churchyard are beautifully executed vernacular exercises in the use of commonplaces or *loci communes,* the mainstay of the old oral–aural culture.

When, however, the rhetorical connections of the vernaculars have all been allowed for, it is still apparent that the vernaculars did not have all the reinforced associations with the old-style polemic structures maintained in the psyche by the Latin tradition. This was especially true insofar as the vernaculars were controlled out of the growing commercial milieu. If the vernaculars were more directly oral than Latin in their everyday currency, commerce bound their formal use to writing. Factors or commercial agents (salesmen) had to talk, certainly, but seldom in a public setting. When modern advertising did produce a verbalized public message from businessmen, the rhetoric of this form of public address has turned out to be only partially a verbal rhetoric, since it is far more concerned with direct visual stimuli than the older classical rhetoric could be. Early commerce demanded no educational equivalent of the Latin formal oratorical program, no large-scale oral training for businessmen as such, only training in writing.

Hence, of course, the artificiality of the written commercial letter as prescribed in *The Merchants Avizo* and similar works. Such a letter was a production cut off from what would have been its own English oral roots and grafted awkwardly onto the written half of the complex Latin tradition. The commercial mind was here responding to the assumptions fostered by typography, identifying education completely with writing and regarding expression enshrined in writing as the ideal, independently of its association with an oral tradition, classical or vernacular. Nothing shows better than do these commercial letter-writing manuals the ineffectiveness of writing isolated from oral expression. The gauche and pitifully artificial ineptness prescribed in *The Merchants Avizo* persisted in its essentials in commercial letter writing in English quite generally until only two or three decades ago, and probably persists in some quarters still. For commercial letters in many other languages, Spanish for example, something like it is still the general rule.

It may be that at times the irenic drives in bourgeois society combined with devocalizing tendencies in the typographic world and with Christian teaching to foster in other special ways not discussed here a detached, objective, pacifist attitude toward man's life-world. At least one thinks of this possibility when noting the connections between nonpolemic religious beliefs and the bourgeois–typographical milieu of the sixteenth-century printer Christopher Plantin which have been brought to light in a finely researched article by Robert M. Kingdon. Still more work remains to be done in this area.

The movement to give formal schooling to girls was associated with the growing together of the academic and bourgeois worlds, and this movement, too, helped wear down on several fronts the classical polemic structures surrounding the word. First, the very presence of women discouraged the rough and tumble of the disputatious male Latin world. Women were neither physically nor temperamentally equipped for rhetorical and dialectical *agonia*. There is a theory that the operational root of male dominance among human beings lodges less in the male's larger skeleton and muscles than in his more powerful voice—a theory seemingly supported by our earlier observation that sound is itself an indication of the active use of physical power. Without artificial amplification, the normal woman's voice simply cannot reach the thousands who found themselves enthralled by the bellowing of the old-line male orator from antiquity through the nineteenth century. Before the advent of public address systems, women orators were understandably few. Moreover, the openly warlike character of the rhetorical or dialectical arena hardly appealed to most women either because of temperament or training or both.

Secondly, schooling for girls encouraged the use of the vernacular, since women had no tradition of Latin learning and moved into the schools only when Latin was on its way out. They both profited from the diminution of Latin instruction and further diminished it. Before the nineteenth century, when girls were educated in letters (as they not infrequently were), they were educated normally at home and chiefly in the vernacular, sometimes with a modern foreign language. Since the polemic rhetorico-dialectical tradition was, as has been seen, tied so closely to the sociological, cultural, and psychological state of the Latin language itself, the weakening of Latin in favor of the vernaculars associated with the growth of school education for girls itself weakened the polemic structures fostered by academia.

But the feminine presence operated in more complicated ways, too. It disqualified language teaching as a male initiation procedure. As I have shown in an article on "Latin Language Study as a Renaissance Puberty Rite," when Latin from around A.D. 500 to 700 on ceased to function as a vernacular and was retained only in the schools, it became a sex-linked language, a kind of badge of masculine identity. With the appearance of what we have called the sound–sight split in Latin; that stream of the language which developed into the modern romance vernaculars remained in use in the home, but the other stream known as Learned Latin, which moved only in artificially controlled channels through the male

world of the schools, was no longer anyone's mother
tongue, in a quite literal sense. Although from the sixth
or eighth century to the nineteenth Latin was spoken
by millions of persons, it was never used by mothers
cooing to their children. There was no Latin baby-talk
or nursery language, no access in Latin to playfully intimate tones of expression such as we find in Swift's
Journal to Stella. Under these circumstances learning
Latin took on the characteristics of a puberty rite, a
rite de passage or initiation rite: it involved isolation
from the family, the achievement of identity in a totally
male group (the school), the learning of a body of relatively abstract tribal lore inaccessible to those outside the
group and calculated to make one a responsible member
of extrafamilial society, and all this in an atmosphere
marked by hardship and displays of physical violence,
for physical punishment was hardly an accidental
phenomenon so much as a presumedly necessary adjunct
of Latin study. The standard attribute of the schoolmaster through medieval and Renaissance iconography
is the bundle of switches which in actuality formed always
part of his professional equipment. The Latin world was
a man's world.

The move to give formal academic education to women
thus struck a whole complex of forces sustaining the old
polemic orality, where Latin, masculinity, and a cult of
violence ranging from the verbal to the physical made
common cause. As women moved into the schools, the
vernaculars crowded back Latin and the rhetorical and
dialectical polemic structure grown up around Latin,
the teaching of Latin could no longer function as a *rite
de passage* introducing young boys to the aggressive
masculine world, and the value of aggressiveness itself as
an academic virtue was called into question.

As literacy gradually killed off the old oral institutions,

women were able to move into the formal educational system and did. Schooling became not only genteel but also gentle except in a few bastions of artificially sustained masculinity and Latinity such as the British public schools. If women were not necessarily more "objective" than men, they tended to bring education into closer association with bourgeois life. Woman's education had always been more practical than theoretical, and the academic tradition as a whole adjusted to this fact when the women moved in. Vernacular commercial courses for men came in, roughly speaking, pari passu with education for women. Both set themselves against the old oral, contentious, polemic attitudes inherited from classical antiquity.

The demise of the Muses adverted to in chapter 2 was of course tied in with the atrophy of Latin as a sex-linked language and the entry of post-Gutenberg women in notable numbers into the world of literature and public verbalization generally. The Muses, strongly feminine figures, are obviously the projections of the male psyche concerned with generating its "brain children." The implications of their demise, the psychological reorganization entailed, the connection of the demise of the Muses with romantic views of literary composition as "creative" (that is, as producing something out of nothing, like God's act of creation rather than man's act of generation in matter), the change in the psychological and sociological and anthropological meaning of skilled verbalization (whether oral performance or literature as such)— these and related questions are matter for scores of volumes yet to be written.

Romanticism gave the final blow to polemic Latin-sustained oralism. Largely extra-academic, with roots in the vernacular romances composed in the Middle Ages and so often sponsored by women, Romanticism simultaneously emphasized woman's presence on the scene, gave new strength to the vernacular against the classical tradition, devalued oral recitation in favor of private epiphanies achieved alone and in favor of the visually conceived romantic image, which Frank Kermode has furnished with a history, and in its quest of the novel, the strange and unusual, devalued the cult of the commonplaces or *loci communes* which had been the absolutely necessary equipment of the oral performer, whether epic singer or orator and which had persisted through Pope and Gray as a legacy of the shrinking oral–aural world. If Gray's *Elegy* was the last great work in English featuring in its polished reflections the wealth of the commonplace tradition, Wordsworth's Lucy poems, written in Germany in 1799, announced the new direction: "But she is in her grave, and, oh,/ The difference to me!"

In the perspectives we have been sketching these words of Wordsworth's invite a far lengthier commentary than there is space for here. First, they signal plainly the end of the old commonplace tradition, the major literary relict of the old oral tribal cultures. Henceforward, no longer what is "common" to all—arguments applicable to all subject matters and/or appealing to all men—but what precisely is not common, what is *different* (from all other subject matters) to *me* (not for all men), will be the guideline of expression. Secondly, Wordsworth's lines remind us what has happened to the Muses. They, too, are no longer public. Muses had been interiorized and personalized as early as Dante's Beatrice, under the combined influences of the Christian and the courtly love traditions. When they had become personalized, they no longer sang publicly, of course, but simply inspired by their beloved presence. They were private, as expression itself was growing private under the influence of writing, an influence soon to be intensified and brought to maturity by print. Wordsworth's muse has realized a greater privacy than ever—she is hidden away, "a violet by a mossy stone," truly the poet's own, not even allowed to grow to self-sufficient maturity, to flower so that others might possibly notice her, somewhat asexual, too young for her femininity to count much.

For this is no longer the contentious masculine world of the public, rhetorically based epic or of the old rhetorically guided lyrical tradition, thriving on the cultivation of the commonplaces. This is truly a romantic poem, breathing the Lake Country and the cult of nature, miles away from the classical-minded university. "Subjective" in the new sense of this term, the word here has left the polemic world and retreated into the isolation of the individual consciousness which the respondent is invited not to fight with but to share. The old tribal, traditional, extroverted polemic structures here yield in significant fashion to the introverted drives initiated by script, intensified first by the alphabet and later by alphabetic typography, but extremely slow in changing the kind of presence which the word exercised among men. Probably here, in this unstudied repudiation of the overwhelming dialectical and rhetorical tradition lies Wordsworth's basic significance.

The interiorizing trend discernible here continues today, despite other countertrends. A contemporary protraction of Wordsworth's revolution would be the pretentiously introverted beatnik's plotless and seemingly pointless story, followed by the question, expressed or implied, "Do you dig it, man?" The fact that such a performance often conceals, rather poorly, a childishly nagging bid by the narrator for empathy and emotional support does not mean that as a convention of expression it does not have a history.

THE WORD IN A STATE OF PEACE

In technological society today, the word has mostly left behind the old polemic and feudal oral–aural culture which had polarized knowledge, and with it the word, around struggles between heroic figures and thus (by today's standards) had overcharged man's life-world with virtue and vice. Schools today no longer teach verbal communication skills chiefly in the context of rhetorical and dialectical strife, standard from antiquity through the age of Edmund Burke. Instead, we have discussion or dialogue, an irenic airing of differences. Initiation to the formal study of language—basically Latin—used to be a genuine puberty rite, as we have just seen, removing the boy from the safety of home and forcing on him rough-and-tumble adult male existence. Today the academic study of language begins in far less traumatic fashion, for the language initially studied is normally one's vernacular, and to that extent formal linguistic education is continuous with preschool experience and can be entered into without shock.

At the same time, massive supplies of information or "fact" inaccessible to primitive man have taken much of the edge off disputation, which throve on uncertainties or half-certainties. To a significant degree, if not always in perfectly satisfactory fashion, decisions, which earlier societies had to arrive at through acrimonious disputes, all the more agonizing because both sides were arguing from minimal stocks of information, can be prepared for by data processing on computers. The decision still has to be made, but the disputable areas are often narrowed almost out of existence; at least, often one can calculate exactly what risks one is taking. The chances of a rain shower, for example, in a given area at a given hour will be estimated as a percentage. There is still an area of dispute, but it is not about what the chances are for rain, only about whether or not one should take this particular calculated risk.

In some of the developing countries, of course, the old verbomotor culture of overt personal polemics remains, and indeed temporarily runs completely wild as the auditory mass media of radio, public address systems, and recordings are selectively borrowed from other cultures in advance of the other nonauditory trappings which also go with a fully technologized society. From China to Africa and Latin America, in cultures still oral in structure even where partly literate, three-hour and four-hour and longer harangues about capitalist warmongers, imperialists, brigands, murderers, traitors, and other "bad guys" have an appeal which they normally lack today in a society technologically balanced in the sense that it has steel foundries and chemical plants, for example, and not merely imported radios.

It is true, of course, that some old tendencies linger in technological cultures. Virtue–vice analyses of essentially nonmoral forces, often in the form of conspiracy theories of history, crop out here and there even in "developed" countries, particularly among groups composed of psychologically disturbed individuals unable to adjust to technological culture. Moreover, in technologized societies polarization of issues in terms of heroes and villains persists in infantile and retrogressive art forms such as Westerns. But despite these facts and despite the clichés which still form the staple of much politics as well as of advertising and journalism, calculated name calling and its converse, hero-worship, simply do not form the staple of public life in technological societies as they do in the still weakly technologized verbomotor cultures or as they did in Jacksonian America. When something is wrong in the social or economic order, it is hard for technological man to believe that the cause reduces simply to some individual's or some group's villainy. Moral evil exists, as do real virtues and vices, but few of our difficulties trace directly to perfidy.

Roughly speaking, as cultures feel the effects of the chirographic–typographic stage of communications they lose their tendency to overplay the virtue–vice polarity. Russia, for example, where literacy has taken a firm hold and by now has had time to affect psychological structures in depth (time to become "interiorized"), is now emerging from the name-calling, personal-invective stage in politics into a more objectively operating stage. That is to say, it is emerging from a strongly residual oral culture, where general literacy was too new to have had an effect on psychological organization, to the visualist objectivism of writing and print. Russian programmatic name calling, as on the rostrum of the United Nations, is now largely for the benefit of allied, or supposedly allied, countries such as China or Cuba, which are still deep in the residually oral, vituperative stage.

Virtue–vice polarized cultures, when they use electronic media, typically resort to the radio rather than television. Radio is cheaper and easier, but it also keeps the culture more totally in the world of sound. In the hands of a Castro, the radio exploits to the maximum the old oral–aural structures, building up around the hearer the resonances, personalist loyalties, strong social or tribal feelings and responses, and special anxieties (including the berserker syndrome) characteristic of the old oral–aural world. Television tends to fragment the tribe into individuals, even though not very reflective ones. In a study cited above on "L'Oeil et l'esprit," Merleau-Ponty has beautifully shown that vision is a fractioning sense in that the awareness it presents to man consists of a true "field" which invites and enforces dissection. But vision is also fractioning in that it splits up the human group. An assembly of individuals using only their eyes to assimilate what is presented to them—a scene in nature, a silent spectacle—does not form a group as it would in listening to a public speaker or in attending a sports spectacle accompanied by shouting and cheers. The cheerleader instigates the vocalization that makes the individuals cohere with one another. In this way he revives the old polarities of virtue and vice, the feeling for "good guys" and "bad guys," on which public sport depends.

Although it is thus not entirely divorced from the old oral–aural personalized world, of itself technological life ties words in with things rather than with persons. Technology demands verbal description of things visually perceived in space and of visually perceived process far beyond anything known to pretechnological man. The verbal directives accompanying a home washing machine today, frustrating though they may sometimes be, could not even have been attempted in Elizabethan English, much less in ancient Latin. Vocabularies were not yet accommodated even to much simpler artifacts and processes with anything like modern precision, trade manuals were virtually unknown, and skills were learned not by verbal instruction but by apprenticeship, which involved vision but not much conversion of the visualizable into words. Much less could the intricacies of a rocket launching or of modern transformational grammar have been verbalized in earlier times, although in works of art, concrete human relations could be expressed or suggested with nuances which we still have a hard time surpassing, even when we can make our awarenesses of these relations more reflectively explicit than earlier man could.

The word remains, of course, a potential implement of aggressiveness and hostility even in a highly objectified visualist culture. The human word can never be entirely depolemicized. Words move toward others, and to make them weapons one has only to fit them with barbs. Nevertheless, despite the hostile potential of words and whatever the incidence of private hostilities, the technological style of life discourages publicly verbalized strife. The fliting or ceremonial verbal display of hostility common in heroic cultures—the bragging and boasting and verbal muscle flexing one finds from the *Iliad* through *Beowulf* and later—has largely disappeared from the visualist technological world or has been relegated to such comic manifestations as the newspaper strip *Big George*. It is significant that "speech meets" in or between schools in the United States often feature nondecision debates. In these perspectives, Deweyism, the Boy Scout program, and other "progressive" movements appear as typical shifts away from the residually oral–aural educational world: they minimize personal competition and verbalization in favor of work with things and measure even verbal achievement in terms of standards, which belong to the objective world or object-world rather than to a realm of contending persons.

The breakthrough to a new kind of orality, implemented chiefly by electronics, has not restored the public

polemic structures of the old oral–aural world. This may
sound strange when we recall the voices of dissent, which
seemingly have never been raised so high as in the protests, highly vocal most of them, which have swept the
world lately in all technologized countries where repression of free public expression is not the rule. It may
sound strange, too, in view of the sense of immediate involvement which the modern electronic oralism creates
in ways reminiscent of primitive oralism. McLuhan is
quite right in relating our present sense of simultaneity
(Teilhard's noosphere) to the electronic revival of sound
and to the generation of something like a preliterate
tribal village. Newspapers do not create the sense of im-
mediacy and simultaneity produced by radio and television (which latter, we must remind ourselves, is a vocal
medium, its pictures always accompanied by voice and
other sound). Still, as we have seen, unlike early tribal
orality, this present new orality is possible only through
heavy reliance on visual constructs, out of which is generated the sound world of a technological milieu. Electronic computers will never eliminate writing or print—
they will simply change the kinds of things we put into
these earlier media. Beneath the oral–aural mentality
today, a visualist, objective, neutral structure remains, no
longer in complete control, but there.

This is true even when the new oralism erupts in the
institutionalized polemic which oral structures favor.
What other age has known so many protests which have
been so calculatingly peaceful? Passive resistance and
nonviolent civil disobedience, by contrast with comparable movements of earlier ages, are in typical cases
spectacularly restrained. The worst of the violent protests, as for example the Watts riots, are by contrast relatively nonvocal phenomena, where what public vocaliz-

ing there is comes as an afterthought, as it does not for the typical nonviolent protest groups.

Furthermore, the word today is positively mobilized for peace on a scale hitherto unknown. There is no pretechnological equivalent of the massive literature and debate today devoted to the cause of international peace. Early oral–aural cultures or residually oral–aural cultures generally favored peace only rather abstractly. In the ancient Roman Empire the peace of Augustus was an exceptional phenomenon, and it was only relative peace. The Christian message itself was ordinarily not thought of as applicable to the political sphere except in brief-lived truces. Psychological structures were not such that permanent political peace could be planned for realistically even as late as Shakespeare's day, when more or less permanent war was still taken as the normal and continuous state of mankind, as Jorgensen has shown. Peace was regarded, wryly but resignedly, as in reality undesirable: it led to softness and degeneracy, which in turn invited war! Life had to include strife with one's fellows.

Neither is there a pretechnological equivalent for the vast literature and discussion today devoted to the easing of hostilities in society itself and to other forms of social betterment. There were many sincere and effective Christian and other efforts toward peace, but sociological assumptions narrowly circumscribed their effectiveness. Our present-day efforts to minimize and eliminate international misunderstandings by assimilating foreign languages and cultures are new, at least on the scale on which they now operate. Language itself is thus being viewed as a phenomenon which can be managed to ensure peace. Perhaps most typical of our evolving attitudes toward the word is the appearance in modern psychotherapy of verbalization as a much-used and highly advertised route to the easing of personal hostilities and tensions.

This is not to say that all vocalized public protests in highly technologized societies or all cultivated uses of language in such societies are free from hostile overtones or even violent hostility. It is to say, however, that by comparison with the state of affairs several generations ago, the institutionalized mobilization of hostilities around the word itself has unmistakably decreased. In this sense, some kind of foundation for a less polemic human existence appears to have been laid within the uses of the word.

CRISES OF THE WORD AND THE SPLIT IN WESTERN CHRISTIANITY

The cultural developments sketched here in terms of the evolution of the word throw new light on Christianity in its relationship to secular culture and to its own announced message of peace. The polemic setting of much religious activity in the past is a scandal to present-day man, whether he be religious or not in his own personal attitudes. We are made uneasy by the acrimony of religious disputes so widespread through earlier ages, and we are mortally embarrassed at the history of religious wars. We feel that religion thus expressed, through verbal or physical aggression, cannot be real.

Our ultimate embarrassment is the fact that earlier man all too obviously often felt quite the opposite. For him, a polemic stance often manifested not the unreality but the reality of his own religion. Holy wars were fought mercilessly by the Old Testament Hebrews and, although they appear to conflict with the patent spirit of the Gospel, were by no means unknown among Christians. The Middle Ages favored the concept of a "Christendom" whose members were more or less supposed to engage non-Christians in physical combat. At a time when Christians were taking up arms to fight one another, Erasmus was to protest against this unchristian Christendom in a letter (August 14, 1518) to his friend Paul Volz, urging that the Turks be approached with written letters and books (less incendiary than oratory?) which would make Christianity known through the language of the Gospels and of the Apostles themselves, serving much better than futile attempts to spread it by arms. Erasmus' intent is irreproachable. It is too bad that his own letters and his other writings—for example, the much-used and influential *Colloquies*—themselves so assiduously cultivate the hostility and polemic which was part of the personality structure imposed by his culture.

Seemingly, all early cultures (not merely oriental ones, as we have seen) tended to be more or less ontocratic in the sense developed by Arend Theodoor van Leeuwen in his *Christianity and World History:* they tended to identify secular and sacral objectives. In the perspectives we have been developing, this meant that the polemic structures of the psyche connected with the ancient oral tradition affected both secular and religious attitudes simultaneously, despite the long-standing antipolemic set of Christian teaching. Moreover, the ontocratic character of earlier cultures was itself quite of a piece with the oral heritage, if only because the nice distinctions which later cultures can draw between sacral and secular objectives by virtue of elaborately recorded laws and court decisions are impossible in an oral culture and are likely to be unconvincing in a manuscript or typographical culture so long as it is strongly dominated by its oral past. The present church–state relationship in the United States could not have been worked out without writing. Oral modes of existence are synthetic rather than analytic.

Certainly one of the most fruitful periods to examine in terms of the history of the word as related to the history of Christianity is the age of the Reformation. The religious complexities of this age have been subject to endless analyses, but seldom if ever to analysis directly attending to the state of the communications media. Some attention is commonly called to the connection between the development of printing and the spread of literacy and of Bible reading which mark the beginnings of Protestantism. For the most part, however, historians have assessed the effect of printing in quite external fashion: printing "spread ideas," made the text of the Bible "available," put the Bible "into the hands of the people," or "encouraged more people to read." All this is true enough. But the interior change in psychological structures tied in with the shift of the word from a written to a printed culture is at least as important as the physical spread of inscribed texts, for changes in sociological structures are the interior coefficients of developments in exterior history.

Protestant and Catholic differences developed at a time when attitudes toward the word, expressed and subconscious, were undergoing a sea change. In the sixteenth century, as we have seen, the residually oral institutions of dialectic and rhetoric competed strenuously with the new visualism induced by print for control of man's sensibility, forcing a reorganization of the sensorium which was changing man's "feel" for his lifeworld. Given the initial importance of the word in Christian teaching—God's word, written in the Scriptures and spoken in preaching, and the Word of God incarnate in Jesus Christ—it is hardly surprising that many of the critical religious differences among Christians at this time in one way or another, directly or indirectly, register the changing structures surrounding the word. This can be seen in a multiplicity of developments, among which we can select four groupings: (1) attitudes toward Scripture and tradition, (2) attitudes toward the sacraments, (3) attitudes toward the preaching of the word, and (4) attitudes toward authority. All these developments are complex. The literature about them is too massive to admit of detailed citation here. But the issues are classic and can be treated in a way which is both general and meaningful regarding Protestant and Catholic differences. I propose to examine them here only in the most general fashion as they relate to the evolution of the media of communication. Books through which the issues and the classic sources can be traced and the present discussion enlarged include standard historico-dogmatic treatments such as those of Ernst Troeltsch, Roland Bainton, Henri Daniel-Rops, Philip Hughes, Joseph Lortz, Wilhelm Pauck, Jaroslav Pelikan, and George H. Tavard, as well as collections of documents such as those of Denziger and Schaff or Leith and standard manuals of Catholic and Protestant dogmatic theology. Individual works like these are referred to only in passing, for my present purpose is merely to suggest lines of thought. To examine in full historical detail the relationships here touched on would be work for volumes.

Attitudes toward Scripture and tradition. It can hardly be doubted that the Reformers' insistence upon the primacy of the Scriptures was closely connected with the invention of print and a consequent shift in feeling for the position of inscribed communication in man's life-world. As we have seen in some detail, the orientation of the psyche toward the inscribed text was by the end of the Middle Ages far more intense than anything classical antiquity had known. Although through the classical Greek and Roman world and even more through the ancient Hebreo-Christian world the inscribed word had commanded respect and awe, the shift from the orality of antiquity to the intense chirographic preoccupations of the Middle Ages made some kind of shift in the attitudes toward the Scriptures inevitable. Medieval manuscript culture had culminated in the passionate textual studies which mark the Renaissance and the birth of print, and which affect secular and sacred texts equally.

The medieval state of affairs, as has been earlier explained at length, was somewhat ambivalent, with strong oral institutions (dialectic, rhetoric, and all that went with them) competing actively with intense concentration on writing. In particular, attitudes toward the Scriptures are puzzling when measured by post-Tridentine standards, which are also post-Gutenberg standards. The mass of theological literature reviewed with great competence by Gerald Van Ackeren in his study "Is All Revelation in Scripture?" (especially pp. 251–54) pays almost no attention to the change in the media as a possible clue to the puzzling relationship between medieval concepts of Scripture and tradition to those of antiquity on the one side and those of the typographical era on the other. Theologians are puzzled by the absence of the term oral in medieval writers and by the apparent assumption, common to medieval scholastic theologians generally, that "theology itself was but a commentary on Scripture." On the other hand, as Father Van Ackeren reports, De Vooght finds that the scholastic theologians did not really read the Scriptures and used its texts (which they had not read!) uncritically. Finally, modern historians are thoroughly put out by the fact that the Decretalists in their more frenzied states of mind could occasionally extend to the written decretals of the popes something of the nature of the Sacred Scriptures themselves.

Without pretending to account for all the details of the complex picture here, we can supplement other explanations, such as that of George H. Tavard in his *Holy Writ or Holy Church,* by thinking in terms of the state of the word and its media. We are faced with the presence of the two traditions, one oral and the other chirographic, and both strong. The assumption that theology was simply a commentary on Scripture was thoroughly consonant with the medieval fixation on texts as such. The obverse of this assumption was medieval inattention to the problem of a complementary oral tradition. This problem emerged full force only with Trent and today is undergoing vigorous development, no longer simply among Catholics but also among Protestants, as Jaroslav Pelikan, for example, testifies in his *Obedient Rebels* (pp. 42–53). Despite the medieval chirographic set of mind, only with print would the text as such reach high enough definition to begin to draw attention to the oral as oral by way of contrast, and only in our own day, as we move beyond print into electronic communication, would the question of the oral as oral be decently refined. The intense studies of the background and meaning of Trent's decree on scripture and tradition belong not to the age immediately after Trent but to our present generation.

Medieval neglect of the oral, however, was due not merely to the age's fixation on the text as such. It was also due to the fact that, by contrast with the post-Gutenberg age, the Middle Ages were themselves overwhelmed with orality. They did not advert to the problem of oral tradition largely because they never considered the possibility of anything other than a culture as oral as their own. Acquaintance with the orality of medieval culture helps us understand why the scholastics did not read the Scriptures (relatively speaking, that is, by comparison with post-typographical theologians). The Greeks did not read Homer much either. They recited him. As we have seen, medieval man was more intently textual than the classical Greeks or Romans, but he still gave himself even to texts in highly oral fashion, as we have also seen. The Bible was indeed present to the Middle Ages, but present in the way it could be present to a society still, to our way of thinking, impossibly oral despite its possession of and fixation on writing.

In such a culture by contrast with print culture, the number of copies of a work, even of the Bible (which was multiplied far beyond any other text), was of course severely limited. But quantitative limitation of copies was not so important a determinant of attitudes toward the Bible as was the oral mode of assimilation of the word. Being "in the Bible" in such a culture meant being present via the largely oral tradition through which the society still functioned. If a medieval theological student listened for twelve years (the theology course at Paris once lasted this long) to endless disputations built around the Scriptures and at the same time attended countless sermons quoting incessantly from the Scriptures, he could very well get by without much reading of the Bible, especially since the culture had trained his memory for oral assimilation.

The air was filled with the word of God. It is evident enough from medieval literature generally that, although the percentage of persons who had formally studied the Scriptures or theology was always minuscule, the Bible was quite familiar to society at large—in England, for example through the wide social spectrum represented by the characters in *The Canterbury Tales*. Most of this familiarity came through hearing, which itself was a biblically advocated state of affairs: *fides ex auditu* "faith comes through hearing" (Rom. 10:17). The sermons of Anthony of Padua (1195–1231), perhaps the greatest preacher of the Middle Ages, are another case in point. Filled to the brim with Scriptural quotations but essentially oral performances, they were put into writing only by command of the Holy See shortly before Anthony's death, as Huber explains in his *St. Anthony of Padua* (p. 87), after they had been molded and remolded over and over again by oral delivery. (Of course, we have no guarantee that what Anthony put in writing as his sermons corresponded exactly to what he had said, any more than we have any such guarantee for Cicero's orations—but we know that this was the *sort* of thing he said.)

Under these conditions the Bible was present to people largely in what we can style an oral mode. Some medieval theologians may have favored theories of exact verbal inspiration of the Scriptures, but whatever theological doctrine may have breathed through the schools, the culture as a whole assimilated the biblical word not verbatim but as oral cultures typically assimilate a message, thematically and formulaicly, tribally rather than individually, by contrast with post-typographical culture. There was still relatively little question of the individual's going to the text for himself for much the same reason that in Homer's day no one would have challenged Homer's rendition of the Troy stories in favor of a written original from which he should have been working. The original for Homer was the communal memory more or less suspended in the oral tradition from which he worked. The Middle Ages, I would suggest, felt the Bible, although it was written and although they were strongly textual people, as basically possessed in the communal or tribal memory. By the same token, they of course used texts uncritically. They explicated the communal memory as much as the text itself. (We still do this, but in a different way.) Critical use of a text depends on the kind of control and the kind of historicism which only typography makes possible.

Finally, it should not surprise us to find in the medieval mind little sense of a "deposit" of faith or questions of the sources of revelation treated formally as such. As I undertook to show some years ago in *Ramus, Method, and the Decay of Dialogue,* the sense of knowledge as a commodity contained in some sort of cache, while not unknown to antiquity, is relatively inoperative until the advent of the printed book, which truly "locates" words, locking them once for all in exactly the same place upon the pages of thousands of copies of a work. In earlier ages knowledge could not be thought of as something to be transferred out of books or some other locale into men's minds so readily as it could be in the age of Comenius.

This is not to say that the Middle Ages had no sense at all of textual accuracy. After all, some such sense had inspired the textual work of Jerome as early as the fourth century. It is not to say, either, that in the Middle Ages no man ever controverted the argument of another by calling his opponent back to the exact text of the Bible. Neither is it to deny what has already been discussed in detail above, that the Middle Ages were far more text-conscious than was antiquity. It is to say, however, that a sense of domination by the text as such was much less typical than it was to become after the invention of print. The medieval resort to multiple interpretation and highly allegorical elaboration of texts is evidence in point. These, as much as the book, were the containers in which the text itself was suspended. Of a similar value were such compilations as Aquinas' *Catena aurea* or *Golden Chain* of quotations from the Church Fathers woven together to form a composite commentary on the text of the Scriptures. In the *Catena aurea* the Scriptures could be experienced as possessed largely in terms of what the Christian community had said and was saying in and out of and around them. The commentaries on the *Sentences* of Peter Lombard regularly done by Aquinas and others during their teaching apprenticeship as bachelors of theology—remarks on remarks others had made about the Scriptures or about remarks still others had made about the Scriptures—show this same oral communal possession operating at full tilt. Communal memory, invested with the ability of oral cultures to conserve thematic and formulaic (rather than verbatim) accuracy, could actually serve as a stabilizing textual influence to counteract the weaknesses of written textual transmission endemic in manuscript culture before print.

Under these conditions, the word of God was indeed in the Bible, but in effect this often meant in the Bible as stored largely in the oral reservoirs of a still highly oral culture. Since the word itself was thus not anchored to the silence of the page with the exclusiveness which a typographical society would imagine necessary (reading, we recall, was commonly done aloud or at least labialized, even when done alone), the presence even of the written word was felt to be less confined to the surface of the page and to be more diffused through the whole of the social fabric than would be common after Gutenberg.

With the development of print the polarities of the word shifted as did the psychological structures for assimilating the word. The difference between Protestant and Catholic shows up in our present perspectives as in great part a function of this shift: of the basic options open to make the adjustments necessitated by the advent of print the Protestant mind took one and the Catholic the other.

The Protestant stress on the primacy of the written word of the Scriptures—*sola scriptura*—reflects quite patently the growing confidence in the word-in-space, whatever its foundations in the Christian tradition itself. One of the common critiques of the Protestant stress on Bible reading proffered by Catholic adversaries has been that it is accompanied by a doctrine of private interpretation of the biblical text which fosters divisiveness in Christianity, leading to what Edmund Burke was to call the dissidence of dissent. Neither Catholic adversaries nor Protestant defenders of the practice have commonly been aware of how far reading itself fosters divisiveness to the extent that it isolates the individual from communal structures. So long as reading remained basically recitation—the use of script to foster oral production (even when one is reading to oneself)—as it had remained to a great degree during the Middle Ages, its isolating effect was minimized. When it became silent reading, as it appears to have become by the time of print more commonly than it earlier was, it forced the individual into himself and out of the tribe. In their confidence that private reading of the Scriptures would not divide Christianity, a confidence which they based in principle on the belief that the Holy Spirit would guide each individual reader to the same truth, the Reformers appear to have been in fact thinking also, without being explicitly aware of it, in the framework of a psychology of a non-individualistic oral culture which was fast passing out of existence.

This is not of course to say that from every point of view private reading of the Bible guarantees the dissidence of dissent. The text is, after all, a single thing, the same text open to inspection by all and, in terms of textual criticism, an immeasurably firmer text (despite all its variants, or rather because of them) than any other text we have because of the hundreds of early extant biblical manuscripts; many texts, by contrast, of classical Latin authors are dependent on only one manuscript dating from seven or eight hundred years or more after the author's death and even, as in the case of Catullus, completely lost again after it was printed. Despite its divisions, there is still a very real sense in which all Christianity is unified around a very firm text—the word of God recorded in the Bible.

There was of course also in Protestantism a complementary emphasis counterbalancing the strong stress on the written or printed word. This was the emphasis on oral presentation of the word of God in preaching found from Luther to Calvin and perhaps even more strongly in the minor Protestant sects. Reading the word recorded in the Bible was complemented by listening to the preaching of the word. But this corrective proved to be itself divisive, for typography had introduced forces driving the economy of the recorded word and that of preaching farther and farther apart. It had made possible modern textual criticism, as Erasmus and other humanists were quick to sense. Typography conserved work on texts. To achieve a good text in a manuscript culture was not only a Herculean task but also a frustrating one, for once a good text had been achieved, it might be immediately corrupted in every handwritten copy of it made. With typography, once a good text had been established, copies of it could be multiplied exactly almost without limit, and circulated for still further improvement. This situation gave the text itself in its physical existence a new prominence and value. It also placed a new premium on individual initiative: the work done by one textual scholar working on his own could be put into everyone's hands immediately. In a manuscript culture, individual textual work, like much other work, was always dissipated.

As a result of typography, textual scholarship or philology, as it would soon be commonly called, came into being. In and around the philology of post-Gutenberg humanists, implemented by study of the word locked in typographic space, all sorts of new knowledge took form. Just as grammar (basically the study of the written word) had done in the Middle Ages, so now philology would come to include a vast diversity of learning. The philologist was the new savant. The new attention to textual accuracy in documents coming out of the remote past generated a consciousness of the differences between past and present in man's life-world such as had never before been known. This life-world, up to this point hardly attended to in organized intellectual fashion, would be given closer and closer attention, and such attention would give birth to the modern sciences of economics, sociology, ethnography, and so on, including (most important of all) "scientific" history, with all their attendant disciplines. The new revolution in the quantity and mode of knowledge storage implemented by typography was comparable in depth to that effected by literacy in Plato's day as detailed by Havelock, and it was in many ways even more sweeping.

It drew the study of the Scriptures, already highly

analytic as a result of scholasticism, into a new world of great cultural complexity and profound historical depth at the very point when some Protestant preachers, abetted by the developments of which Ramism was the center, were most insistent about the "plain" sense of the Scriptures. From one point of view, the quest for the plain sense of Puritan and other "methodist" preachers continued the medieval quest for clearly articulable meaning in everything. But from another point of view, the plain sense returned one to the old traditional oral–aural culture where meaning was largely held in common as the heritage of a past which was not subject to individual inspection but only to communal continuation. The plain sense was felt as what everyone in the community could be relied on to take the sense to be. The disconcerting fact that no longer could everyone be so relied on showed that communal structures and psychological structures had changed.

The split between the economy of the written text of the Bible on the one hand and the economy of oral preaching on the other reaches a maximum today in the gap which divides the literalist interpretations of highly oral fundamentalist Protestant groups from the best scriptural scholarship. The Fundamentalist groups, oral in their insistence on the preaching of the word, show also a competing influence of script and print, for overvaluation of the literal meaning is associated, as we have seen, with exposure to these media. On the other hand, some of the assurance among such groups that the quest for literal meaning is straightforward and socially unitive connects with the oral heritage, too. For in an oral–aural culture, meanings are typically tribal, which is to say that they are by definition meanings shared to a degree that would become outmoded in a typographical culture.

The Catholic answer to the Protestant *sola scriptura*

equally registers the new structures of the typographic age. This answer was basically the definition in the Council of Trent that divine truth and teaching is contained in the written books of the Bible and in "unwritten traditions" (*sine scripto traditionibus*—Denziger 783). Since the relationship of the Scriptures and tradition has been further discussed in the Second Vatican Council, it has become commonplace knowledge today that, as Josef Rupert Geiselmann had earlier shown, Trent had put aside the formula "*partly* in the Scriptures and *partly* in tradition" in favor of the more simple statement "in the Scriptures and in unwritten traditions." By doing so, it was made possible for Catholics to hold, as do Geiselmann, Gerald Van Ackeren, and many others reported in Van Ackeren's study "Is All Revelation in Scripture?" that all revelation is contained in each of the two, because the two are different modes of expression and communication. The partly ... partly would have encouraged thinking of revelation as portioned out in two different places or depositories, conceived to be of more or less the same kind. In short, the partly ... partly formulation would have encouraged thinking of tradition itself by analogy with writing, rather than as something of a different order. It would have encouraged thinking of tradition as a kind of second volume of the Bible which Catholics somehow kept hidden from their Protestant brethren.

Trent's actual formulation was less favorable to such thinking, but to no avail. For, by and large, post-Tridentine Catholic theologians, who were also post-Gutenberg men, conceived of tradition just this way: by analogy with a written text. Recent studies by Charles Baumgartner and Walter J. Burghardt have made it clear that post-Tridentine Catholic theologians experienced great difficulty in conceiving of tradition as truly unwritten. The drive under which we still labor today to consider communication as ideally written was already making itself clearly felt.

Thus, in a curious way, Catholic theologians registered the impact of typography in their thinking quite as discernibly as did Protestants, but in a different fashion. If the Protestant insistence on the recorded word (the Bible) reflected the organization of the post-Gutenberg sensorium, the Catholic theologians' explanation of Trent's position reflected the same organization (which Trent's position had actually transcended). The word appeared to the age to be necessarily at its best when anchored in space.

Attitudes toward the sacraments. Another initial division between Catholics and the Reformers had concerned the doctrine of the sacraments. Protestants commonly held two sacraments, baptism and the Eucharist, whereas Catholic doctrine, as defined by Trent, stated that the sacraments were seven. Catholic teaching, however, gave a kind of primacy to the two sacraments accepted by Protestants, and the differences between the two views in a way turned much more centrally on the kind of efficacy which the sacraments were believed to have. Here once more Catholic–Protestant differences can be plotted quite clearly in terms of attitudes toward the word.

Medieval theologians had been highly conscious of the place of the spoken word in the Christian sacramental economy. Aquinas notes in the *Summa Theologica* (III, 60, 5) that, as contrasted with their nearest equivalents in Old Testament times (such as circumcision and the sacrifices prescribed by the Law), the seven sacraments of the Church all had spoken words as their "form" (or the equivalent of spoken words, since the normally verbal-

ized consent in matrimony might be given by some other
sign). Thus in baptism, the "matter" of the sacrament
consists of water (remote matter) and the washing itself
(proximate matter), and the "form" is the words, "I
baptize you in the name of the Father, and of the Son, and
of the Holy Spirit." Since the sacrament in its totality
is essentially a sign of a spiritual reality beyond the sensible world, the matter itself is of course a part of the signification of the sacrament—that is to say, is itself symbolic
(water and washing symbolize the spiritual cleansing of
the soul). To the degree that it is a symbol, the matter
is itself therefore already a kind of word. Taking the
words of the sacrament as the form, however, enhances
the verbal element in the sacramental signification, since
in the matter–form relationship it is the form that domi-
nates.

Consideration of the words of the sacraments as somehow Aristotelian form (forma in Latin, like the original
Greek morphē, signifies form, shape, outline, appearance) certainly represents a drift away from the oral–
aural to the visual–tactile, an adaptation of the Hebrew
mentality to the Greek. In one way, indeed, reinter-
preting words as "forms" means no longer to take them
precisely as words. And yet, as we have seen, the use of
visualist concepts makes for explicitness and clarity, and
treatment of the words of the sacraments as form attests
an increasingly explicit, if at times impoverished, consciousness of the role of the word in the Christian economy. Aquinas is thus explicitly aware that the New Law,
following on the Incarnation of the Word of God, the
Son, Second Person of the Trinity, is a dispensation even
more dominated by the word of God and analogues of
the word, than was the previous Hebrew dispensation.
The use of words in the Christian sacraments is the con-

sequence of the presence among men of the Incarnate
Word of God.

The word in the sacraments (the formal element of
the sacraments themselves) is, in Aquinas' teaching as
in that of Trent, an efficacious word. For the sacraments,
in Catholic teaching, operate *ex opere operato,* which is
to say that the sign itself does something. Certain conditions are indeed required. If a person is not sorry for his
sins, the sacramental sign of penance does him no good
at all; quite the contrary, for he is guilty of misusing it as
a sacred thing. But if he is duly sorry, it is through the
sign itself, dominated as it is by the words involved, that
is, by the form, that God acts to forgive sins.

It is not difficult to translate this into the terms we have
earlier used to describe attitudes toward the word in oral
cultures. Such cultures think of the word as spoken word.
The spoken word is necessarily an event, an action, an indication of the present use of power (since it is something
going on), and thus is of a piece with other physical
actuality. The word is "behavioral," that is to say, in
Carothers' terminology. The Catholic doctrine of the
efficacy of the sacraments suggests this sense of the word
as something belonging to the world of physical power.
This of course does not mean that the effect achieved by
the sacraments is in Catholic doctrine of a piece with
natural physical effects. In the common Catholic doctrine
for which Aquinas is the spokesman, the effect of the
sacraments is of another and transcendent order. It depends on direct divine activity and has its effect basically
not in the sensible world at all but insensibly upon the
interiority of the human person, his soul, in the economy
of grace and redemption. Nevertheless, the efficacy of the
sacraments in Catholic teaching is certainly more readily
comprehensible to oral–aural man—or to modern man

who understands oral–aural cultures and the actuality behind them in depth—than it would be to cultures tyrannized over by the alphabet and more particularly by print.

In these perspectives, the extreme Protestant view appears by contrast to be thoroughly in accord with the typographic state of mind, which takes the word to be quite different from things. To the extreme Protestant mind of the sixteenth century and later, Catholic teaching here, as elsewhere, is "superstitious." There are many elements involved in such a charge, but one certainly is an uneasiness about associating words or signs (which are visualized words) with any kind of physical efficaciousness. Words must affect the heart or interior consciousness of the hearer as something isolated from the exterior world. We have earlier seen how, paradoxically, it is only when words are removed from their natural habitat of sound and made to appear something that they are not, namely marks on a visualizable surface, that they appear to be set off from exterior things. The classic Protestant sensibility seems strongly influenced by this feeling for words as processed through writing and, even more, print. In these perspectives, the well-known Protestant stress on literacy has deeper psychological roots than those allowed for when this stress is taken to be due simply to the desire to have as many as possible read the Bible for themselves. More profoundly, this stress appears to come from an unarticulated feeling that without reading one does not have quite the proper feel for words or for God's word itself.

As in many other points of difference between Protestant and Catholic, the issues here can be caught in sharp focus in terms of eucharistic theology. Protestant and Catholic are both agreed that the Eucharist has its effect in the interior of man and that somehow the sacramental sign here—bread, wine, the words of consecration—relate to this effect. In typical (although not universal) Protestant teaching, the words of consecration are commemorative but do nothing to the bread and wine as such. In Catholic teaching, they actually change the bread and wine, insensibly of course, into the body and blood of Jesus Christ, so that one must say that this is no longer bread and wine but his body and blood (and thereby, since this is his body and blood in their present, living state in his resurrected living body, there is present here under each sacramental species all that goes with his living body and blood, namely, the full person of Jesus Christ himself, as man and God). The words of consecration are, in Carothers' terms again, behavioral. In other terms, they are physically (if supernaturally and insensibly) efficacious. This is so because of God's power, of course, a power so often expressed in terms of God's word: "He spoke, and it was made; he commanded, and it stood forth" (Psalm 32 [33]:9). Catholic theology regards the use of human words for purportedly magic effects as misguided and morally wrong. But the kind of efficacy accorded by Catholic teaching to the words in the consecration of the Eucharist, most Protestants, true to a typographic sensitivity, would consider somehow magical and would not allow even to the words of Christ.

Attitudes toward the preaching of the word. Protestant sacramental theology as described here has as its complement the strong stress on the efficacy of the word of God in preaching which has been characteristic of Protestantism from the beginning and which is reviewed, for example, in Gerhard Ebeling's recent *Word and Faith*. Issues here are extremely complicated—in Luther's discussion, for example, of the relationship of the

Church to the Word or of the relationships of the Word, the Gospel, and the Law. But through all the centuries of theological discussion from the origins of Protestantism to the present, the Protestant sense of the power of the word is unmistakable, as is also the fact that when the word of God is thought of as powerful, the sensible analogue for it tends clearly to be the spoken word, whether that actually heard in sermons or prayer or that heard in the imagination of the believer reading the Scriptures in print. The old oral–aural sense of the power of the word strongly asserts itself here.

One can ask why the advent of print, which brought attention to bear on the visually recorded text as never before and thereby isolated the individual from the tribe before the silent page, could see also this rise in explicit attention accorded the spoken word. A part of the answer is of course that in making the text of the Bible more physically accessible by sheer multiplication of copies, print heightened the attention accorded to words themselves by comparison with the attention accorded other elements in the Christian heritage (such as nonverbal symbolism, liturgical gesture, and the like) and thus opened the way to develop further the Christian (and Hebrew) feeling for the power of words, and especially of God's word. The successive stages in the development of the media can be reinforcing, as has been seen, even when they alter balances in the sensorium. The typographically conditioned Protestant assertion of the power of the word reinforces oral–aural attitudes in the Bible. It also alters them by insisting much more *explicitly* on the power of the word than does the early Church. This was the Protestant way of coping with the tendency of print, subconsciously sensed, to weaken the feeling that words themselves possess power, a feeling clearly losing

ground in the age influenced by Francis Bacon. Because
the Catholic Church retained its strong sense of the power
of sacramental signs, it did not need this particular kind
of adjustment to the new state of affairs.

Attitudes toward authority. Contrasting attitudes toward authority among Catholics and Protestants are due
to a great many factors, some of them basically doctrinal
as others are cultural. It would be fatuous to suppose that
these differences can be reduced simply to shifts in the
media of communication. Yet it is not unlikely that they
are related to such shifts, and it appears quite possible to
suggest, if only in passing, some of the relationships.

The fact that the crisis of authority marking the rise
of Protestantism appeared at the time it did is itself interesting. The movement from an authoritarian to an
objectivist state of mind, as has been earlier explained
here, in great part correlated with the shift from habits
of predominantly auditory synthesis to habits of predominantly visual synthesis. An oral culture tends to be
communal, nonindividualistic, and authoritarian. It will
be recalled from Scholes' and Kellogg's description in
The Nature of Narrative that in oral narrative the narrator is typically both anonymous and totally authoritative: the communal tradition speaks through him, and
there is no appeal. An oral culture stores information in
memory and thus maximizes the word of others as an
avenue to truth, stressing the reliance of mind on mind,
of person on person. By contrast, a typographic culture,
because it is strongly visualist, isolates the individual
from the tribe even in much of his verbal activity, mutes
and minimizes interpersonal communication, and elab-
orates the visual in all its aspects, including "observation"
and "objectivity," as the preferred route to truth.

Here the remark sometimes heard that Luther simply

substituted a paper pope, the Bible, for the pope in Rome conveys as much misinformation as truth. A paper pope and a pope in the flesh relate quite differently to the psyche. Even apart from an expressed doctrine of private interpretation, the printed text throws the individual back on himself, away from the group or tribe. Psychological structures supporting the corporate sense of the Christian are weakened, as we have just seen, when private reading of the Bible is moved to the center of Christian life, although the corporate sense may of course be strengthened concomitantly by other developments. Private reading of the Bible is to this extent de-authoritarianizing in its general psychological bearing. Insofar as the pope is a personal symbol, his authority is felt in quite another fashion, as bearing on the Church as a whole and, indeed, as proceeding from the Church and his place in the Church's structure. It is at root public and communal. Literacy may interfere with the sense of communality here.

In this connection it is interesting to note that the Catholic and Protestant views regarding authority are subjective and objective in opposite ways. Both Catholics and Protestants stress authority and in doing so maintain special contact with the oral–aural world where, in one way or another, authority has its roots because authority is reductively always personal and the oral–aural world is a primary ground for personal relations. In Catholic teaching, the voice which is heard as the voice of authority is God's voice speaking through the Church, in which the Bible has a unique and preeminent place. In classical Protestantism, the voice speaks through the Scriptures alone, to the accompaniment of preaching. The Catholic is objective in that he has resort to the word of an objectively existing Church, recognizable, Catholic doctrine insists, in its "visible" members, and he is subjective in the sense that the tradition on which this Church relies does not in its entirety have the visually discernible presence which the Bible as a written document does have. The Protestant has been charged by Catholics with being subjective in the sense that his interpretation of Scripture, which at basic points departs from that of his neighbor, is not objectively controlled. On the other hand, in basing his position on a written and printed document, the Protestant is objective in the sense that he fixes on the visible word.

This description of Catholic–Protestant differences in terms of the presence of the word in the reorganized sixteenth-century sensorium could of course be extended to many other areas of the religious crisis of the sixteenth and subsequent centuries. The massive question of faith and good works in particular needs examination in the present perspectives. Perhaps we are too little conscious that the Latin term for faith, *fides,* like the corresponding Greek *pistis,* belongs to the old oral–aural economy in a quite specific way. It was the term which since antiquity had been used for the conviction which the rhetorician, hierarch of the old oral–aural culture, was supposed to arouse in his audience. But enough has been said to suggest relevant aspects of the crisis which the word was undergoing at the beginning of the typographical era.

In the contentious climate of the Reformation, which we have seen in chapter 5 was neither exclusively nor distinctively religious, the use of print served in great part to fix theological positions more irrevocably than might have been the case in pretypographical ages. Positions were made firm by massive investments of time and energy in research such as that of the Protestant teams of Centuriators at Magdeburg and of Catholic apologetes typified by Canisius and Bellarmine and Melchior Cano. Once the lines were drawn in widely circulated books, they were harder to revise than they might have been in a more oral, less typographically bound age. This is not to say that some of the differences were not real, for they certainly were and are. But it is to say that not all of them were so radical as the controversial literature, which mounted to incredible volume and acrimony through the sixteenth and seventeenth centuries, made them out to be. The men of the age of the Reformation were, of course, quite unable to appreciate fully what was happening to their religious world in terms of the transformations of the word. We are better able to understand the situation today because our world is no longer theirs. We stand at a distance not only from their residually oral (dialectico-rhetorical) and incipiently typographical culture but also at a distance from the minimally oral typographical culture of the eighteenth and nineteenth centuries. Having entered into the electronic age, where a new oralism served by technology reigns, we can begin to understand the earlier age in some depth. But we need more research and reflection to understand it adequately.

6

Man's Word and God's Presence

GOD'S "SILENCE" AND THE MEDIA

Those who attend to the word of God today do so in a world where the human word—which man must use as his analogue for the divine—has been complicated to a degree unthought of by those who in biblical times responded to God's word or those sixteenth-century Christians who came to blows over it. Writing and print are not merely on hand, available for use; they have become more insistent than ever. Before the early 1700s lettered signs were virtually unknown even in cities; establishments needing identification were still marked by emblematic devices such as our strangely persistent American barber poles. Today lettered words thrust themselves up like shouting monuments not only in the cities but along country highways as well, and are inscribed in the heavens by skywriters. New media have supplemented the alphabet, giving words utterly new kinds of currency. On the radio, the voice of one man can really be heard around the world. Symbols which in the last analysis are words (in that at some point they must be verbalized) are fed into computers and emerge from them after passing through operations which only the specially initiated can understand and only computers can carry out.

Seriously religious persons, not always aware of the background of the present state of affairs, have argued that today's media distract from the word of God. As suggested in chapter 1, the state of the media may lie back of this persuasion as well as back of the Nietzschean protest that God is dead. Others, such as the late Martin Buber, have spoken of our age as one in which God is "silent." In his *Eclipse of God,* taking up a statement of Sartre and giving it a more profound meaning than Sartre had intended, Buber refers to Isaiah 45:15 to suggest that God is one who not only reveals himself but conceals himself as well. Without impugning the depth and truth of Buber's insight, we might recall that concealment and silence, though alike, are not exactly the same thing. Communication by voice thrives on concealment, for voice emerges from the interior, which is essentially concealed. One might ask whether a feeling that God is silent might not on the one hand mean that God is communicating to man very much today, since his word is also like our silence, as noted in chapter 3, and on the other hand might not be intimately connected with the reorganization of the sensorium which technological man has undergone and which is signaled by the countless transformations to which the word has been subject. If God's presence is to be known, it must be found while man is living in a newly arranged constellation of sensory apprehensions.

The story told in the foregoing chapters suggests that a certain silencing of God may have been prepared for by the silencing of man's life-world. The ability to respond directly to the word enjoyed by early oral–aural man has been attenuated by objectifying the human life-world through hypertrophy of the visual and the obtrusion of the visual into the verbal itself as man has moved through the chirographic and typographic stages of culture. In Buber's terminology, we have maximized the "it" and minimized the "I" and the "thou." But we have not done this perversely, or even very deliberately, for this maximizing and minimizing was the inevitable result of the evolution of the media. Maximizing the it, the objective, visual–tactile aspect of existence necessarily accompanies the restructuring of the sensorium and of the psyche demanded by the evolving relationship of man with his communications system and its environment which we have traced here.

In these perspectives, the religious problem of modern man is far deeper than secularization, or, if the problem is conceived of as secularization, then secularization is a far more complex and elusive problem than it is commonly made out to be when it is seen as due simply to the buildup in knowledge concerning the natural, secular world with a consequent diminution of attention to what is transcendent. Secularization has connections not merely with our increment of natural knowledge but also with changes in psychological structures which are the coefficients of man's pilgrimage through time. It corresponds in great part to the shift from a life-world polarized in sound and person to one polarized around sight and object. This shift, moreover, is intimately related to the buildup of knowledge concerning the material world, and, for that matter, concerning the transcendent insofar as this can be investigated philosophically and theologically by means of abstractions. For unless the shift into the visual modes of conceptualization had been achieved—that is, unless the world had been apprehended more and more as a kind of object—the present advances in science could not have been made, nor could the fund of knowledge on which even philosophy and theology today must build have been accumulated. But the present advances have exacted a price. To gain the insights which they assure, certain other awarenesses have had to be curtailed, including those fostered by habits of auditory synthesis.

We have seen that, with the development of electronic communication, sound has been acquiring a new currency in the present day after its previous devaluation through the development of script and print. The new attention to sound includes of course greater implementation of voice and of spoken words, as on the telephone, radio, and television. How much promise is there here of a counterbalance to the hypertrophy of the it, of the objective, of the quantified and impersonal and mechanistic? Despite computerization, thus far the last stage in the quantification of man's life-world, is it possible that we are moving toward some new realization of the personal and·thus new opportunities for Christian living and giving in our time?

A common persuasion is that we are not, because the electronic media are mass media in which the use of verbiage does not entail true sensitivity to the word. The genuine spoken word relates person to person. Mass media, we are urged to believe, do not do so even when they are sound media such as radio or television. They follow crowd-manipulatory recipes. They know no true person-to-person contact. Thus, in effect, in the mass media even the use of voice itself continues in its own way the depreciation of the word which hypertrophy of the visual had first fostered.

There is, of course, much to this view, but it does not do justice to the total state of affairs today by contrast with preceding ages. Crowd-manipulatory recipes are not recent inventions. The orators of ancient Rome were already past masters in using them. The doctrine of the commonplaces (*loci communes*), which Cicero and thousands of orators practiced and which rhetoricians like Quintilian taught, provided just such recipes. The fact is, mass media begin not with the press and radio but with the mass languages. When—after several hundred thousand years during which languages had been each the property of a group of a few hundred or few thousand persons at the most—urbanization and empire produced languages shared ultimately by hundreds of thousands and millions of persons, the stage for manipulation of masses of men had been set. Without a mass language, as some of the developing countries are painfully aware, typographic and electronic media are inoperable. These media extend the range of the always basic mass medium, language, beyond the wildest dreams, or nightmares, of earlier man, but always in dependence upon the language. In doing so, they of course alter the languages, establishing new vocabularies, tones, and feelings (without necessarily entirely eliminating earlier ones). But the base of the mass verbal medium remains language itself. To this verbal medium even pictorial media are secondary. Moving pictures themselves call for sound.

Moreover, it is not always true that person-to-person contact is nonexistent in today's mass media, particularly in those using the spoken word. The telephone has certainly helped maintain many close personal relationships at a pitch otherwise impossible. So has rapid transportation, which, we must remember, is largely a communications device (probably most traveling is done to talk to others) and is also in fact a part of our electronic communications system, for without electronics neither airways nor modern turnpikes could be brought into existence or operate. One could argue that the telephone and rapid transport, though dependent on electronics, are not really mass media: they are too individualistic in actual use. Radio and television are more representative of true mass media. But even radio and television are not entirely lacking in intimacy (particularly television), because of the degree of audience involvement it fosters. The experiences shared by millions after the assassination of President Kennedy provide a test case, poignantly real, however exceptional. Here public affairs themselves became intimate with a reality and intensity quite impossible without electronic mass media. Part of the overwhelming personal effect was precisely the knowledge that so many others were also personally affected, as they would not have been without television.

But we can go farther still. There is manifold evidence that technological cultures give rise, sometimes directly and sometimes by way of reaction indirectly, not merely to external devices favoring the use of voice but to a deep sensitivity to all that voice and person mean. Indeed, unless we are under falsely romantic illusions that early man was totally "adjusted" and at home in his highly unfavorable and hostile environment, we can find that in many quarters today's sensitivity to voice and person far surpasses that of early man.

The oral quality of language has commanded widespread, explicit attention only in the electronic age. Language as such had formerly been approached through grammar, which is to say, through writing (*grammata*, we remember, means letters of the alphabet, so that *grammatica*, grammar, is the study of "letters"). Today, language is studied directly as spoken, through the new science of linguistics, a massive field of knowledge of which grammar can be considered a part, somewhat as Euclidean geometry is part of a field of geometry much greater than itself, or as Aristotelian logic is a part of a larger field of logic. Linguistics is closely related to electronic technology, without which data could not effectively be gathered or stored. Grammar needs no comparable equipment—only script.

Philosophy has undergone a parallel development. The old oral culture had lingered in the West well through the Renaissance in the arts of dialectic and rhetoric, which finally yielded to Descartes' logic of inquiry, a private, ideally nonverbal procedure. But today philosophers are intimately aware of the social character of thought—one hears expressions such as "the sociology of knowledge." The interest in dialogue both as a technique of learning and as a focus of philosophic interest is a distinctive phenomenon of our age, indeed, so common in places as to be a fad.

The old dialectic of the schools had devoted itself to exploring delimited questions in formalized, sequential, deliberately polemic styles which over the centuries showed more and more the influence of writing. Dialogue works in a less delimited, freer, more oral fashion. Dialectic belonged to a culture in which issues were relatively simple and could be presented convincingly in linear or sequential form, one after the other. Dialogue, with the discussion groups and brainstorming sessions accompanying it, belongs to a culture which typically experiences problems as interconnected or simultaneous and which thus lives with a sense of the present, typical of oral, sound-synthesizing cultures rather than of visual, quasi-extratemporal states of mind. Earlier concern with language often proceeded by extreme formalization of linguistic and logical structures. This formalization continues today, but concern with dialogue and communication as such has also converted the study of speech as never before into a study of the entire human life-world. Such study, perhaps best shown or best known in Heidegger, appears in the work of countless other scholars, as can be seen by a glance through the bibliography in Verhaar's monograph, *Some Relations between Perception, Speech, and Thought.*

Parallel interests are found in theology, where express preoccupation with the spoken word is probably keener today than at any time in history. The theological interest in the spoken word appears paradoxical, for it has arisen largely as Scripture scholarship, the study of the written word, has matured in today's keen awareness of the long oral tradition in which the text of the Scriptures is encapsulated and out of which it grows. The current renewal in the Roman Catholic Church decreed by the Second Vatican Council in its Constitutions on the Liturgy and on the Church stresses the use of the spoken word as never before, in keeping with the spirit of the times.

But does this attention to the spoken word in any way counteract what has been called the silencing of God? In one sense of course it does not. It does not force God to manifest himself. If God's manifestation of himself is something real, a personal encounter, as Hebrew and Christian tradition has made it out to be, it is of course beyond the power of man, as one person to the encounter and the finite one at that, to dictate on what occasions God will conceal himself and on what occasions he will make his presence felt, whether to an individual person or to any group of persons. Encounter is an action à deux. Insofar as it is a giving of person to person, it is a free act. In this sense, attention to the spoken word, however intent, cannot bring God to manifest himself. But this results in no crisis particular to our age. It is totally foreign to the Hebreo-Christian tradition to think in any age man has been able to make God manifest himself. To attempt to do so would be to substitute magic for faith. The scriptural term for such an action is "tempting God" —trying to work an experiment with him.

There is, however, the matter of man's preparedness for encounter with God. Here it would appear that recent attention to the spoken word and the present state of the media of communication offer, in addition to much confusion, some promise. For, amid all our technological armor today, all our hardware, we live with a sense of personal presence which is a new and invigorating human experience and which without our modern communications media would be impossible.

HUMAN PRESENCE TODAY

To be present to himself, man must find the presence of another or others. Man's life-world is the opposite of solipsist: it is a world not of presence but of presences. In presences we mature. Each individual I finds himself by dealing with a thou, and another thou, and another. The presence of other persons fills man's consciousness, as objects cannot. Situated among objects, a person may indeed find them interesting, but he responds only to other persons, other presences, who are not objects. In a whole universe filled with countless objects and occupied only by one other man alone, it would be to the man alone that I could present myself, establish a relationship of presence.

The kind of presence which early man was able to establish in the universe was vastly different from the presence enjoyed by technological man today. Despite what personalizing effects may have been realized in his immediate environment, for early man the globe was not truly peopled. Human contacts, by any twentieth-century standards, were severely circumscribed. Man was scattered in tiny isolated populations which had lost memory of each other's existence. To salve his sense of isolation, in his religious rites primitive man frequently reassured himself, as we have seen, that he was truly at the *omphalos* or navel of the world, the midpoint of things, where whatever presence he could experience was by definition maximal. There is something poignant about this quest for centrality, as there is also about the host of animate or semianimate beings with which primitive man invests the relatively unpeopled world around him. From totemic figures to the more sophisticated polytheisms of ancient Egypt or China or Greece or Rome, these projections appear from one point of view as attempts, terrifying insofar as they were not subject to rational control, to populate a world too lacking in presence for comfort.

Modern technological man is in a different state. Our sense of the presence of others in the world is overpowering. For us the world is thoroughly "hominized"; human presence bears in on us from Europe and America to Russia and Japan and China, from Siberia through Cape Town and up from Tierra del Fuego to Hudson Bay. Indeed, our sense of almost total or closed human presence is so strong as to bring us readily to assume that it was always part of human experience. Of course it was not. Modern man's sense of global presence, of a peopled world, is entirely novel, until recently an unheard-of thing, both a new burden and a new boon for our consciousness.

Man's sense of the presence of his fellows is desperately assertive. Even with the strictest taboos and caste systems it is impossible for any two groups of human beings to

remain isolated from each other, for no group that has
known of another's existence has ever remained truly
isolated. Today everyone knows of everyone else. The
unification of the human race has lately become an inescapable public issue, so intense is the presence of man
to man. Flight from other groups only involves one with
them more. The white racist or the Black Muslim is
more preoccupied (even if negatively) with members of
the other race than are most of those who favor integra-
tion. In the present situation, such a society as the whites
of the Republic of South Africa is not only a retarded
culture but a self-deceived one. The white South African
psyche is structured around and enslaved to the Negro.

The assertiveness of human presence and the deep
drive toward the unity of man is today so strong that the
one who is farthest from us is likely to command the
keenest interest. Elsewhere, in *The Barbarian Within,*
I have attempted to point out some reasons why this age
is the age of the outsider. Outgroups generally, who
formerly were often spurned, feared, and even massacred,
have today become in many if not all sectors of technological society the objects of unprecedented positive concern, even though the concern is not always effective.
Foci of interest run from racial minorities to voluntary
or quasivoluntary outsiders like beatniks, to such tragic
rejects as juvenile delinquents and on even to active military foes. Never before was the outsider the object of
such attention as he is given today. Unfortunates were
often treated with great kindness by individuals or religious associations in the past, but society was not organized to tolerate outgroups to the extent possible in open
societies today, with their vast and interlaced communications media. Outsiders have reverse status—to be "far
out" today actually means being "in."

THE PRESENCE OF MAN AND THE OPENNESS OF THE WORD

The presence of man to himself over the face of the globe is basically a presence of the word. It is not a peripatetic presence. Individual men do not all journey to the ends of the earth and back to encounter each other. The presence is realized within the human communications media. These media affect us in two ways which are important here. First, they make the past present by implementing accumulation and storage of historical and other knowledge about man and by giving us relatively ready access to this knowledge as needed. Secondly, they post us on the present, keeping us more or less constantly aware of urgent problems in all sorts of groups around the world, outgroups as well as ingroups. The sense of an urgent present in which technological man now lives is due, as we have seen, not merely to the growing efficiency of our computational and information-retrieval techniques (computers, electronic indexing, etc.) but also in a special way to direct use of sound, particularly for voice. Hearing engages and enforces the present as no other sense can. Electric impulses on a telegraph wire travel at the same speed as electric impulses on the telephone or as radio waves. But the live human voice on telephone or radio creates a sense of presence and the present which goes far deeper than the transcribed telegraph message ever can. Voice is "real." And voice is on the air today more than ever before.

One test of presence is spontaneity or openness, for the presence of man to man is the openness of one consciousness to another in trust and love. The sound media create in quite evident, if limited, ways a more fully open society. Radio and television bring with them the open-end discussion, the dialogue, the unrehearsed program, a whole new economy of spontaneity in production unknown to writing and print. Spontaneity is not merely accepted but also cultivated. Programs such as "Candid Camera" week after week systematically trap unsuspecting participants into unrehearsed reactions to totally unprecedented situations.

An open-end style of activity characterizes our entire existence. Public airing of unresolved questions has become a way of life, from the Second Vatican Council to the countless discussion groups proliferating in the wake of electronic communication (of which rapid transport, the precondition for large-scale discussion groups, is a product, since it is inoperable without telecommunication). In the individual's private world, open-end discussion has been made therapeutic in psychiatric treatment, and it has proved equally useful in the half-private, half-public operation of group dynamics. Even such hard-nosed activities as science, technology, and commerce have found open-end discussion invaluable for the research and development (R and D) teams which undertake to explore new and unthought-of possibilities for scientific or technological work or for the operation (which often means the diversification) of commercial empires. A large manufacturing corporation today is often excruciatingly aware that in a few years it may be directing its resources to producing utterly different lines: nylon hose may be supplanted by steering wheels.

The openness in the religious milieu across the world today is so spectacularly evident as to need no comment. Here the most recently effective moves have been made by the Second Vatican Council, following the lead of Pope John XXIII, who in turn, it is becoming more and more evident, was opening outlets for drives long at work in the Church. Christian groups hitherto isolated from one another have entered into fruitful contact, and conversations between Christians and non-Christians have become more frequent and meaningful.

In terms relating directly to the verbal media of communication, it is interesting to note how the catechism has made way for dialogue as a technique for presenting religious truths. Although there were weak pretypographical antecedents, the catechism as we know it is the product of typography. The pioneers in the production of catechisms, such as Martin Luther and Peter Canisius, were post-Gutenberg men, reared in a print culture. More oral ages had received religious instruction by catechesis in the precatechism sense of this term, "resounding," "back-echoing," reiterating by word of mouth what had been delivered to them by word of mouth without the intervention of stereotyped questions incident to writing and print. Repetition (catechesis) belongs to the primary oral stage of communications, question-plus-answer belongs rather to writing matured in print, where information is more codified and "answers" are "looked up." The catechism extended to religious teaching the feeling for exact textual control encouraged by alphabetic typography. Today, even to disseminate the teachings it itself contains, the catechism is no longer the effective instrument it once was. Discussion is essential for assimilation in the post-typographically oral age.

For these and the countless other instances of openness in the contemporary sensibility, dialogue is a normal accompaniment. Today's openness is unmistakably associated with vocal exchange. Dialogue constitutes the basic use of the spoken word, and in its normal stage dialogue is entirely unrehearsed. It moves from determined points of departure toward an undetermined goal, for in dialogue the utterance of each individual is decided not merely by the individual himself but by the preceding remark of the interlocutor to whom his remark is a reply. And sound itself is open in that it moves into the future. It is never present all at once as a printed text can be. Writing and print effect closure. The written word means constriction. This constriction has been newly liberated by a new flow of speech.

In the perspectives suggested here, the curious irenic tone given to society, both secular and religious, by the present insistence on dialogue is of major interest, for it suggests that through the reorganization of man's worldview, enforced by development in the media, some kind of new prospect of peace and understanding is indeed dawning. If we recall what we have reviewed of the overwhelming anxieties connected with earlier habits of auditory synthesis—the berserk Scandinavian warrior, the Southeast Asian warrior run amok, the rioting Congolese —and the highly polemic cast of training in the arts of expression which marked the central Western tradition so long as it retained its oral orientation through centering around rhetoric and dialectic or debate, the present détente in the approach to oral communication is surprising and paradoxical. The old orality had not been this open.

The present state of affairs makes it clear that the new orality is not basically a reconstitution of the old sensorium but rather a new organization which the present electronic media of communication have enforced, bringing the whole globe into continual contact with all of itself at once and thus tending to minimize ingroup feelings. The present orality is post-typographical, incorporating an individualized self-consciousness developed with the aid of writing and print and possessed of more

reflectiveness, historical sense, and organized purposeful-
ness than was possible in preliterate oral cultures.

Of course, not every manifestation or paraphenome-
non of the new oralism is irenic by any means. Some of
the old oral tendencies to frenzied outburst recur all too
evidently, for modern oral man, like early oral man,
lives in a world of happenings rather than in the more
exclusively cause-and-effect world favored by writing and
print. We like to be "turned on" or to act turned on, to
be "with it." The demonstration or even the riot has
achieved a new prominence and effectiveness. But, although we have unplanned outbursts, what is typical of
our culture is the planned demonstration or riot. Our
oralism is linearly controlled as early oralism was not.

To suggest that even our orality is curiously irenic or
at least controlled is not of course to say that today man's
anxieties or hostilities are gone, much less that they ever
will be. It is to suggest, however, that they are displaced
and that perhaps some of our anxiety about anxiety is
due to the fact that the present forms of anxiety are relatively new and surprising. The extroverted hostility of
the old tribal family feud would perhaps be more com-
forting to us than our hostilities turned in so resolutely
on ourselves. We should note however that a recent study
by Raymond B. Cattell in the *Scientific American* has
produced a great deal of evidence that individuals from
highly technological cultures are actually less prone to
anxieties than those from less technological cultures.

I do not mean to overstress the openness and irenic
qualities in present-day technological society, which has
grimmer aspects aplenty, too. Man's present openness to
himself is full of ambiguities, but it has promise insofar
as it is personal in cast, as often enough it seriously undertakes to be. The depersonalizing elements in technologi-

cal society are often exaggerated, even by fine scholars such as Jacques Ellul, not infrequently by supposing that personalism today should be the same sort of thing it was in earlier cultures. The ability of urbanized man, a salesclerk, for example, to relate to large numbers of individuals pleasantly but without deep involvement is at least as humanizing as it is dehumanizing. It makes possible the multiple contacts between large numbers of individuals absolutely necessary in today's world while not breaking down the privacy which modern man has finally achieved and which, as we have noted, even the most privileged did not enjoy in the tribal structures formerly engulfing the individual day and night. Modern technological man necessarily has a far wider variety and choice of personal contacts than had tribal man, whose world was kept intimately personal largely by default, since he knew of the existence of only a small fraction of mankind. Today intimacy must coexist with greater openness. It is distinctive of matured technological man that he must and can maintain a large number of contacts which are decently personal and yet relatively noncommittal. One of the achievements of technological, urban society has been to develop personality structures capable of doing just this. Visitors from other cultures are likely to find that their style of life knows only personal relations which are irremediably so close and exhausting as to make it impossible to deal graciously with the number and variety of persons that technological society demands they relate to.

But, granted that the variety of relationships with others demanded by technological society are duly personal, can they for the most part truly be invested with love? Or is love reserved for our most intimate relations with others alone? Can love be shown only within a family? Christian teaching, as seen in the parable of the Good Samaritan (Luke 10:30–37) would say no: love can and should be shown not only to those close to us but also to casual acquaintances and strangers, to those one merely stumbles upon. There is no indication in the parable of the Good Samaritan that after his rescue a close friendship between rescuer and rescued flowered. The Samaritan's benefactor, with a casualness which prophets of doom might ascribe only to a late techno-logical society, did all he could to restore him to health, paid for his care, and left. In the light of this parable, the vast network of somewhat casual personal relationships fostered by technologized urban living can provide ground for Christian charity and for true openness of man to man. It is affectation to pretend otherwise. And why can such relationships also help to keep man open to God? There is no indication that the kind of com-munication fostered in our electronic world is particu-larly dehumanizing or antireligious if one compares it with the actuality of earlier communication between man and man, and not with some symbolic transforma-tion of early human relations.

PRESENCE IN THINGS

Man's increased and intensified presence to himself has had a profound effect on the world of things as these have entered into and implemented this presence. De-spite the nostalgia we can suffer for a simpler life pur-portedly close to nature, man appears on the whole far closer to things today than ever before, and in a more human, because a more informed and potentially more understanding way. It is true that technological man does not assimilate the nonhuman world to his own as desperately as did early animistic cultures which imputed to inanimate nature itself a lifelike glow. But he does draw things to himself by his far more manifold and matured insights. Technological man brings things under his more complete and intimate control. In doing so, he infects things with his own human presence.

Technological man is frequently pictured as dehumanized by simple immersion in the world of things, the world of "it." He is overwhelmed with hardware, with mere equipment, from his bath through breakfast (electric refrigerator, toaster, percolator, and waffle iron) and on out of the house into the airconditioned laboratory or scholar's study or off to the automated outing in the woods. Everywhere he entangles himself in equipment, which the ancient Romans long ago had had the prescience to style *impedimenta,* luggage, things lugged along. The astronaut typifies the plight of technological man: emerging from his *Gemini* capsule to float "freely" in space, he finds himself less a free, naked swimmer than a knight in full armor would be. He is in direct contact with nothing but the hardware that encases him. Everything else comes to him mediated, filtered through layers of gadgetry. His arrangements to confront the universe have seemingly only mechanized and dehumanized his own being. The astronaut's situation is a paradigm of the total situation of technological man, for the whole of human society has become infested with the mechanical and impersonal.

Technological hardware has indeed dehumanized man, but only to a degree. Gadgetry promotes humanization as much as it threatens it. Early man was terribly brutalized by his lack of gadgetry in an often hostile and murderous environment. The kind of control over things which technology has given man, subjecting to the intellect the material world in which human consciousness

exists, has made this world less and less alien, more of a
piece with man himself, more like man's own body, a
material thing-like existent which man can control and
which is indeed part of himself. Technology has enabled
man to move about and to take possession of all the
world as of his home. The astronaut's space suit is an
extension of himself, however cumbersome.

The world of material things as such of course remains
in itself still a world of objects, of things, psychically inert.
It is not of itself a world of presences. And yet objects can
be more or less infected with presence, provided that they
are somehow used or appropriated by man. The chair in
which my father sat is invested with his being. Today
the penetration into the material world of mere things,
of "it," which man has effected through the great human
achievement we know as science, does as much to invest
the world of it with human presence as it does to threaten
man's own world with the dead impact of the infrahuman
world. If the meager architectural ruins of antiquity are
inhabited by the presence of man so fully as we find them
to be, what a massive presence the creations of our technological culture exude. Were all of New York or of
St. Louis to be suddenly emptied of people, the presence
of man in the things left behind would remain overwhelming.

The presence of man is a presence of the word. This
is true not merely for the presence of man to man; it is
also true for the presence with which things themselves
are invested. For things become part of the human world,
not insofar as they are known simply to one or another
person but rather as the knowledge of them becomes a
part of shared human experience, which as we have seen
is so critically focused in the word. We have no exact
comparative studies of the difference between the

amounts of knowledge concerned with material things commonly shared in a primitive preliterate community and in modern technological society. The difference is too multidimensional to be measured. But it can be sensed. One thinks, for example, of the early semiscientific knowledge of the world of nature sparsely disseminated in antiquity as represented in Pliny's *Natural History* and, by contrast, of the vast float of knowledge concerned with the physical universe which fills the schools, the newspapers, the other mass media, and ordinary conversation. In Pliny's day the world of things was so little known that it could provide only the most tenuous ground for verbalized encounter between man and man. Ancient man talked chiefly about man, in part because he had been unable to find out the "secrets" of anything else. He was often a humanist by default. The proper study of mankind was man only because little else had become available in depth. Today the world of things has itself grown dismayingly accessible, a vast field of discourse, and hence a vast meeting place for minds.

The impersonal nature of the world of things should not blind us to the fact that man's understanding dealing with the world of things can produce or reinforce a sense of human community. Nowhere in pretechnological society can one find instances of human cooperation so massive and intense as that required for countless technological projects today, from the commonplace to the most spectacular, from the construction of another airconditioned skyscraper (involving intricacies of cooperative engineering and thus of discourse unimagined in preelectronic cultures) to the launching and recovery of a pair of astronauts. Technological society is team society. Its major achievements are communal, its most idiosyncratic performance the countdown, which brings the devoted labor of thousands to bear on the instant present, a matter of life or death.

But the teamwork engendered by human concern with the world of things is not found only in work concerned with directly technological achievements such as space travel. It is equally in evidence at another pole, if we consider the modern scholar preparing, for example, an edition of a medieval work from microfilms of manuscripts. Between the original documents and his final edition there stands a similar cooperative network of countless persons, from chemists and photographers to postal clerks, airline employees, highly trained librarians, linotype operators, and publishers' sales departments. And the end result is the better for it. Man today everywhere is supported in a vaster and vaster network of communal life, none the less social because its intricacies most often conceal themselves. We take the cooperative structures of present society for granted and forget that only a few hundred years ago an edition of a work was commonly produced by taking a pen (cut by oneself) and ink (made by oneself) and parchment, and copying out the work alone. The result could be a remarkable achievement, but it still left much to be desired.

PRESENCE OF MAN AND PRESENCE OF GOD

One of the reasons we fail to sense more keenly the cooperative structures of technological society is that we succumb to the temptation of technological man to consider the universe as a world-in-space and only a world-in-space, as essentially something picturable. Picturability is not the measure of actuality. For the universe, or at least our part of it, is filled with presences, which form the real stuff of our awareness but which of themselves cannot be pictured. Being-in-space is not of itself pres-

ence in the full sense of presence, that is, the sense of
simultaneous at-oneness and otherness which another
human being can bring to me. A presence is an interiority
bearing toward and calling to another interior, an inwardness which is simultaneously an utterance or "outer-
ance" or "outering" insofar as the other is outside. And
yet this outering is not merely an outwardness, not an
abandonment of interiority for exteriority. My voice
really goes out of me. But it calls not to something outside, but to the inwardness of another. It is a call of one
interior through an exterior to another interior.

Because presence is itself interior, it is involved in the
world of sound with which we have here been concerned
more intimately than in the world of space. Sound, as we
have seen, reveals interiors. For man the paradigm of
sound is voice, in which communication between man
and man (man is the deepest of interiors) flowers as in no
other sensory manifestation. Voice is alive.

Voice is alive because sound is alive. The relation of
the cosmos to sound actively evolves, whereas its relationship to space remains relatively static. With the advent
and diffusion of man, the world is no more involved in
space than it was at its beginning. Space holds objects
today in the way it always has. Even man, insofar as his
body is an object (as it is under one of its very real aspects), is in space the way things themselves have always
been. In this sense, the role of space in the universe does
not change. Man finds out more about it, often with the
help of designs; that is all.

The world of sound, however, does change. Only with
the advent of man does sound peak in the human voice,
producing the word. From this point on, sound is in the
cosmos in a new way. We have seen earlier how the use
of sound becomes, generally speaking, physically more

and more interiorized as animals evolve to higher or more interiorized forms. The world of sound is essentially cumulative, culminating. Whereas space has the same cosmic import now as before, sound plays a new and decisive role after the long evolution leading up to man.

Moreover, the role of sound continues to grow and diversify after the advent of man as society evolves through its successive stages. With writing and print, sound enters into more direct traffic with space, and with the advent of the electronic media it acquires more currency than ever through the telephone, radio, and television (including Telstar), as well as through the immediate confrontation of person with person made possible, as we have seen, by a rapid transport system (itself dependent on electronic communications media) which within a matter of hours can bring together for conferences persons separated by the maximum distances on our globe.

The evolution of human society and the "hominization" of the world (man's entering into possession of the world, filling it up, becoming the active focus of more and more of its operations) can thus be understood in a basic, though by no means an exclusive sense, as a triumph of voice, of the word, through which man comes to an understanding of actuality and through which he constructs human society. For the word, as we have seen, is not only the repository of intelligibility and intelligence; it is also the basic agent holding society together. The word, which is essentially sound, unites not just one man and another; it forms men into groups. It is the expression and incarnation of community.

In keeping with its profound relationship to the word, the community itself exercises a kind of presence. The presence of a human group can enhance a sense of other

presences as well. Even the most intimate unity of husband and wife, their mutual presence, gains strength and
indeed depends on a sense of a larger community to which
they belong. The sense of the larger community pressing
in on man everywhere today is truly a sense of the presence of man to man.

Such a presence is hardly of itself, however, the presence of God, for many of those who experience a sense of
man's presence in one or another way do not take any
evident interest in the presence of God or may even
dispute or write off or ignore its possibility. Yet the
presence of man to man is doubtless the matrix in which
the sense of God's presence grows for the present-day man
of faith as for no earlier human beings. In the Hebrew
and Christian dispensation at least, love of God and love
of man, while not the same thing, are complementary:
the command to love one's neighbor is like the first com-
mandment, to love God (Matt. 22:36–40). And for Christians the presence of Jesus Christ is tied to a sense of
human community: "Where two or three are gathered in
my name, there am I in the midst of them" (Matt. 18:20).
It is not merely the gathering which makes for Christ's
presence: the "in my name" is crucial. His presence cannot be concocted by magic or by any scientifically acquired skills. The gathering must call to him. But when
it does, the gathering itself furnishes the matrix, the
womb for his coming, as Mary's body once did. If the
group calls and waits on him, he is there.

For believers, the increased sense of human presence
enjoyed by man today is thus filled with promise. Earlier
man knew theophanies at certain times and places. But
time and place have become neutralized for modern man,
largely because of the technological tendency to neutralize space mathematically. If man is to retain sanity

through affirmation of his past, as he must, certain times and places—Hanukkah or Easter, the interior of a church —will retain to a degree a special sacrality. But time and place as foci of the human life-world have been complemented and in part supplanted by the sense of conscious interchange of man with man, a sense of human presence, of intersubjectivity, of psychic participation even with persons in the most distant lands. This is the situation that gives reality to present-day internationalized political and civic action—marches concerned with Vietnam, the activity of the Peace Corps—whether or not such action in a given case is foolish or wise. Formerly, religious international concern had little of this political and civic concern to work with.

This is what in truth is meant when we say that modern means of *communication* (this includes, we must remember, rapid transport) have annihilated *time* and *space*. It is not merely that time and space are lesser handicaps than they used to be. More than this, time and space no longer carry the psychological weight they once carried. Presence has penetrated through them and come to outweigh them as never before. In the totality of being which is the universe, physical and conscious conjointly, despite the known immensity of this universe, time and space bulk smaller and the sense of human presence and of shared consciousness immeasurably larger than ever before. Time and space are of course by no means inimical to Hebrew and Christian values: for the Hebrew and Christian God is attentive to temporal and spatial occurrences, concerned with temporal and extended actuality (the Christian doctrine of the Incarnation is cardinal here), but he is so because of the relationship of time and space to man's consciousness, which is involved in time and space while at the same time it transcends them.

Within time and space, the human consciousness and with it man's word remains a primary point of entry for the divine. As it expands its purchase in the universe, enlarges itself, the ground on which grace operates and God's presence is felt is enlarged.

REFLECTIVENESS OF THE WORD

The word evolves not merely into intersubjectivity but also into reflectiveness. Through the development of the verbal media the word creates history and throws light upon itself. One of the characteristics of our present culture, with its massive control of knowledge through electronic as well as typographic, chirographic, and oral media, is that it has situated man within his own history and thus given him a sense of self-possession previously unrealizable.

With the accumulation of knowledge of all sorts made possible by writing, by typography with its accompanying techniques of printed illustrations (exactly repeatable visual statement), and now by electronic devices, man has built up his awareness of himself and his fellows in all directions: back through political and social and psychological history into the past, in the process bringing to light the remarkable truth that the farther we get from our origins the more we know about them; back into his own intellectual history, bringing this to bear more and more on the present; around him into his natural environment and from it up and out to the edges of the universe and of time. Man must situate himself in the universe today in terms of all this knowledge. He can no longer deal with his life-world so unreflectively as did earlier man. Explicit and highly analytic knowledge of the past rather than emotional commitment to ancestors, the "dead," gives man today his sense of identity. The resulting psychological burden is often overwhelming, and one form of protest is the by now tiresome observation that man is lost or isolated or that God is dead—as though earlier men really had found themselves or God in any more effective ways than those open to us now.

The word is no longer situated in the universe or in man's life-world automatically either. This is the difference between the new oral age today and the old primitive oralism. Early man had a true, if at the same time confused, sense of the mystery, power, and holiness of the word. He lived by the word in its natural habitat, the world of sound, partly because he did not know how to do otherwise. He was undistracted, although at the same time he was relatively undeveloped. Today the oral word, the original word, is still with us, as it will be for good. But to know it for what it is, we must deliberately reflect on it. The spoken word, center of human life, is overgrown with its own excrescences—script, print, electronic verbalism—valuable in themselves but, as is generally the case with human accomplishments, not unmixed blessings. One of the reasons for reflection on the spoken word, the word as sound, is of course not to reject the later media but to understand them, too, better.

The word as sound signals interiority and mystery (a certain inaccessibility even in intimacy) as we have seen, two aspects of existence which we need to keep alive today. It also signals holiness—the holiness of the individual person and, in Hebrew and Christian teaching, the holiness of God. For holiness is inaccessibility, a sense of distance to be maintained, a sense of what is taboo: the Hebrew *kadosh,* generally translated as holy, at root means separated. The spoken word is somehow always radically inaccessible: it flees us, eludes our grasp, escapes when we try to immobilize it. Coming from the deep interior, it comes from a region to which we have no direct entry, the personal consciousness of another, the consciousness which utters the mysterious "I" which means something utterly different from what it means in the mouth of anyone else.

THE WORD BESPEAKS HOPE

Besides interiority and mystery and holiness, the spoken word signals also hope. Knowledge grows by hope. For all knowledge is only arrested dialogue, framed ultimately in speech, in communication. I speak because I hope in others. This is fairly easy to see in the case of philosophical knowledge, for example, since it is easy to feel philosophy as progressing socratically by interrogation and riposte. But it is also true of physical science in its own way: basically, even the latest scientific formulation represents something a scientist has said to some of his fellow men. It is a response to the hope of others, and is itself an expression of hope. It is never mere information. Hope is the difference between information encoded in machines and real knowledge in the consciousness of man.

Because it is framed in dialogue, knowledge even when most carefully formulated, or especially when most carefully formulated, promises more than it explicitly states. Seen as part of dialogue, as communication, as caught in the word, each statement of a truth looks forward to the next stage. It is an invitation to a riposte, a "this is true, but . . ." or a "this is true, and moreover . . . ." Because it is always an invitation as well as a vehicle of information, the word can never be concluded nor put aside: it looks always into the future, ahead, anticipating further growth.

At the level of sound, this state of affairs registers in

the fact, discussed at the beginning of the present work, that the word as sound is never present all at once. Sound exists only when it is going out of existence. This means of course that it exists also only when it is coming into existence. If we stop bringing sound into existence, actively producing it, it is no longer there. Sound is future-oriented, and thus hopeful. And, in accord with its natural habitat in the world of sound, so is the word.

GOD'S WORD TODAY

In the perspectives suggested, if at this stage one can tolerate so visualist a concept as perspectives, we can see some of the complex dimensions of Christianity, which maintains that God's word is given to man in history and that in Jesus Christ his Word is incarnate in history. The point has often been made that as opposed to most (perhaps even all) other religions, the Hebreo-Christian view of time is not cyclic. Matters begin in one state and end in another, in a way comparable to, although not exactly like, events in the evolutionary universe. To contrast the Hebreo-Christian view with other views—the ancient Greek or the Hindu, for example—it is often said that the Hebreo-Christian view is linear. Of course it is not, strictly speaking. In certain ways it is analogous to a straight line which begins at one point and ends at another different point. But, basically, time is not at all linear, for linearity is spatial, and, as we have seen in chapter 2 above (pp. 40–45), time as time is simply not conceivable in terms of space any more than sound is.

If history, which develops in time, is taken as a continuous reorganization of personality structure—which we have here approached in terms of reorganization of the sensorium, although it can be approached in a variety

of other ways—it is obvious how the analogy between
time and a straight line breaks down. Events are not
merely next to each other, like points on a line, each
outside the other. Events are not outside one another at
all. Rather, succeeding events, at least some of them,
include and reconstitute earlier events without being
identified with them. In the terms in which we have been
working, script includes and reconstitutes speech. Alphabetic typography includes and reconstitutes alphabetic
script and its antecedents, and electronic communication
includes and reconstitutes alphabetic typography and its
antecedents. Moreover, as the successive media develop,
while man finds himself progressively farther away from
past events lying closer to the beginning of time, something happens to these past events themselves. Through
the constitution of history which the expanded media
make possible, the past events become more alive and
effective in our immediate present. The details of human
origins are more real to us today than they were to
Paleolithic man. What we know of our past tells us where
we are at present and molds our plans for our future.

In Christian teaching, developing from its Hebrew
legacy as we can see this teaching and legacy now, the
word of God comes to man in history which culminates
in the coming of the Word in the person of Jesus Christ,
and this necessarily means not simply after a given
number of events have followed each other upon an imaginary line of time, but after the psyche has in certain
ways reorganized itself in its relationship to the events
and to the world around it. The word of God comes to
man and is present among men within an evolving communications system.

The strongly oral cast of the Hebrew and Christian
Scriptures bespeaks a culture not only temporally but

temperamentally quite different from ours, with a sense of the world and a psychological structure which is different not merely by reason of position in time and of social institutions generally but also specifically by reason of the way in which it is oriented toward the word itself. The alphabet had not been so thoroughly interiorized in biblical times as it was to be centuries later, particularly after the development of alphabetic typography. The sensorium was differently mobilized vis-à-vis the exterior world.

Oversimplified thinking might suggest, and has suggested, that it is the business of Christians today simply to get back to this original state of affairs in their response to the word of God. They should somehow or other recapture the mentality of the Hebrew people at the time of Christ and of Isaiah and David, too. Of course there can be no doubt that Christians must so far as possible try to understand and to enter into the mentality of these earlier times, particularly the mentality and culture of the primitive Church. To put it another way, we can say that for the informed Christian today, and the Church must always contain a large core of informed members, a sense of history is inseparable from his religious awareness. For the sensitive twentieth-century Christian a sense of God includes a sense of history.

But to say that we must be aware of the psychological structures and culture of the primitive Church is not to say that we can reconstitute these structures and this culture within ourselves in the way in which they once existed. Our very sense of presence in the universe, which makes us think of thus reconstituting the past, is necessarily different from that of the first Christians, who were related less self-consciously to their own past. Today's

Christians are not the coevals of the first Christians but their successors, bearing the marks of intervening time.

> The trilling wire in the blood
> Sings below inveterate scars
> And reconciles forgotten wars.

As these lines from T. S. Eliot's *Burnt Norton* suggest, our cultural struggles have left their marks on us for good. Our very ambition to reconstitute the past, which implies the communications devices we take for granted but which earlier man did not know, shows a state of mind impossible for earlier man even to conceive. With a differently organized sensibility, a more oral–aural culture, a more marked tendency toward primary auditory synthesis and the world-view which this entails, the early Christians, like the Hebrews before them, even when they were most cognizant of the past and reverent toward it, did not study it "objectively," and they lived, moreover, in the present in ways that are no longer feasible or realistically imaginable for us. We can profit from knowing their state of mind, but we can possess their state of mind only within the context of our own, which they did not know.

In other words, to dream of "demythologizing" the Scriptures, if by this we mean paring away excrescences to get at some innocent state of the Word which they contain, is a delusion of the most unhistorical sort. Certainly we must pursue the study of literary form, *Formgeschichte,* in the Scriptures, seeking to determine what the conventions and intent of the individual writers may have been; but let us not think that we are thereby finding for the first time what the Scriptures "really" mean. We are, more humbly, doing what we have to do to inter-

pret them to *ourselves*. Earlier man needed no demythologizing. He found myth neither opaque nor distracting.
We find it both. We feel obliged to rationalize, to explain
symbols which by definition and intent are themselves
explanations. In doing so we are establishing, by study,
between the Scriptures and ourselves the continuity
which is the continuity of the spoken word, a living continuity in which all other meanings have their home.

This, I might mention as a Catholic, suggests the meaning of the Roman Catholic Church herself. The existing
Church is the antidote to mere archaeologism in religious
history. True contact with the past can never be archaeo-
logical in the merely objective sense. Ultimately, contact
with the past is contact with the living present, continuous with that past, precisely because it has realized
all the developments that intervene between the past and
its present, the developments that make the past present
to it. The Catholic Church, accessible to all man's senses
through her identifiable members, is, I believe, the focus
in the present in which the word of God given to man in
the past most eminently lives and in which the person
of the Word is most eminently present. The Catholic
Church *is* the continuity of revelation with its past,
which, so far as the word is concerned, is necessarily an
oral continuity, for, as we have seen, the meaning of anything written in the past can be ascertained only in terms
of the present spoken word. The Catholic Church is
sacred history. For those who live within her, she is the
presence of the Word.

Particularly in studying the presence of the word to
man, whether the human word or God's Word, we must
beware of the elusive quest for a lost Eden. There is no
road back into history: we can only relate the past to the
present. The spoken word, as we have seen, is primary,

and yet from the start it was destined—or, in another way, doomed—to be supplemented with all the devices and even gadgetry which have reduced it more and more to space. The predicament of the human word is the predicament of man himself. Its very flowering bears within itself evidence of its own limitations and eventual transmutation. The evolution of the media of communication, with the continuous psychological reorganization which this evolution entails, was implied from the very beginning by the very structure of actuality. Because of its impermanence, the spoken word needs supplementing. Writing, particularly the alphabet, supplemented it while at the same time denaturing it, as we have seen. The fragmentation of consciousness initiated by the alphabet has in turn been countered by the electronic media which have made man present to himself across the globe, creating an intensity of self-possession on the part of the human race which is a new, and at times an upsetting, experience. Further transmutations lie ahead.

In this context, Christianity as a religion of the Word is necessarily entering today into a deeper understanding of itself and of the unity of man in God. God's Word is not man's word, whether we take God's Word in the sense of God's communication to man through the Scriptures or the Church or through some special visitation, or in the sense of the person of Jesus Christ, who for the Christian is God's own Word and his final communication. And yet man must think of God's word in accordance with what he can make of the word in his own life, even though at the same time he is aware that God's Word transcends his own, for God's word is God's *word,* not a projected visual image.

Despite its seeming reduction to space, the spoken word remains in actuality irreducible. For man, intelligibility has never been entirely dissociated from sound and can never be. The output of a computer becomes meaningful ultimately at the point at which it can be reintroduced into the world of sound, at least in the imagination, where what is read leaves the world of space and enters its proper domain. We are going to have to continue to "objectify" knowledge, to consider it in the visual or visual–tactile frames which every attempt to explain anything inevitably projects. But we have, or should have, sensitivity enough to know the limitations which such objectification entails, even while we are cultivating it. Among philosophers of science, Milič Čapek shows this sensitivity to an admirable degree in *The Philosophical Impact of Contemporary Physics* (pp. 170–71) when, as earlier noted, he urges physicists to supplement their visualist approach to the universe (the universe thought of primarily as something picturable) with a frankly auditory approach (the atom not as an assembly of picturable particles but as a harmony, the physical universe as an orchestration—of course, without a *written* score!). This is the dizzying kind of conceptualizing enterprise we may have to embark on. Visualism can become a port of refuge for the insecure.

The fact is that the permanent correlative of human knowledge in the world of sense, as we have reiterated so often, is not primarily visual or tactile or gustatory or olfactory but auditory. When man first broke into speech, the universe flowered and the knowledge explosion maturing in our own age really began. The picture must always be elucidated by the word more than the word by the picture. All reductions of the spoken word to non-auditory media, however necessary they may be, attenuate and debase it, as Plato so intensely felt.

Our insensitivity to the auditory character of the word

and of understanding is due in great part to the conditioning which has brought us to think of the word as primarily a sign. In the strict sense, the word is not a sign at all. For to say it is a sign is to liken it to something in the field of vision. *Signum* was used for the standard which Roman soldiers carried to identify their military units. It means primarily something seen. The word is not visible. The word is not in the strict sense even a symbol either, for *symbolon* was a visible sign, a ticket, sometimes a broken coin or other object the matching parts of which were held separately by each of two contracting parties. The word cannot be seen, cannot be handed about, cannot be "broken" and reassembled.

Neither can it be completely "defined." To want to define the word (or the concept associated with it is somehow to want to remove it (or the concept) from its natural habitat and place it in a visual field. Definition is useful and true, but never ultimate. The very notion, define, is arrived at by considering understanding in terms of vision: *definire* is to draw a line around, to mark the borders of something. There are of course analogies between the spoken word and visually apprehended objects, but the one is not the other, and no object in the visual field can possibly function as does the word. It is impossible to relate two visual objects as we relate subject and predicate.

Thus the word remains for us at root a mystery, a datum in the sense-world existing in closest association with that other mystery which is understanding itself. The word is a datum with a history, and a complex one, only a tiny part of which has been examined here. Through the spoken word—supplemented by the devices of the alphabet, typography, and electronic communication to which it itself ultimately gives rise—man's capacities for reflection are actualized as he enters into further and further communion with the universe around him, with his fellow man, and with himself.

In presenting himself to man in his Word, God as known in the Hebrew and Christian tradition has thereby entered into man's process of self-awareness, of reflective presence in the world, into the interior structure of history within the human psyche. The word of God in the Old Testament was his manifestation and his action and his power. In the New Testament it is all this and also more specifically his Son, Jesus Christ, God himself, whom Thomas the Apostle addressed as "My Lord and my God" (John 20:28). The Incarnation itself is an event not only in the objective world but also in the history of communication, in the mystery of sound.

Those with faith read history differently—and, as I believe, more completely—than do others, but faith or no, we must all deal with the same data, and among these data we find not only the elaborate transformations of the word which follow upon its initial spoken existence but also the permanent irreducibility of the spoken word and of sound itself. The mystery of sound is not the only mystery among the senses. There is boundless mystery, of another sort, in vision, too, and further mystery in touch, as well as in taste and smell. But the mystery of sound is the one which in the ways suggested here is the most productive of understanding and unity, the most personally human, and in this sense closest to the divine.

Readings

When an author is referred to in the text of this book, if the relevant title or other reference is not cited or easily ascertainable it can be located in this list of readings, which supplies full bibliographical information. This list also provides, where necessary, fuller bibliographical information on titles which are named in the text. Such information is not considered necessary, for example, in the case of standard reference works or the works of standard authors available in standard editions (for example, Homer, Plato, Aristotle, Virgil, Augustine, Alexander Pope), which are listed here only where the length of a quotation or other special circumstances demand.

Page numbers for references cited in the text of the present book are given directly in the text itself when needed—that is to say, when the relevant material cannot be readily found through the table of contents or index or other apparatus in the work in question.

This list is alphabetical by author. To find material in it on a given subject, the reader can use the general index at the end of this volume. The desired subject heading in the index will lead to the place or places in the text of the present volume where the subject is discussed and where the authors who treat the subject are cited.

To keep this list within bounds in an age when works on which a book such as this relies are numbered by the hundreds or perhaps thousands, no attempt has been made in the text of the present book or in the references to mention all relevant works. It has been deemed adequate to cite one or another work as a point of entry into a particular field where additional studies can be located either through the work cited or through ordinary bibliographical sources. The list includes a few relevant works not referred to specifically in the text.

Some items in these readings are briefly annotated when annotation is especially called for.

Achebe, Chinua. *No Longer at Ease.* New York: Ivan Obolensky, 1961.

Adamson, John William. *Pioneers of Modern Education, 1600–1700.* Cambridge: The University Press, 1921.

Albright, William Foxwell. *The Archaeology of Palestine.* Harmondsworth, Middlesex: Penguin Books, 1949.

Andrewes, Lancelot. *Sermons on the Nativity* [editor unnamed]. Grand Rapids, Mich.: Baker, 1955.

———. *Works.* Ed. by J. P. Wilson and James Bliss, 11 vols. Oxford: Parker, 1841–1854.

Ariès, Philippe. *Centuries of Childhood: A Social History of Family Life.* Trans. by Robert Baldick. New York: Knopf, 1962.

Auerbach, Erich. *Literary Language and Public in Late Latin Antiquity and in the Middle Ages.* Trans. by Ralph Manheim. Bollingen Series, 74. New York: Pantheon, 1965.

———. *Mimesis: The Representation of Reality in Western Literature.* Garden City: Doubleday, 1957.

Bainton, Roland H. *The Age of the Reformation.* Princeton: Van Nostrand, 1956.

Baker, Herschel. *The Wars of Truth: Studies in the Decay of Christian Humanism in the Earlier Seventeenth Century.* Cambridge: Harvard Univ. Press, 1952.

Baldwin, T. W. *William Shakspere's Small Latine and Lesse Greeke,* 2 vols. Urbana: Univ. of Illinois Press, 1944.

Balthasar, Hans Urs von. *Word and Revelation.* Trans. by A. V. Littledale and Alexander Dru. *Essays in Theology,* I. New York: Herder and Herder, 1965.

Barbu, Zevedei. *Problems of Historical Psychology*. London: Routledge and Kegan Paul, 1960.

Baron, Gabrielle. See Jousse, Marcel.

Barr, James. *The Semantics of Biblical Language*. London: Oxford Univ. Press, 1961.

Baumgartner, Charles, S.J. "Tradition et magistère," *Recherches de science religieuse, 41* (1953), 161–87.

Benesch, Otto. *The Art of the Renaissance in Northern Europe: Its Relation to the Contemporary Spiritual and Intellectual Movements*. Cambridge: Harvard Univ. Press, 1947.

Bergson, Henri. *Time and Free Will: An Essay on the Immediate Data of Consciousness*. New York: Harper, 1960.

Bertholet, A. "Die Macht der Schrift in Glauben und Aberglauben," *Abhandl. deutsch. Akad. Wiss. Berlin, Phi.-hist. Klasse* (1948).

Bessinger, Jess B. "Oral to Written: Some Implications of the Anglo-Saxon Transition," *Explorations* (Toronto), [No.] 8 (1957), pp. 11–15.

Bloomfield, Morton W. *The Seven Deadly Sins: An Introduction to the History of a Religious Concept with Special Reference to Medieval English Literature*. East Lansing: Michigan State College Press, 1952.

Bolgar, R. R. *The Classical Heritage and Its Beneficiaries*. Cambridge: The University Press, 1954.

Boman, Thorlief. *Hebrew Thought Compared with Greek*. Trans. by Jules L. Moreau from *Das hebräische Denken im Vergleich mit dem Griechischen*, 2d ed. (1954) with the author's revisions to January, 1960. Philadelphia: Westminster Press, 1961.

Boring, E. G. *Sensation and Perception in the History of Experimental Psychology*. New York: Appleton-Century, 1942.

Bouyer, Louis. *The Word, Church, and Sacraments in Protestantism and Catholicism*. Trans. by E. V. Littledale. New York: Desclee, 1961.

Bowra, C[ecil] M[aurice]. *Heroic Poetry*. London: Macmillan, 1952.

———. *Primitive Song*. Cleveland and New York: World Publishing, 1962.

B[rowne], I[ohn]. *The Merchants Avizo:* Very necessary for their sons and servants, when they first send them beyond the seas, as to Spaine and Portingale, or other countries. Made by their heartie welwisher in Christ, I. B. Merchant. London: John Norton, 1607.

Bruner, Jerome S. "The Course of Cognitive Growth," *American Psychologist, 19* (1964), 1–15.

———, Jacqueline J. Goodenow, and George A. Austin. *A Study of Thinking*, with an Appendix on Language by Roger W. Brown. New York: Wiley, 1956.

Brunner, Emil. *Truth as Encounter*, new ed., enlarged. Philadelphia: Westminster Press, 1964.

Buber, Martin. *Eclipse of God: Studies in the Relation between Religion and Philosophy*. New York: Harper, 1957.

Bullein, William. *Bulleins Bulwarke of Defence against All Sicknes, Sornes, and Woundes*. London: J. Kyngston, 1562.

Burghardt, Walter J., S.J. "The Catholic Concept of Tradition," *Proceedings of the Catholic Theological Society of America* (1951), pp. 42–76.

Caillois, Roger. *Man and the Sacred*. Trans. from *L'Homme et le sacré* (1930), by Meyer Barash. Glencoe: Free Press, 1959.

Čapek, Milič. *The Philosophical Impact of Contemporary Physics*. New York: Van Nostrand, 1961.

Carothers, J. C. "Culture, Psychiatry, and the Written Word," *Psychiatry, 22* (1959), 307–20.

Carter, Thomas Francis. *The Invention of Printing in China and Its Spread Westward*. Rev. by L. Carrington Goodrich, 2d ed. New York: Ronald Press, 1955.

Cassirer, Ernst. *The Problem of Knowledge; Philosophy, Science, and History since Hegel*. Trans. by William H. Woglom and Charles W. Hendel. New Haven: Yale Univ. Press, 1950.

Cattell, Raymond B. "The Nature and Measurement of Anxiety," *Scientific American* (March 1963), pp. 96–104.

Chadwick, H. Munro, and N. Kershaw Chadwick. *The Growth of Literature,* 3 vols. Cambridge Univ. Press, 1932–1940.

Chastel, André. "L'Épitre et le discours," *Bibliothèque d'Humanisme et Renaissance, 16* (1954), 381–85.

Chaytor, H[enry] J[ohn]. *From Script to Print: An Introduction to Medieval Literature.* Cambridge: The University Press, 1945.

Claudel, Paul. *The Eye Listens.* Trans. by Elsie Pell. New York: Philosophical Library, 1950.

Comenius (Komensky), John Amos. *Janua linguarum.* London: J. Redmayne for J. Williams, 1670.

Croll, Morris William. *Style, Rhetoric, and Rhythm: Essays by Morris W. Croll.* Ed. by J. Max Patrick and Robert O. Evans, with John M. Wallace and R. J. Schoeck. Princeton Univ. Press, 1966.

Crosby, Ruth. "Oral Delivery in the Middle Ages," *Speculum, 11* (1936), 88–110.

Cubberley, Ellwood P. *The History of Education: Educational Practice and Progress considered as a Phase of the Development and Spread of Western Civilization.* Boston: Houghton Mifflin, 1948. Treats the use of the vernacular in schools, including dissenters' academies and dame schools, and for scientific writing.

Curtius, Ernst Robert. *European Literature and the Latin Middle Ages.* Trans. by Willard R. Trask. Bollingen Series, 36. New York: Pantheon, 1953.

Daniel-Rops, Henri. *The Protestant Reformation.* Trans. by Audrey Butler. London: Dent; New York: Dutton, 1961.

Day, Angel. *The English Secretorie.* London: R. Walde-grave for R. Jones, 1586.

DeMott, Benjamin. "Comenius and the Real Character in England," *PMLA, 70* (1955), 1068–81.

Denziger, Henricus, Clemens Bannwart, Ioannes Umbero,

and Carolus Rahner, S.I. (eds.). *Enchiridion symbolorum, definitionum, et declarationem de rebus fidei et morum,* 31st ed. Barcelona: Herder, 1957.

Diringer, David. *The Alphabet: A Key to the History of Mankind,* 2d ed. rev. New York: Philosophical Library, 1953.

————. *The Hand-Produced Book.* New York: Philosophical Library, 1953.

————. *The Story of Aleph Beth.* New York and London: Yoseloff, 1960.

————. *Writing.* "Ancient Peoples and Places," vol. 25. London: Thames and Hudson, 1962.

Donohue, John W., S.J. *Jesuit Education: An Essay on the Foundation of Its Idea.* New York: Fordham Univ. Press, 1963.

Drachmann, A. G. *The Mechanical Technology of Greek and Roman Antiquity: A Study of the Literary Sources.* Madison: Univ. of Wisconsin Press, 1963.

Durand, Gilbert. *Les Structures anthropologiques de l'imaginaire.* Bibliothèque de Philosophie Contemporaine, 2d ed. Paris: Presses Universitaires de France, 1963.

Ebeling, Gerhard. *Word and Faith.* Trans. by James W. Leitch. Philadelphia: Fortress Press, 1963.

Eby, Frederick. *The Development of Modern Education: In Theory, Organization, and Practice,* 2d ed. New York: Prentice-Hall, 1952. Discusses vernacular education as it grew in the various countries of Europe.

Eliade, Mircea. *Birth and Rebirth: The Religious Meaning of Initiation in Human Culture.* Trans. by Willard R. Trask. New York: Harper, 1958.

————. *Patterns in Comparative Religion.* Trans. by Rosemary Sheed. New York: Sheed and Ward, 1958.

————. *The Sacred and the Profane: The Nature of Religion.* Trans. by Willard R. Trask. New York: Harcourt, Brace, 1959.

Ellul, Jacques. *Technological Society.* Trans. by John Wilkinson. New York: Knopf, 1964.

Erasmus, Desiderius. *Opus epistolarum.* Ed. by P. S. Allen, H. M. Allen, and H. W. Garrod, 12 vols. Oxford: Clarendon Press, 1906–1958.

Erikson, Erik H. *Childhood and Society,* 2d ed. rev. New York: Norton, 1963.

———. *Young Man Luther.* New York: Norton, 1958.

Febvre, Lucien, and H. J. Martin. *L'Apparition du livre.* Collection Évolution de l'Humanité, *II,* 8, 3. Paris: Michel, 1950.

Finley, M. I. *The Ancient Greeks: An Introduction to Their Life and Thought.* New York: Viking Press, 1963.

Freud, Sigmund. *Civilization and Its Discontents.* Trans. by Joan Riviere. The International Psycho-Analytic Library, No. 17. London: Hogarth Press, and Institute of Psycho-Analysis, 1949.

———. *Group Psychology and the Analysis of the Ego.* London: Hogarth Press, and the Institute of Psycho-Analysis, 1948.

Fugger, Correspondents of the House of. *The Fugger News-Letter, Being a Selection of Unpublished Letters from the Correspondents of the House of Fugger during the Years 1568–1605.* Ed. by Victor von Klarwill, trans. by Pauline de Chary. New York: Putnam, 1924.

Fullwood, William. *The Enimie of Idlenesse.* London: Henry Bynneman for Leonard Maylard, 1568.

Ganshof, François L. *Wat Waren de Capitularia?* Verhandlingen van de Koninklijke Vlaamse Academie voor Wetenschappen, Letteren en Schone Kunsten van België, Klasse der Letteren, No. 22. Brussels: Paleis der Academien, 1955. This book is reviewed by Bryce Lyon in *Speculum, 33* (1958), 87–88.

Gebert, Clara (ed.). *An Anthology of Elizabethan Dedications and Prefaces.* Philadelphia: Univ. of Pennsylvania Press, 1933.

Geiselmann, Josef Rupert. "Scripture, Tradition, and the Church: An Ecumenical Problem," in *Christianity Di-*

vided: Protestant and Roman Catholic Theological Issues,
ed. by Daniel J. Callahan, Heiko A. Oberman, and Daniel
J. O'Hanlon, S.J. New York: Sheed and Ward, 1961, pp.
39–72. In this work the author reports earlier work by himself and others.

Gelb, I[gnace] J. *A Study of Writing: The Foundations of
Grammatology.* London: Routledge and Kegan Paul, 1952.

Geldard, Frank Arthur. *The Human Senses.* New York:
Wiley, 1953.

Gibbons, Sister Marina, O.P. *Instructive Communication:
English Renaissance Handbooks 1477–1550.* Ph.D. dissertation, Saint Louis University, 1966. Ann Arbor: University Microfilms, 1967.

Gibson, James J. *Perception of the Visual World.* Boston:
Houghton Mifflin, 1950.

Gombrich, E[rnst] H[ans]. *Art and Illusion: A Study in the
Psychology of Pictorial Representation, 1960.* London:
Phaidon Press, 1960.

Guarna, Andreas. *Bellum Grammaticale: A Discourse of
Great War and Dissention between Two Worthy Princes,
the Noune and the Verbe Contending for the Chief Place
or Dignity in Oration.* Trans. from the Latin (Strasbourg,
1512) by W. Hayward. London: 1569.

Gwynn, Aubrey, S.J. *Roman Education from Cicero to
Quintilian.* Oxford: Clarendon Press, 1926.

Hajnal, István. *L'Enseignement de l'écriture aux universités
médiévales.* Budapest: Academia Scientiarum Hungarica
Budapestini, 1954.

Hanson, Norwood Russell. *Patterns of Discovery: An Inquiry
into the Conceptual Foundations of Science.* Cambridge:
The University Press, 1958.

Hardison, O. B., Jr. *The Enduring Monument: A Study of
the Idea of Praise in Renaissance Literary Theory and
Practice.* Chapel Hill: Univ. of North Carolina Press, 1962.

Harris, James. *Hermes, or A Philosophical Inquiry Concerning Grammar.* London: J. Nourse and P. Vaillant, 1751.

H[art], J[ohn]. An Orthographie, Conteyning the Due Order and Reason, How to Write or Paint Thimage of Mannes Voice, Most Like to the Life of Nature. Composed by I. H. [i.e., John Hart] Chester Heralt. London: W. Serres, 1569.

Havelock, Eric A. Preface to Plato. Cambridge, Mass.: Belknap Press, 1963.

Hawkes, Jacquetta [Mrs. J. B. Priestley] and Sir Leonard Woolley. History of Mankind, vol. I. Prehistory and the Beginnings of Civilization. New York and Evanston: Harper and Row, 1963. Rather good but not always up-to-date chapter on "Languages and Writing Systems: Education," chapter vi in Part II.

Hayes, Cathy. The Ape in Our House. New York: Harper, 1951.

Heidegger, Martin. Being and Time. Trans. by John Macquarrie and Edward Robinson. New York and Evanston: Harper and Row, 1962.

Hoffmann, Ernst. Die Sprache und die archäische Logik. Tübingen: Mohr, 1925.

Hollander, John. The Untuning of the Sky. Princeton Univ. Press, 1961.

Hopkins, Gerard Manley, S.J. [Comments on the Spiritual Exercises of St. Ignatius Loyola], in The Sermons and Devotional Writings of Gerard Manley Hopkins, ed. by Christopher Devlin, S.J. London: Oxford Univ. Press, 1959, pp. 105–209.

Howe, Reuel L. The Miracle of Dialogue. New York: Seabury Press, 1963.

Howell, Wilbur Samuel. Logic and Rhetoric in England, 1500–1700. Princeton Univ. Press, 1956.

Howes, Raymond F. (ed.). Historical Studies of Rhetoric and Rhetoricians. New York: Cornell Univ. Press, 1961.

Huber, Raphael. St. Anthony of Padua. Milwaukee: Bruce, 1948.

Hughes, H. Stuart. Consciousness and Society: The Reorientation of European Social Thought. New York: Knopf. 1958.

Hughes, Philip. *The Reformation in England,* 3 vols. New York: Macmillan, 1963.

Huizinga, Johan. *The Waning of the Middle Ages.* New York: Longmans, Green, 1948.

Humphrey, George. *Thinking: An Introduction to Its Experimental Psychology.* London: Methuen; New York: Wiley, 1951.

Innis, Harold A. *The Bias of Communication.* Univ. of Toronto Press, 1951.

————. *Changing Concepts of Time.* Univ. of Toronto Press, 1952.

————. *Empire and Communications.* Oxford: Clarendon Press, 1950.

Ivins, William M., Jr. *Art and Geometry: A Study in Space Intuitions.* Cambridge: Harvard Univ. Press, 1946.

————. *Prints and Visual Communication.* Cambridge: Harvard Univ. Press, 1953.

Jacobs, Melville. *The Content and Style of an Oral Literature: Clackamas Chinook Myths and Tales.* Viking Fund Publications in Anthropology, No. 26. New York: Wenner-Gren Foundation for Anthropological Research, 1959.

Jaeger, Werner. *Aristotle: Fundamentals of the History of His Development.* Trans. with the author's corrections and additions by Richard Robinson, 2d ed. Oxford: Clarendon Press, 1948.

————. *Early Christianity and Greek Paideia.* Cambridge, Mass.: Belknap Press, 1961.

————. *Paideia: The Ideals of Greek Culture.* Trans. by Gilbert Highet, 3 vols. New York: Oxford Univ. Press, 1944.

Jaspers, Karl. "On My Philosophy," trans. by Felix Kaufmann and published in English for the first time in *Existentialism from Dostoevsky to Sartre,* ed. by Walter Kaufmann. New York: Meridian, 1956, pp. 131–58.

Jayakar, Pupul. "The Girl and the Dark Goddess," in *New World Writing: Ninth Mentor Selection.* New York: New American Library of World Literature, 1956, pp. 166–73.

Jespersen, Otto. *Language: Its Nature, Development, and Origin.* New York: Norton, 1964.

Jones, Richard Foster. *The Triumph of the English Language.* Stanford Univ. Press, 1953.

Jorgensen, Paul A. *Shakespeare's Military World.* Berkeley: Univ. of California Press, 1956.

Jousse, Marcel, S.J. "La Mimique hébraïque et la rhythmo-pédagogie vivante" (a résumé by Etienne Boucly of the course in "La Psychologie de la parabole dans le style oral palestinien" given by Père Jousse in 1935 in Paris at the École des Hautes-Études de la Sorbonne), extrait des *Cahiers juifs,* No. 15 (May–June, 1935), pp. 1–13. Because Père Jousse himself was so oral in his mode of existence and teaching, his work is ill accommodated to a typographical culture and for that reason may never have the currency it should. Typical oral phenomena in this and other works of his include the following: (1) authorship is uncertain and/or shared (how much of this is Jousse and how much Boucly?); (2) ability to verbalize description is limited; (3) typographic space is used not typographically but as a field for something like gestures, texts are thrown onto the page in variously colored inks (red and black in his *Les Récitatifs rhythmiques*) with no sure printed directions as to what it all means. This is not to disparage his work; quite the contrary, it is to show its genuineness and to show how true understanding of an oral culture pulls one out of our typographic culture.

————. *Les Récitatifs rhythmiques de Jésus et de ses apôtres,* reconstitués par le R. P. Jousse, S.J. Présentation sous la haute patronage de son Eminence le Cardinal Dubois, Archevêque de Paris, par les élèves de Mlle H. Georget, Directrice de l'Institut Pédagogique de Style Manuel et Oral. Theatre program: Théâtre des Champs-Elysées, 25 avril 1929; Paris, 1929; 10 pp. (unnumbered). See note with Jousse's "La Mimique hébraïque . . . ." Here again, as one of Père Jousse's "works," we have the program of an oral performance, which was itself his "work."

————. *Les Récitatifs rhythmiques: I, Genre de la maxime.* "Études sur la psychologie du geste." Paris: Editions Spes, 1930. Père Jousse's brief Introduction, pp. ix–xliv, discusses "la loi psychologique du parallelisme," "balancement," "schèmes rhythmiques," etc. Most of this book (pp. 1–212) is a series of maxims, printed in red and black ink to indicate rhythmic structure, etc., though there is no commentary on the texts printed here. See note with Jousse, "La Mimique hébraïque . . . ."

(Jousse, Marcel, S.J.) Baron, Gabrielle. *Marcel Jousse: Introduction à sa vie et à son oeuvre.* Paris: Casterman, 1965. Contains bibliography of Père Jousse's works.

————. Lefévre, Frédéric. *Marcel Jousse: Une Nouvelle psychologie du langage.* "Les Cahiers de l'occident," ed. Gérard de Catalogne and Émile Dufour, Vol. I, No. 10, pp. 1–116. Paris: Librairie de France, 1926. [Lefévre's text itself is dated (p. 116) August 1927.]

Keckermann (Keckermannus), Bartholomaeus. *Opera omnia quae extant,* 2 vols. Geneva: Aubert, 1614.

Keller, Abraham C. "Pace and Timing in Rabelais's Stories," *Studies in the Renaissance, 10* (1963), 108–25.

Kellogg, Winthrop N. *Porpoises and Sonar.* Univ. of Chicago Press, 1961.

Kepes, Gyorgy. *The New Landscape in Art and Science.* Chicago: Theobald, 1956.

Kermode, Frank. *Romantic Image.* New York: Vintage, 1964.

Kingdon, Robert M. "Christopher Plantin and His Backers, 1575–1590," *Mélanges d'histoire économique et sociale: En hommage au Professeur Antony Babel.* Geneva: 1966, pp. 303–16.

Kisiel, Theodore J. "The Reality of the Electron," *Philosophy Today, 8* (1964), 56–65. Treats overvisualization of physics, citing Čapek's work referred to above and Whitehead's "fallacy of misplaced concreteness."

Larwood, Jacob, and John Camden Hotten. *The History of Signboards: From the Earliest Times to the Present Day,* 11th ed. London: Chatto and Windus, 1900.

Lavelle, Louis. *La Parole et l'écriture*. Paris: L'Artisane du Livre, 1942.

Lechner, Sister Joan Marie, O.S.U. *Renaissance Concepts of the Commonplaces*. New York: Pageant Press, 1962.

Leeuw, Gerardus van der. *Religion in Essence and Manifestation*. Trans. by J. E. Turner, with appendices to the Torchbook edition incorporating the additions of the second German edition by Hans H. Penner. New York: Harper, 1963.

Leeuwen, Arend Theodoor van. *Christianity and World History*. London: Edinburgh House, 1964.

LeHiste, Ilse, and Gordon E. Peterson. "Vowel Amplitude and Phonemic Stress in American English," *Journal of the Acoustical Society of America, 31* (1959), 428–35. The authors found that in judging explicitly the relative loudness of vowels, "almost invariably the listeners identified the vowels that were produced with a greater amount of effort (such as /i/ and /u/ recorded at zero VU) as louder than vowels having greater intrinsic amplitude but produced with normal effort (such as / ɑ / and / ɔ /)" (p. 431).

Leith, John H. (ed.). *Creeds of the Churches: A Reader in Christian Doctrine from the Bible to the Present*. Garden City: Doubleday, 1963.

Lewis, Wyndham. *Time and Western Man*. Boston: Beacon Press, 1957.

Locke, John. *Works*. Ed. by J. A. St. John. Bohn's Standard Library. London: Bohn, 1854.

Löwith, Karl. *Meaning in History*. Univ. of Chicago Press, 1958.

Lohfink, Norbert, S.J. "The Inerrancy and the Unity of Scripture," *Theology Digest, 13* (1965), 185–92 (trans. from the German). An excellent summary of Catholic thought on the inerrancy of the Scriptures, inspiration, and related subjects.

L'Orange, H. P. *Studies in the Iconography of Cosmic Kingship*. Instituttet for Sammenlignende Kulturforskning,

Ser. A: Forelesninger, 23. Oslo: Aschehoug (W. Mygaard);
Cambridge: Harvard Univ. Press, 1953.

Lord, Albert B. The Singer of Tales. Harvard Studies in
Comparative Literature, 24. Cambridge: Harvard Univ.
Press, 1960.

Lortz, Joseph. The Reformation: A Problem for Today.
Trans. by John C. Dwyer. Westminster, Md.: Newman
Press, 1964.

McCarthy, Dennis J., S.J. "Personality, Society, and Inspiration," Theological Studies, 24 (1963), 553–76.

McCulloch, Florence. Medieval Latin and French Bestiaries.
University of North Carolina Studies in the Romance Languages and Literatures, No. 33, rev. ed. Chapel Hill: Univ.
of North Carolina Press, 1962.

Machiavelli, Niccolò. Letter to Francesco Vettori, Dec. 10,
1513, as quoted in André Chastel, The Age of Humanism:
Europe 1480–1530, trans. by Katherine M. Delavenay and
E. M. Gwyer. New York: McGraw-Hill, 1963, p. 82.

McKeon, Richard. "Rhetoric in the Middle Ages," Speculum,
17 (1942), 1–32.

McLuhan, Marshall. The Gutenberg Galaxy: The Making
of Typographic Man. Univ. of Toronto Press, 1962.

————. Understanding Media: The Extensions of Man. New
York: McGraw-Hill, 1964.

McNamee, Maurice B., S.J. "Literary Decorum in Francis
Bacon," Saint Louis University Studies, Ser. A, 1, No. 3
(March 1950), 1–52.

Marcuse, Herbert. Eros and Civilization: A Philosophical
Inquiry into Freud. Boston: Beacon Press, 1955.

Marler, Peter, and William Hamilton. Mechanisms of Animal Behavior. New York: Wiley, 1966.

Marrou, Henri-Irénée. A History of Education in Antiquity.
Trans. by George Lamb. New York: Sheed and Ward, 1956.

Merleau-Ponty, Maurice. "L'Oeil et l'esprit," Les temps
modernes, 18, Nos. 184–85 (1961), Numéro spécial: Maurice Merleau-Ponty, pp. 193–227.

Mill, John Stuart. "What is Poetry?" and "The Two Kinds of Poetry," reprinted with slight revisions from the *Monthly Repository*, Jan. and Oct., 1833, in John Stuart Mill, *Dissertations and Discussions: Political, Philosophical, and Historical*. New York: Holt, 1874–1882, *1*, 89–120.

Miller, Edwin Haviland. *The Professional Writer in Elizabethan England: A Study of Nondramatic Literature*. Cambridge: Harvard Univ. Press, 1959.

Nicolson, Marjorie. *Science and Imagination*. Ithaca: Cornell Univ. Press, 1956.

Nielson, Eduard. *Oral Tradition: A Modern Problem in Old Testament Introduction*. London: SCM Press; Chicago: Allenson, 1954.

Nogué, Jean. *Esquisse d'un système des qualités sensibles*. Paris: Presses Universitaires de France, 1943.

Ong, Walter J., S.J. *The Barbarian Within*. New York: Macmillan, 1962.

———. *In the Human Grain*. New York: Macmillan, 1967.

———. "Latin Language Study as a Renaissance Puberty Rite," *Studies in Philology, 56* (1959), 103–24.

———. "Oral Residue in Tudor Prose Style," *PMLA, 80* (1965), 145–54.

———. "Ramist Method and the Commercial Mind," *Studies in the Renaissance, 8* (1961), 155–72.

———. *Ramus and Talon Inventory*. Cambridge: Harvard Univ. Press, 1958.

———. *Ramus, Method, and the Decay of Dialogue*. Cambridge: Harvard Univ. Press, 1958.

Opler, Marvin K. *Culture, Psychiatry, and Human Values*. With a foreword by Thomas A. C. Rennie. Springfield: Thomas, 1956.

Owens, Joseph. *The Doctrine of Being in the Aristotelian Metaphysics*, 2d ed. Toronto: Pontifical Institute of Medieval Studies, 1963.

Owst, G. R. *Preaching in Medieval England*. Cambridge: The University Press, 1926.

Panofsky, Erwin. *Early Netherlandish Painting, Its Origins and Character,* 2 vols. Cambridge: Harvard Univ. Press, 1953.

————. *Meaning in the Visual Arts: Papers in and on Art History.* Garden City: Doubleday, 1955.

————. *Renaissance and Renascences in Western Art.* Stockholm: Almqvist and Wiksell, 1960.

————. *Studies in Iconology: Humanistic Themes in the Art of the Renaissance.* New York: Oxford Univ. Press, 1939.

Pauck, Wilhelm. *The Heritage of the Reformation,* rev. ed. Glencoe: Free Press, 1961.

Pedersen, Holger. *The Discovery of Language: Linguistic Science in the Nineteenth Century.* Trans. by John Webster Spargo. Bloomington: Indiana Univ. Press, 1962.

Pelikan, Jaroslav. *Obedient Rebels: Catholic Substance and Protestant Principle in Luther's Reformation.* New York and Evanston: Harper and Row, 1964.

Peter of Spain. *Petri Hispani Summulae logicales.* Ed. by I. M. Bochenski, O.P. Torino, Italy: Casa Editrice Marietti, 1947. For discussion see Walter J. Ong, *Ramus, Method, and the Decay of Dialogue,* pp. 55–74.

Petersson, Torsten. *Cicero: A Biography.* New York: Bilbo and Tannen, 1963.

Piaget, Jean, Bärbel Inhelder, and Alina Szeminska. *The Child's Conception of Geometry.* Trans. by E. A. Lunzer. New York: Basic Books, 1960.

————. *A Child's Conception of Physical Causality.* Trans. by Marjorie Gabain. New York: Harcourt, Brace, 1930.

————, and Bärbel Inhelder. *The Child's Conception of Space.* Trans. by F. J. Langdon and J. L. Lunzer. London: Routledge and Kegan Paul, 1956.

————. *The Language and Thought of the Child,* 3d ed. rev. Trans. by Marjorie Gabain. London: Routledge and Kegan Paul, 1959.

Pollard, Hugh M. *Pioneers of Popular Education, 1760–1850.* Cambridge: Harvard Univ. Press, 1957.

Reif, Sister Mary Richard, I.H.M. *Natural Philosophy in Some Early Seventeenth Century Scholastic Textbooks.*

Ph.D. dissertation, Saint Louis University, 1962. Ann Arbor: University Microfilms, No. 64–3764, 1964.

Riva Palacio, Vincente. "El Buen ejemplo," in *Imaginación y fantasía*, ed. by Donald A. Yates and John B. Dalbor. *Cuentas de las Américas.* New York: Holt, Rinehart, and Winston, 1960, pp. 89–93.

Robins, R. H. "Noun and Verb in Universal Grammar," *Language, 28* (1952), 289–98.

Róheim, Géza. *Magic and Schizophrenia.* Posthumously ed. by Warner Muensterberger and S. H. Posinsky. Bloomington: Indiana Univ. Press, 1955.

Rosenstock-Huessy, Eugen. *Soziologie*, 2 vols. I, *Die Übermacht der Räume;* II, *Die Vollzahl der Zeiten.* Stuttgart: Kohlhammer, 1956.

Ryle, Gilbert. *The Concept of Mind.* London and New York: Hutchinson's University Library, 1949.

Sapir, Edward. *Language: An Introduction to the Study of Speech.* New York: Harcourt, Brace, 1921.

Schaff, Philip. *Creeds of Christendom,* 3 vols. New York: Harper and Bros., 1919.

Scholes, Robert, and Robert Kellogg. *The Nature of Narrative.* New York: Oxford Univ. Press, 1966.

Schumpeter, Joseph Alois. *Capitalism, Socialism, and Democracy.* New York and London: Harper, 1942.

————. *Imperialism and Social Classes.* Trans. by Heinz Norden, ed. by Paul M. Sweezy. New York: Kelley, 1951.

Schwartz, Joseph, and John A. Rycenga (eds.). *The Province of Rhetoric.* New York: Ronald Press, 1965.

Siertsema, Bertha. *A Study of Glossematics: Critical Survey of Its Fundamental Concepts.* The Hague: Martinus Nijhoff, 1955. The author solidly establishes her point that sound is primary in language. The point could be made even more cogent by noting the fact that the author and those she quotes regularly convert sound into spatial categories in the very process of defending sound—so fragile is its being.

Smalley, Beryl. *English Friars and Antiquity in the Early Fourteenth Century.* Oxford: Blackwell, 1960.

————. *Study of the Bible in the Middle Ages*, 2d ed. rev. Oxford: Blackwell, 1952.

Smith, J[oe] W[illiam] Ashley. *The Birth of Modern Education: The Contribution of Dissenting Academies, 1660–1800.* London: Independent Press, 1954.

Smith, Sir Thomas. *De recta et emendata linguae Anglicae scriptione.* Paris: 1568.

Spitzer, Leo. *Classical and Christian Ideas of World Harmony: Prolegomena to an Interpretation of the Word "Stimmung."* Ed. by Anna Granville Hatcher with a preface by René Wellek. Baltimore: Johns Hopkins Press, 1963.

Tanqueray, Adolphe, with J. D. Bord. *Brevior synopsis theologiae dogmaticae*, 7th ed. New York: Benziger, 1943.

Tavard, George H. *Holy Writ or Holy Church.* New York: Harper, 1959.

Teilhard de Chardin, Pierre. *The Phenomenon of Man.* Trans. by Bernard Wall, introduction by Sir Julian Huxley. New York: Harper, 1959.

Tinbergen, Niko. *The Herring Gull's World: A Study in the Social Behavior of Birds*, rev. ed. New York: Basic Books, 1960.

Troeltsch, Ernst. *The Social Teaching of the Christian Churches.* Trans. by Olive Wyon, 2 vols. New York: Harper, 1960.

Turner, E. S. *The Shocking History of Advertising!* New York: Dutton, 1953.

Tuveson, Ernest. "Locke and the Dissolution of the Ego," *Modern Philology*, 52 (1955), 159–74. Discusses Locke's extreme visualism.

Van Ackeren, Gerald, S.J. "Is All Revelation in Scripture?" *The Catholic Theological Society of America: Proceedings of the Seventeenth Annual Convention.* Yonkers, N.Y.: Catholic Theological Society of America Editorial Offices, St. Joseph's Seminary, 1962, pp. 249–61.

Verhaar, John W. M., S.J. *Some Relations between Perception, Speech, and Thought: A Contribution toward the*

Phenomenology of Speech. Assen, Netherlands: Van Gorcum, 1963.

Vico, Giambattista. *The New Science.* Trans. by Thomas Goddard Bergin and Max Harold Fisch. Ithaca: Cornell Univ. Press, 1948.

Waelhens, Alphonse de. *Existence et Signification.* Louvain: Nauwelaarts; Paris: Béatrice-Nauwelaerts, 1958.

Waldron, Ronald A. "Oral-Formulaic Technique and Middle English Alliterature Poetry," *Speculum, 32* (1957), 792–801.

Waterman, John T. *Perspectives in Linguistics.* Univ. of Chicago Press, 1963.

Werner, Heinz, and Bernard Kaplan. *Symbol Formation: An Organismic–Developmental Approach to Language and the Expression of Thought.* New York: Wiley, 1963.

White, Lynn. *Medieval Technology and Social Change.* Oxford: Clarendon Press, 1962.

Whitehead, Alfred North. *Modes of Thought:* Six Lectures delivered in Wellesley College, Massachusetts, and Two Lectures in the University of Chicago. New York: Capricorn, 1958.

———. *Process and Reality: An Essay in Cosmology.* Gifford Lectures Delivered in the University of Edinburgh during the Session 1927–1928. New York: Social Science Book Store, 1929.

Whorf, Benjamin Lee. *Language, Thought, and Reality: Selected Writings.* Ed. with an introduction by John B. Carroll. Cambridge: Technology Press of Massachusetts Institute of Technology; London: Chapman and Hall, 1956.

Wilder, Amos N. *The Language of the Gospel: Early Christian Rhetoric.* New York and Evanston: Harper and Row, 1964.

Wilkins, John. *An Essay towards a Real Character and a Philosophical Language.* London: Sa. Gellibrand and John Martin, 1668.

Wilson, Richard Albert. *The Miraculous Birth of Language.*

Preface by George Bernard Shaw. New York: Philosophical Library, 1948. Wilson's book is better than Shaw's preface, annoyingly superficial as usual.

Wynne-Edwards, V. C. *Animal Dispersion in Relation to Social Behaviour.* Edinburgh and London: Oliver and Boyd, 1962.

Yates, Frances A. *The Art of Memory.* Univ. of Chicago Press, 1966.

Zilzel, Edgar. "The Genesis of the Concept of Physical Law," *Philosophical Review, 51* (1942), 245–79.

Zuckerkandl, Victor. *Sound and Symbol: Music and the External World.* Trans. by Willard R. Trask. Bollingen Series, 44. New York: Pantheon, 1956.

Index

Abraham, 12, 113

Abstraction, limited in oral culture, 23

Académie Française, 65

Achebe, Chinua, 136

Achilles, 133, 204

"Actuality" compared to "reality," 172

Adamson, John William, 245

Addison, Joseph, 72

Adler, Mortimer, 87

Advertising, 221–22, 242–43, 248, 256, 287

Aeneas, 204

African cultures, oral quality of, 75, 131–36, 256

Aide-mémoire devices, 35–36

Albee, Edward, 208

Alphabet, ix, 7, 35–53, 68–69, 111, 135–39, 189, 207, 229, 318; Greek, 34; Hebrew, 189; International Phonetic, 46; nonce origin, 38–39; sense of order fostered by, 45; spatializes sound, 42–53. See also Scripts

Ambrose of Milan, St., 52–53, 58

American cultures, oral quality of, 131–36

American Philosophical Society, xi

Ames, William, 217

Amok, 132, 301

Analysis, causal, fostered by writing, 203, 206–07

Andrewes, Lancelot, 187

Animism, 206–07, 228, 296, 304–05

Anthony of Padua, St., 269

Antihero, 205

Anxiety–hostility syndromes, 131–32, 219, 257, 302–03

Aphthonius, 84

Aquinas, St. Thomas, 46, 59, 140, 156, 211, 213, 222, 271, 277–79

Arab culture, oral quality of, 30, 75, 233–34

Ariès, Philippe, 197–98

Ariosto, Ludovico, 133

Aristotle, 26–27, 31, 52, 55–56, 82, 85, 212–14, 216–18, 222, 224, 232, 278

Armstrong, John, 5

Artes sermocinales, 209

Asian cultures, oral quality of, 131–36

Audience of writer is a fiction 116–17

Auditory, new stress on the, 9, 174–75. See also Sound

Auditory synthesis, 111–38, 162–63, 200, 206, 290; meaning, 126–27

Auditory, vs. visual. See Auditory synthesis; Greeks, ancient; Hebrews; Oral culture; Visualism; Voice

Auerbach, Erich, 12

Augustine of Hippo, St., 40, 47, 58, 96, 177, 187

Aural. See Oral–aural

Authoritarianism, 50–53

Authority, 231–36, 283–86; narrator's, in oral narrative, 70

Awe, religious, 168

Aztec script. See Script

Bacon, Francis, 87, 237, 283

Bainton, Roland, 265

Baker, Herschel, 239

ABOUT THE AUTHOR

WALTER J. ONG, S.J., is professor of English at Saint Louis University. A native of Kansas City, Missouri, he studied at Rockhurst College (B.A.) and worked in commercial positions two years before entering the Society of Jesus (Jesuit order), continuing his studies thereafter at Saint Louis University (M.A., S.T.L.) and Harvard University (Ph.D.). He was ordained a priest in 1946. Twice recipient of a Guggenheim Fellowship, he has also been a Fellow at the Center for Advanced Studies at Wesleyan University (Connecticut). He has served as visiting professor at the University of California and Indiana University, visiting lecturer at the University of Poitiers in France, Macdonald lecturer at McGill University in Canada, Terry lecturer at Yale University in 1963–64, and Berg Professor of English and American Literature at New York University in 1966–67. His many publications include the books *Frontiers in American Catholicism* (1957); *Ramus, Method, and the Decay of Dialogue* (1958); *Ramus and Talon Inventory* (1958); *American Catholic Crossroads* (1959); *The Barbarian Within* (1962); *In the Human Grain* (1967).